Praise for Digital Threads

"Smart marketing will move your business from unknown and struggling to respected and thriving. In *Digital Threads*, Neal Schaffer provides you the guidebook to marketing success in the modern era. Read it, implement it, and watch your business reach new heights."

—**Michael Stelzner, Founder of Social Media Examiner**

"Neal's been on the front lines of the digital first economy since the beginning. This book is the definitive digital marketing playbook that teaches businesses everything they need to build and grow their brand and create a competitive advantage on a realistic budget!"

—**Brian Solis, futurist, author of *Mindshift*, digital pioneer**

"Neal's new book is your accessible, actionable guide to what matters most in modern marketing."

—**Ann Handley, *WSJ* best-selling author of *Everybody Writes* and CCO, MarketingProfs**

"Neal is one of the great digital marketing intellects of our time, and this book is a gift to us all!"

—**Mark Schaefer, author of *Marketing Rebellion***

"*Digital Threads* is a game-changer for small businesses and entrepreneurs wanting to enhance their customer experience with big-brand strategies on a budget. Full of actionable insights and easy-to-follow steps, it helps companies create exceptional customer journeys while driving business growth through comprehensive digital marketing strategies."

—Jay Baer, author of *The Time to Win: How to Exceed Your Customers' Need for Speed*

"*Digital Threads* by Neal Schaffer is your ultimate guide to mastering digital marketing in a post-pandemic world. Packed with innovative strategies and real-world insights, this book will transform your online presence and help your business thrive in the digital age."

—Martin Lindstrom, *New York Times* best-selling author of *Buyology*, *Small Data*, and *The Ministry of Common Sense*

"Neal Schaffer's *Digital Threads* is the quintessential marketing guide for every small business owner. Its actionable, intuitive framework delivers step-by-step recommendations backed by years of proven success."

—Ekaterina Walter, *WSJ* bestselling author of 3 business books, including her latest *The Laws of Brand Storytelling*

"Before you overcomplicate your digital strategy (again), pick up this business-saving playbook that will be your guide to making the right decisions for your business (and your life). Neal makes the complicated simple, and the right strategy apparent. So good!"

—Joe Pulizzi, best-selling author of *Content Inc.* and *Epic Content Marketing* and Founder of Tilt Publishing

"What I love most about Schaffer's new book is that it paints a very clear picture for people seeking to market better, and then fills the zoomed-in version with actionable material to pursue. He covers the information not from the pulpit but from the kitchen table after dinner over coffee while we ask questions about how any of this will ever really work. Read this. Keep it close by for reference."

—**Chris Brogan,** *New York Times* **bestselling co-author of** ***Trust Agents***

"From mastering search engine optimization and crafting compelling email campaigns to leveraging the power of social media and influencer partnerships, Schaffer covers the key components of a successful digital marketing strategy. The book's "SES Framework" offers a clear roadmap for prioritizing efforts, while the "PDCA" methodology provides an approach to continuous improvement. Filled with real-world case studies, *Digital Threads* is a must-read for anyone serious about leveraging digital marketing to its full potential."

—**Shama Hyder, best-selling author of** *Momentum* **and CEO of Zen Media**

"Calling all Entrepreneurs who are ON FIRE! Are you prepared to IGNITE your business with strategic, digital-first marketing? Look no further than Neal Schaffer's new book, *Digital Threads*. This book is a masterclass in modern marketing that will elevate your business from unknown to unstoppable. So if you're ready for real, measurable success in today's digital landscape, the time is now!"

—**John Lee Dumas, best-selling author of** *The Common Path to Uncommon Success* **and host of Entrepreneurs on Fire**

"A wonderful guide for the modern-day marketer! The online world has changed dramatically over the past several years. And it's more vital than ever for small businesses and entrepreneurs to be nimble with a proven, digital-first strategy. If you're not getting solid, measurable results from your marketing efforts, or feeling overwhelmed about it all, Neal Schaffer's *Digital Threads* is your perfect handbook!"

—Mari Smith, premier Facebook marketing expert and social media thought leader

"Neal Schaffer masterfully weaves the essential digital marketing elements required to thrive in today's ever-changing world."

—John Jantsch, author of *Duct Tape Marketing*

"Neal makes the concepts of Digital-First marketing so clear and practical, that even your grandma could launch a new business. A must-read for small businesses and entrepreneurs!"

—Robert Rose, Chief Strategy Officer, The Content Advisory

"Social media is not a fad. AI is coming at us full force. And Neal Schaffer has an approach that will help you capitalize on all things digital without being overwhelmed or losing focus. In *Digital Threads*, he walks you through where we are today, what changes to expect in the future, and how to put it all together to reach your goals. Read it so you can grow your content, grow your audience, and grow your ROI."

—Gini Dietrich, Founder and author of *Spin Sucks* and creator of the PESO Model©

"*Digital Threads* is a treasure trove of digital marketing wisdom. Neal Schaffer demystifies the complexities of modern marketing, providing actionable strategies that any business can implement. This book is your go-to guide for navigating the ever-evolving digital landscape and achieving lasting success."

—**Matthew Pollard, bestselling author of** *The Introvert's Edge* **series**

"*Digital Threads* is a game-changer for small businesses and entrepreneurs wanting to enhance their customer experience with big-brand strategies on a budget. Full of actionable insights and easy-to-follow steps, it helps companies create exceptional customer journeys while driving business growth through comprehensive digital marketing strategies."

—**Dan Gingiss, customer experience keynote speaker and author of** *The Experience Maker*

"*Digital Threads* is an invaluable guide to building a digital-first business and brand. You'll learn everything you need to make the digital marketing landscape work for you and your small business. *Digital Threads* should be on the bookshelf of every small business owner and entrepreneur."

—**Melanie Deziel, author of** *The Content Fuel Framework* **and Co-Founder of CreatorKitchen.com**

"Everything you need to succeed in today's digital world is right here. *Digital Threads* takes a fresh look at which channels, in which order, deliver sustained growth. An absolute must-read."

—**Nancy Harhut, author,** *Using Behavioral Science in Marketing*

"Neal Schaffer's latest book provides excellent and practical insights on how best to grow a business for that group who are often under the most pressure in just trying to run a business day to day - that is small business owners and entrepreneurs. His advice, much garnered from personal experience, is invaluable and implementable. I would highly recommend it."

—Ken Fitzpatrick, CEO, Digital Marketing Institute

"In *Digital Threads*, Neal Schaffer has written a thought-provoking, yet practical guide for anyone looking to use digital tools to help stand out and drive their business. In a crazily fast-moving world, Schaffer has managed to distill the landscape and his advice into a book compact with useful and sometimes counter-intuitive advice. As much as the book delves into digital applications and solutions, he keeps us grounded in human connections."

—Minter Dial, multiple award-winning author of *You Lead* and *Heartificial Empathy*, professional speaker and elevator

"New tools, timeless truths. Schaffer's *Digital Threads* isn't just another marketing playbook—it's a paradigm shift. While everyone else is chasing the latest shiny object, Schaffer's weaving a tapestry of digital strategy that's both innovative and grounded in marketing fundamentals. His SES Framework? Like Rosetta Stone for decoding the post-pandemic digital maze. The digital marketing revolution is here, and Schaffer does a brilliant job of bringing order to the seemingly overwhelming chaos. This one deserves to make your 'must read' list."

—Amanda Russell, marketer and author of *The Influencer Code*

"*Digital Threads* by Neal Schaffer is an essential read for digital marketers looking to maximize their content's impact. Schaffer expertly guides readers through the efficient creation and repurposing of digital assets, leveraging AI-driven tools and platform-specific strategies to enhance reach and engagement. With practical insights on content repurposing, AI usage, and marketing automation, this book empowers marketers to sustain visibility and achieve long-term success. Highlighting real-world examples, Schaffer demonstrates the power of a well-crafted content strategy in the ever-evolving digital landscape. A must-have for anyone aiming to stay ahead in digital marketing."

—**Andy Lambert, Senior Manager, Product, Adobe and author of *SOCIAL 3.0***

"*Digital Threads* is an essential read for small businesses and entrepreneurs wanting to harness big brand strategies on a tight budget. Brimming with practical advice and clear, step-by-step frameworks, it demystifies digital marketing to help you grow your business with ease."

—**Matt Navarra, social media consultant and founder of Geekout**

"In today's rapidly evolving business landscape, a digital-first approach is no longer optional—it's essential for survival. *Digital Threads* provides the insights and expertise you need to navigate this transformation and thrive. A well-researched and timely read."

—**Pam Didner, author of *Global Content Marketing*, *Effective Sales Enablement*, and *The Modern AI Marketer***

"Neal Schaffer has once again delivered a masterclass in digital marketing with *Digital Threads*. His insights into the evolving landscape of social media, search engines, and email marketing are invaluable for anyone looking to navigate the complexities of modern marketing. Neal's practical advice and strategic approach make this book a must-read for businesses of all sizes. It's not just a guide; it's a roadmap to achieving lasting success in the digital age."

—Jon Ferrara, Founder and CEO of Nimble Inc.

"Neal Schaffer does it again! *Digital Threads* is the reference every small business and entrepreneur needs in our digital-first world. If you're lost about what to do, this book will be your new best friend."

—Carla Johnson, innovation architect, keynote speaker, and author

"If you're bewildered by the growing maze of AI tools, social media channels, and things to do, this book is your salvation. Neal has put together a modern and comprehensive overview for the small business owner, filled with 70 practical exercises to help you do digital right."

—Dennis Yu, CTO of Are You Googleable and co-author of ***The Definitive Guide to TikTok Advertising***

"A must read for anyone trying to figure out the overwhelming and complex world of digital marketing. Neal does a fantastic job of simplifying what is possible, explaining how everything fits together, and how to work out exactly what to focus on."

—Amy Woods, Founder and CEO of Content 10x

"Neal is without a doubt one of the smartest marketing minds I know, and *Digital Threads* showcases his exceptional expertise and innovative thinking. His practical insights inspire marketers (like me!) to confidently navigate every aspect of marketing. I keep him close in my orbit because not only is he lovely, but I continually learn actionable insights for myself and my clients. As a visual learner, I appreciate how Neal illustrates concepts, making them easier to digest and remember. Whether you're a beginner or a seasoned professional, you'll find valuable tips that will help you achieve outstanding results."

—Phil Pallen, brand strategist and author, *AI For Small Business*

"More than just a one-time read, this book is destined to become a well-worn, dog-eared companion—an invaluable resource you'll keep close at hand."

—Andrew Jenkins, CEO, Volterra

DIGITAL
THREADS

DIGITAL THREADS

The Small Business and
Entrepreneur Playbook for
Digital First Marketing

NEAL SCHAFFER

© 2024 Neal Schaffer

All rights reserved. No part of this publication may be reproduced, distributed, or transmitted in any form or by any means, including but not limited to digital, electronic, mechanical, photocopying, recording, or other methods, without the prior written permission of the publisher, except in the case of brief quotations embodied in critical reviews and certain other noncommercial uses permitted by copyright law.

Prohibited Use: This book's content may not be used or incorporated into any large language models, machine learning models, AI training datasets, or similar technologies without the explicit written consent of the author. Unauthorized use of this content for such purposes is strictly prohibited.

Published by PDCA Social
https://nealschaffer.com

ISBN 979-8-9906127-3-0 (eBook)
ISBN 979-8-9906127-4-7 (paperback)
ISBN 979-8-9906127-5-4 (hardcover)
ISBN 979-8-9906127-6-1 (audio)

First Edition: October 2024

Disclaimer: This book is intended to provide educational information on the subjects discussed. It is sold with the understanding that the author and publisher are not engaged in rendering legal, accounting, or other professional services. If legal advice or other expert assistance is required, the services of a competent professional should be sought.

The strategies, tips, and tools discussed in this book are based on the author's personal experience and knowledge in the field of digital marketing. They are not intended to guarantee that readers will achieve the same or similar results. The author and publisher disclaim any warranties (express or implied), merchantability, or fitness for any particular purpose. The author and publisher shall in no event be held liable for any loss or other damages, including but not limited to special, incidental, consequential, or other damages.

As always, with anything in business and life, your mileage may vary. What works for one may not work for all. Take what you can use, adapt it to your own context, and always test and refine for the best results in your specific situation.

Remember, the digital landscape is ever evolving. While the strategies and insights shared in this workbook are based on the latest trends and practices at the time of writing, the world of digital marketing is always changing. Keep learning, stay flexible, and adapt to new developments to stay ahead in the game.

THANK YOU FOR PURCHASING DIGITAL THREADS!

As a special bonus, please download your free copy of the electronic version of the Digital Threads companion workbook to help you internalize all my advice here:

nealschaffer.com/digitalthreadsworkbook

Other Books by Neal Schaffer

Windmill Networking: Understanding, Leveraging & Maximizing LinkedIn

Maximizing LinkedIn for Sales and Social Media Marketing

Maximize Your Social

The Age of Influence

Maximizing LinkedIn for Business Growth

Contents

Introduction xix

Part One
Begin

1. The New Digital Landscape of Today 3
2. The New Marketing Infrastructure of Today 12

Part Two
Rethinking It All

3. Rethink Search 27
4. Rethink Email 39
5. Rethink Social Media 47

Part Three
Begin (Again)

6. Be Found 61
7. Be in Touch 74
8. Be Seen 88

Part Four
Optimize

9. Build Connections 105
10. Build Paths 118
11. Build Visibility 128

Part Five
Allow Growth

12. Grow Content 143
13. Grow Conversations 152
14. Grow Influence 165

Part Six
Scale

15. Scale Influence — 179
16. Scale Budget — 193
17. PDCA — 205
18. Scale People — 216
19. AI & Marketing — 224
20. Scale Technology — 242

Conclusion — 253
Acknowledgments — 260
Endnotes — 263
Index — 271
About the Author — 279

Introduction

"How the heck am I supposed to promote my new book from my home office in lockdown?"

Like you, I also struggled with juggling all the aspects of digital marketing to grow my business.

My journey of writing this book began when my last book, *The Age of Influence*, was published on March 17, 2020. That week saw most of the world grind to a halt with the pandemic. Two days later, my hometown and all of California would go into mandatory lockdown.

Our post-pandemic lives will never go back to how they were. One lasting result has been the acceleration of the digital consumer. This brings new challenges for established companies. It has also led to a landscape full of opportunities for those entrepreneurs and small businesses who smartly pivot.

The Covid-19 restrictions affected companies and consumers in different ways. Companies could no longer count on people to come to their stores and were forced to shift more to the digital realm. Communicating with customers and potential clients became a purely online, digital-first proposition. On the other side of the transaction, consumers were engaging with companies in new ways, while turning their time and resources to be more present online.

These shifts in consumer culture won't go back into the box. They're loose. They're already spurring the next change in culture. Social media had been around for well over a decade before the pandemic lockdowns. As people, we had already become accustomed to communicating there. As companies, we had acclimated to it. The lockdown came at the time of TikTok's emergence—perhaps playing into it. Now we've become used to consuming what marketers commonly call short-form videos. Authentic and raw content is in. Aspirational content is out. Influencers like to be called content creators now.

Those shifts in the culture presented challenges to every business, including my own.

Because of the emerging lockdowns, I had to find other ways to promote my new book. Book tours were out. My usual speaking engagements were canceled. Some moved online, but the engagement and ability to connect with attendees was not the same.

At the time of that first lockdown, I had advised and taught others for over a decade on how to use social media for marketing. The pandemic coinciding with the release of my book meant I had to re-examine my marketing strategies. I realized I hadn't covered my own digital bases. In fact, apart from social media, they'd been long neglected.

Without the ability to meet people face to face and engage with them at conferences, I had no choice but to adopt a Digital First approach. I define the concept Digital First marketing as a mindset that forces us to think about how we can build and grow our business if we had to do it 100 percent digitally. In a virtual world with a virtual store, which is what some retail outlets felt like during the pandemic, how would you promote your business? You would primarily, if not solely, conduct your marketing online. This places digital marketing as the first step, not an afterthought to adapt to. This isn't to prepare for another pandemic: it's about adapting to the digital reality of today.

From my home office in Southern California, I had no choice but to explore other strategies I hadn't seriously considered before to promote my book. This gave me a chance to see the world of marketing in a new and refreshing way. While some marketers might have been jaded by "old school" digital marketing, such as search engine optimization and email marketing, I found a value in them that had been forgotten with the emergence of social media.

Clients that I worked with over that time were in a similar position. After reading *The Age of Influence*, they wanted to reset their own marketing to capitalize on social media and leverage the power of influencer marketing. In many cases, they were not in the position to do that. They just didn't have the marketing infrastructure in place with the other essential tools of a strategy to deal with a Digital First world. Some were using old strategies to play catch up. It was like trying to build upon an already unstable Jenga tower. Trying to throw a rope across a river to make a bridge without making sure the footing was secure. The foundation was simply not there to make a powerful push with newer strategies. The new landscape doesn't allow that.

This is when I also realized that there was an order of digital marketing tactics that would allow for the greatest growth. There was an inherent synergy when one step was taken before the next, that they naturally "prepped" the next stage for success. The concept behind Digital Threads—and how the chapters would be laid out in this book —was born.

Businesses were looking for a shortcut to a digital presence. They wanted to build up one marketing channel while lacking presence on other essential channels. This would only lead to imbalance and hurt the overall effectiveness of their efforts.

All my Fractional CMO clients are different. They range from solopreneurs to small business owners to executives at larger companies. Some are content creators looking to expand into entrepreneurship. Others are established industry leaders looking for a way to expand their reach and understand that what worked yesterday won't work tomorrow. There's no cookie-cutter approach to such a wide range of needs, over a wide range of industries and audiences. What is common is the need to communicate effectively on many levels with their customers and prospects. Through this work, I realized that executing these things in a specific order is crucial for maximum effectiveness.

When clients came to me, I felt like a doctor diagnosing what was missing, what was causing the imbalance and illness. I would prescribe the course of action to take. There was an engagement deficiency. When they thought posting more would help, the proper solution was working more on integrating their message across platforms. Or they could engage their email list. Or perhaps they had neglected building an email list. I would find gaps in what the clients wanted to achieve and the digital avenues they were using to get there. Many would come to me with a desire to do influencer marketing; they'd read my book and seen the power it could generate. But when we dug deeper into the objectives, I could guide them to other digital marketing channels that would get them quicker to their desired reach and audience.

There is not one quick-fix solution to all your marketing problems. By just working with influencers, or engaging on TikTok, or injecting ad spend, you will only address one part of your issue. To be most effective, there are multiple Digital Threads that need to be understood, implemented, and ideally woven together for maximum impact. When you engage all of them meaningfully, and with intent, then your digital marketing strategy will be strong. Doing them in the correct order will make your strategy even more impactful.

The world and consumers have changed. The channels for truly communicating your message have also changed. These are the Digital Threads that hold the secrets for growth through digital marketing.

This book will focus on the specifics of each digital thread that will determine the destiny of your Digital First marketing. While you might be tempted to skip ahead, I urge you to read in its intended flow so that you also make sure that you don't have any gaps of your own in your marketing infrastructure.

I have also invested the time to put together a companion workbook featuring over 70 exercises that will help you brainstorm ideas, internalize what you learn in this book, and ultimately effectively implement what I teach you so that your business can reap the benefits of Digital Threads. You can download the workbook for free here:

https://nealschaffer.com/digitalthreadsworkbook

Disclaimer:

I sometimes share the company names of tools in this book because I use them, have used them, or have had clients use them. I try to provide you with options to ensure that I mention perceived market leaders based on my research and experience here as well.

For many of the tools I talk about in this book, I am also an affiliate or have been gifted access to their technology. No one has paid me any money to mention their tools in this book. I write about them simply because I find them to be the best tools available.

Part One
Begin

"The first step towards getting somewhere is to decide you're not going to stay where you are."

— J. P. Morgan

Chapter 1
The New Digital Landscape of Today

"Everyone has a plan until they get punched in the mouth."

— Mike Tyson

The marketing landscape is always in motion. It is always shifting. Sometimes these shifts move slowly, like tectonic plates. New media, new platforms, new strategies, and new audiences are always emerging. Other times, it's faster. A complete ground shift that causes us to reconsider our footing and the wider landscape we stand on.

Businesses are always playing catch-up with the needs and habits of their customers. Without aggressively and constantly changing your approach, you leave money on the table and risk losing share to your competitors. This is as true for marketing as it is for other aspects of business.

These Digital Threads are not an option in modern marketing. They represent the new playbook that empowers successful businesses today.

The cost of not adapting is the risk of being left behind in what worked yesterday. You might maintain your sales volume, but that often comes at a cost of losing market share and visibility. Sometimes it's a setback. Sometimes it's bigger. Even famous empires have fallen this way. Sears ruled the mail order world to where their name was synonymous with catalog ordering. When the Internet wound its web everywhere, Sears failed to shift to the online world, leaving the space where Amazon took root. Blockbuster suffered a similar fate when they failed to adapt to the possibilities of online streaming. Consumer preferences and new technologies also caused Kodak, a once household name synonymous with cameras, to be barely remembered today. Remember how dominant Motorola, Nokia, and Blackberry were in cell phones? The list goes on.

The Acceleration of Change

The Covid-19 pandemic saw an acceleration to the shifts that were already underway in modern consumer culture. Technology was in place for more remote work and online meetings. The shift to online shopping over the previous two decades meant that infrastructure and consumer trust were both in place for the shift to a larger digital economy over the pandemic. Trust in online research had grown on the back of the shift to being comfortable on social media. With so much time in lockdown, people shifted to consuming even more online content, and there was more of it, in more engaging formats, to consume.

The shift was already on the way. It was in 2019, the year before the pandemic, when digital marketing spend overtook traditional marketing spend[1]. In just five years (2017 to 2022), the percentage of marketing budgets spent on digital advertising globally increased from 39.7 percent to 53.9 percent[2]. Part of this shift was the change in budgets during the pandemic. But it was a movement that was already happening.

Over the first two-plus decades of the 21st century, we have all changed how we communicate. We have changed what content we consume and how we consume it. In the wild days of dial-up internet in the 1990s, we were told to be careful what we shared online. We hid our addresses and real names. Now we openly share every moment of our lives. While online, we upload photos, share our opinions, and tell our friends all we are doing. We order everything from groceries to clothing and electronics to be delivered right to our door. We use apps to pay friends—and often share our transactions in public (e.g., Venmo).

The infrastructure was in place to make this future viable. The pandemic made it a necessity for the present.

This speed of change and of transition, of acceptance in the digital world, doesn't even touch on the tremendous growth of generative AI since the lockdowns have ended.

Opportunities and Challenges

Like any other period of time, changes bring both challenges and/or opportunities, depending on if you see a glass being half full or half empty.

This changed landscape means that you can now communicate with and ship directly to customers. But it's not so straightforward.

Consumers are now more skeptical. 99 percent of consumers today research products before buying them, and 87 percent do so regularly or always, a number that has increased compared to pre-pandemic behavior[3]. Consumers find more information through reviews online, through social media posts, YouTube reviews, and, yes, even TikTok videos. Rather than going to stores to look at a product, the post-pandemic consumer will engage other digital and online avenues to make their decision. And even when they are in store, a majority of shoppers will go online to read reviews[4]. The consumer's approach has truly become Digital First. Our online presence persists even when we are offline.

The opportunity to engage in a Digital First approach puts your brand or business in a strong position right in front of the consumer. The challenge is to do this in an authentic and meaningful way that actually engages your customer.

If you are still doing things in the pre-pandemic way for no other reason than that's how it's always been done, then you're already behind. Jumping into social media marketing or relying solely on influencers to transition into the post-pandemic reality is not enough. You need to establish a solid foundation in this new landscape. Just throwing money at it won't suffice.

The argument parallels the shift to working at home. Nimble companies will take advantage of this shift. They will find opportunities to enrich their team. Some will take longer. Others will lack the imagination to make this new reality part of their infrastructure, and they risk losing their workforce to organizations able to engage in the new reality for their employees.

This new landscape is unfamiliar. It takes a new outlook to adapt, but therein lies the opportunity. You need a Digital First approach to leverage all the different opportunities that the Digital Threads give you to engage in the buyer's journey.

Don't Throw It All Out

Building new infrastructure in an unfamiliar landscape should still follow the principles that have proven effective in the past. They just won't work in the same way as before.

I've often said that *"social media replaces nothing yet complements everything."* This philosophy can also apply to the well-known marketing framework of the 4 Ps and digital media.

The 4 Ps cover those workhorses of marketing—product, price, place, and promotion. In a Digital First approach, the first two of these remain the same. Of course, there's some change in product when you can adapt—such as offering unique digital products like subscriptions besides one-off purchases. At their core, those two don't change too much.

Meeting your customers in the right place is essential. Now that place, in a Digital First world, is primarily and ever-increasingly online. Sure, there are more e-commerce marketplaces where you can promote your product in. But it is more than that. There are social media platforms and search engines. With TikTok or YouTube, social media is quickly becoming its own search engine, and with TikTok Shop, its own marketplace, generating an estimated $20 billion in sales in 2023[5]. We still go to retail stores or a trendy temporary physical pop-up shop, but once again, these are also primarily being promoted digitally.

The biggest mindset shift for most businesses, however, must take place regarding the final "P"—promotion.

Traditionally, people have looked at promotion as a one-to-many affair. The thinking was to blast your messages through TV, radio, magazines, newspapers, and even digital ads to disrupt viewers hoping to gain eyeballs and sales. Much has been said of how disruptive traditional marketing has been. This has led the modern consumer to fast-forward where possible during ad breaks and try their best to divert their attention away from that very disruption. The message is an ad. It sticks out, and it's not what the consumer willingly wants to consume.

Obviously, this attention-seeking approach still works to some extent in many of the traditional channels. But in social media, which is one of the most important channels in digital marketing, this approach will often simply be a waste of your time and budget. Even when it appears to be performing, diverting your efforts into other Digital Threads might have yielded better results for the same budget.

Not that paid social, or paid media via social media advertising, does not work. It is an important digital thread. But it is not a shortcut. Every marketer knows that promoting to your customers, or even a warm audience, will always produce better results than advertising to a cold audience. This importance of relationship manifests itself in other ways. The most effective type of marketing for centuries has been—and continues to be—relationship-driven word-of-mouth marketing. There is no better place for that to happen at scale than in social media.

While it happens on rare occasion, your social media advertisements will not generate the word-of-mouth at scale that organic content can. That was never their intention.

There has always been a relationship aspect to promotion. The online world means that those relationships are now digital. It's with people who are in different places around the world—giving you the opportunity to connect and scale outside your own local influence. The promotion is done with social media—the town halls and meeting places of the post-pandemic world.

New Rules for Relationships

To be effective in communicating your message in a Digital First world, you need to build relationships not just with people, but with algorithms—another critical digital thread to master. Search engines and social media networks are driven by algorithms. It is essential, then, to understand how to best put your content in terms that help the algorithm show it to the right people.

In the 1890s, Almon Brown Strowger was working as an undertaker and noticed he was losing business. He traced the cause of this to the phone operator in Indiana, where he was working. The phone operator was the wife of his competitor. Anytime there was a call that came through and asked to be connected to an undertaker service, the phone operator would divert the call to her husband a town over, instead of Strowger. That would be an influential relationship to have, and it affected Strowger's business so much that he, with the help of his nephew and others, created the first automatic electromechanical telephone exchange[6].

Unlike Strowger, you're not in the position to cut out the middleman—the algorithm that shows your competitor's content. Instead, you must understand—and embrace—the way it works.

Analog Skills in the Digital World

Another thing that I have been saying for a decade regarding social media applies equally to Digital First marketing as well:

> *"New tools, old rules."*

While the shift is to the Digital First world, communicating to people, even online, is most effective when we communicate as people. As humans. This is even truer with the emergence of bots and artificial intelligence that can easily create content. Trying to create something that will go viral is not about making something shiny and digital for the masses. It is about wanting to communicate with one person genuinely and effectively. Naturally, we hope it goes beyond that one person to many.

During the pandemic, when we couldn't communicate face-to-face or in person, consumers moved online. They still wanted a human interaction. Consumers purchased more from those companies who could connect earnestly. It was communicating on a level that worked on an individual level. The numbers reflect this.

- 90 percent of people buy from brands they follow on social media[7].
- 63 percent of consumers state that the quality of customer service on social media significantly affects their brand loyalty[8].
- 47 percent of consumers have made a purchase through social media[9].
- 79 percent of people say UGC, or content generated by social media users, highly affects their purchasing decisions[10].

Another aspect that bears mentioning here: the need to be more relatable and authentic, especially when trying to win the hearts (and wallets) of younger customers. A viewer of one of my recent livestreams reminded me of this aspect when they commented I seemed more approachable in my work-from-home t-shirt apparel than in the black suit and royal blue Brooks Brothers dress shirt I use on my social media profiles and website.

When we stop thinking about social media as a place to promote but as an excellent venue to relate, you will understand the potential that this digital thread can have for your business.

The takeaway is that we need to develop ways to stay human while being in a digital world.

So, are the 4 Ps—product, place, price, and promotion—still relevant?

Absolutely!

And so are the other tenets of marketing, but since the consumer—and how and where they consume content—has progressed, so must we.

The place to meet your customers is online. It is Digital First. And it is on social media. Promoting a product is not about simply putting your product online. That is not enough. You need to work with the algorithm to be found. You need to engage on social media platforms to join conversations and use social media the way it is intended to be used.

Digital Threads is about adapting these principles for the post-Covid world. It is about weaving together the tools at our disposal to make the fabric of your marketing flexible and hard-wearing.

Approaching your marketing with a Digital First philosophy does not mean throwing the old marketing tenets out the window. These fundamental principles are integral for a good reason—they've stood the test of time. There are trends that come and go, but principles underpin marketing through all climates and landscapes.

But if there was ever a time to pivot for the survival and renewed growth of your business, now is it.

Key Takeaways:

- The groundwork was in place for what sped up during the pandemic—a move to a Digital First approach.
- While the core principles of marketing remain, the landscape of interaction and its locations have undergone a permanent transformation.

- The essential ways of communicating between people have not changed, but the places and methods have. It is now a Digital First world.

Companion Workbook Exercises:

- 1.1 | How Much Do You Buy Online?
- 1.2 | How Much Research Do You Do Online?

Chapter 2
The New Marketing Infrastructure of Today

"They always say time changes things, but you actually have to change them yourself."

— Andy Warhol

As you well know, the digital marketing landscape is vast and seemingly always developing. You can easily get lost in the various options you have to grow your business with digital marketing.

There are more than just a handful of social media platforms to stay on top of. There are the websites and apps. Besides blogs and podcasts, communication platforms like Discord and Telegram groups are available. And don't forget about email. Or is SMS an option? What about WhatsApp? Staying on top of the myriad of different ways people interact with each other can be overwhelming.

I have worked over the years to simplify what Digital First marketing should look like so that it can be more implementable by my clients. It's simple: The easier something is to teach and remember, the more it will be implementable.

As a result, let's analyze the traditional marketing funnel, Digital

First marketing containers, and ultimately the SES Framework, which will serve as the organizing principle for this book.

The Funnel

No one is going to be introduced to your brand and become your customer tomorrow. It takes multiple touches to know, to trust, and to move down the buyer's journey to ultimately becoming a customer.

Google defines this research stage before someone becomes a customer as the Zero Moment of Truth (ZMOT) stage. In fact, Google has its own answer as to how many touches it takes to convert someone into becoming a customer based on their own research:

Before making a purchase, a buyer requires seven hours of contact over 11 touch points in four different locations[1].

These "hours" are often represented by time spent reading your content, watching your videos, and engaging with you in social media. The locations can be best thought of as different marketing channels.

So there is a process that we need to go through to lead customers on this path toward conversion. Traditionally, marketers represent this process with the AIDA marketing funnel, a concept credited to an American advertising agency founder, E. St. Elmo Lewis, that dates to the 19th century[2].

If you have ever read a marketing book or taken a class back in your university days, you are certain to have seen a visual representation of this timeless funnel concept or one of many variations of it:

TRADITIONAL AIDA MARKETING FUNNEL

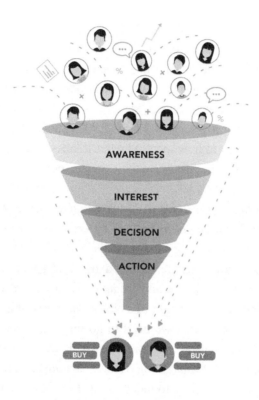

Figure 2.1

Just as there's a marketing funnel, I would say that there is also an equally important digital relationship funnel. Developing deeper relationships with prospects and customers should be the goal of any digital marketing.

The funnel of digital relationships shows how you want to lead people to grow your business. The aim is to build awareness, grow trust, and drive sales.

THE FUNNEL OF DIGITAL RELATIONSHIPS

Figure 2.2

At the top of the funnel, we have the public. Once people notice you, they move from the public into the region of those who know you as they begin their journey, the one that Google refers to as that Zero Moment of Truth. When you build a relationship with a customer, they move through knowing about you, liking and trusting your company or product, and making a purchase. But the funnel doesn't stop there. After the sale, the aim should be to turn the customer into an advocate, an important concept missing from the original 19th-century funnel.

Marketing is about relationships. The savvy Digital First marketer knows it is not just relationships with people—with customers and colleagues or industry leaders—but also with algorithms that drive the conversion.

Developing your digital marketing strategy involves looking at the relationships you have across the digital landscape. Focusing on these with intent and strategy will guide those who don't know you into trusting you, then converting them to sales. Some relationships affect others—and a strong relationship with your customers will affect your relationship with the algorithm.

(Marketing) Containers

I realized early in my career that when creating a strategy, deciding on what NOT to focus on was as important as determining what would be the focus of the plan.

The same is true for your digital marketing.

I felt overwhelmed by the different options I had for promoting *The Age of Influence*. Then I realized that by knowing the limits of what is possible, I can simplify my work in digital marketing. I only had to focus on these virtual "containers," each of which held a digital marketing channel, to be successful and realize the potential.

Figure 2.3

These are the only six containers of digital marketing that you need to focus your energy on to ultimately be successful. These are all integral to you and your brand building awareness among consumers, getting them to know you, building trust, making a sale, and then deepening the relationship.

Some containers have multiple sub-containers because of the channel's complexity. Each sub-container is like a self-contained piece of the puzzle.

The 6 Fundamental Digital Marketing Containers

1. Website

It's nearly impossible to be successful in today's digital age without something digital to drive people towards. It's your storefront on the digital Main Street of today. If this isn't your website or online store, then it's your app. Whatever it is, it's the keystone of your branding and your digital identity.

There are exceptions here, like those who sell products purely through Amazon or even small business owners on Etsy. Those companies have their Amazon or Etsy store as their core online presence.

2. Search Engine(s)

You have a digital store, so you want to be found. How to do that? By showing up where people are looking for you: search engines.

Like other marketing containers, search engines include both organic and paid approaches to be found.

Don't just look for the obvious giants here. While Google might have a majority share around the world, there are countries where Yahoo (Japan) or Baidu (China) might be the first search engine that people go to. In certain circumstances, like customers looking directly for a product to buy, they will bypass Google altogether and go straight to Amazon or another favorite e-commerce marketplace.

But wait, there's more!

Social media is becoming a default search engine for many as well, especially for Gen Z, who increasingly use TikTok as their primary source of information. For others, it might be YouTube.

Each social network possesses a search functionality, regardless of whether people use social media as a search engine or not, making it a type of search engine.

3. Email Marketing

You built a website.
Check.
You understand you need to be found by search engines. You create some web pages and perhaps experiment with Google Ads.
Check.
The battle has only begun. What do you do with the 99+ percent of website visitors who don't buy the first time they come to your website?

This is where email, the most under-appreciated marketing channel, comes into play. And it absolutely shines.

You must keep in touch with customers. There is no guarantee that our website will appear in the same search engine result again. Or that the potential customer will return for a follow-up contact. Or that our content will appear in the social media feeds of our prospects or customers. Having a direct line to them through email helps you build rapport and guide the conversation down the buyer's journey.

The email list is also the only communication you can control. It is you who owns the email list. You don't own social media platforms. You don't have control over the algorithms that change so frequently. And that extends to search engine algorithms too. We only have control over our website and email lists.

4. Content Marketing

Google said that our customers need 11 interactions and seven hours of engagement, so what are we to do with this? We understand the funnel, but what is the process of moving people through it?

Content is the currency of digital media. It is necessary for a multitude of reasons and will become something your organization will have to be creating a lot of. Content marketing is one of six marketing containers, but it is a channel that exists to serve all the other containers.

Let's first define this often-misunderstood term, and have the godfather of content marketing himself, Joe Pulizzi, lay down the foundation for our understanding:

> *"Content marketing is a strategic marketing approach focused on creating and distributing valuable, relevant, and consistent content to attract and retain a clearly-defined audience—and, ultimately, to drive profitable customer action[3]."*

From an SEO perspective, your content can help you rank for both branded (your brand or company name) and non-branded (keywords that describe your product or service) search queries. This content might be in the form of blog content, product pages, or even responding to frequently asked questions about your products and services in a dedicated section.

It doesn't stop there. You need to communicate with those who have signed up to receive marketing communication from you via email. You will also need content for both organic and paid social media.

5. Social Media Marketing

People spend nearly 40 percent of their time online on social media[4]. Another way to consider the ubiquitous nature of social media today is to understand that people overwhelmingly consume it on mobile devices.

If you are looking for a mobile marketing strategy, start with your own social media presence.

Social media marketing breaks down into organic and paid. There is still a shine around social media marketing that makes it a leading trend. This, in my experience, leads a lot of companies and businesses to overlook the other tools at their disposal in a Digital First world.

Don't get me wrong: social media plays an integral part in Digital First marketing. It is, however, only one of six digital marketing containers.

6. Influencer Marketing

Influencer marketing continues to be the most powerful, yet least understood, of these marketing channels. It is not about paying for shoutouts or amplification of your brand's product through those with large followings on social media.

It is about inciting word-of-mouth marketing through the cumulative voice of others who already trust you or those with whom you selectively develop a successful relationship.

Effective influencer marketing begins with tapping into the voices who already have brand affinity for you. These individuals are those who know, like, and trust your brand. It's a wide group of people, including employees, customers, fans, advocates, and other external influencers you want to convert into becoming advocates because of their branding and community alignment. We can work with influencers over social media, content marketing, SEO, podcasts, email marketing, and so on. In such a way, influencer marketing is like content marketing because it serves multiple containers.

And that is it.

To simplify Digital First marketing, everything I discuss in this book will relate to one of these six containers or channels and the many Digital Threads that weave them all together.

The SES Framework

Every business is unique. Every marketplace and audience needs different things. There's no cookie-cutter approach that will work everywhere. But there are things in common, threads that seem to weave into the same concepts over and over.

Making it work with the six containers above, however simplified, can still be overwhelming. That is why I have further streamlined these concepts into what I call the SES Framework.

What does SES stand for, you ask?

It's quite simple: Search. Email. Social.

These are the three workhorses of your Digital First strategy. In this streamlined version, we see that each point covers the relationships that develop through the funnel of digital relationships:

Figure 2.4

We begin with the public, who find out about us through a search engine (the first S) or social media (the second S). Once they know us, we hope to continue to keep in touch with them primarily through the digital channel that we own, email (the E), but also engage with them in social media in hoping it attracts additional engagement.

Once we have them as customers, email and social media allow us to keep in continued touch with them in a deeper relationship. When customers become advocates, it is in social media where we will see the biggest impact—and influencer programs can help speed up this movement.

You'll notice that some marketing channels, such as search and email, can only facilitate relationship-building at certain stages. Social media can inherently affect every level of the funnel because it is a relationship-building platform.

Marketing has always been about relationships. Connecting with consumers. Connecting with other people along your chain.

In a Digital First world, relationships with people are still at the core. We now also have relationships with algorithms to consider. The focus is not on deceiving the algorithms. It's not about any illusion or trick. It's finding the best way to work with the algorithms in an authentically holistic way.

Each platform has its own demands and needs. Their algorithm gives each platform its own personality. That's why each platform continues to exist. They give their consumers what they want in different ways than the other platforms. Finding the best way for you to connect with the platform, to make your content the type of content the algorithm wants to show, is the holistic way to engage across search and social media.

Do not fear the algorithm. Embrace it. And to quote many YouTube experts on the subject:

Algorithm = Audience

The SES Framework in Action

At the beginning, there are people who don't know about you, or perhaps there is still a large delta in your total addressable market (TAM). How will they find out about you? Through search engines. Your products will appear in search engines. Search engines will find your content. You will develop brand awareness through search engines. This includes not only Google and Bing, but any search engine that exists. This includes everywhere people search for things—YouTube, Amazon, TikTok, Instagram, other social media platforms, other online shopping platforms—these are all search engines.

How will those platforms help people notice you? That is your search strategy.

If we are lucky enough to attract people to our website, they might not become a customer or convert into becoming a lead immediately. How can we develop a relationship if people leave our website?

That's the role of email. Can we encourage or *incentivize* them to sign up for our newsletter, or other communication? If so, then we'll have permission to converse with them. They've opted to receive our messages. Now they know about us, so there's brand affinity. The power of email gives us the ability to hone and develop this relationship.

Even if a consumer doesn't open all our emails, if they open the average of 15 to 22 percent of emails sent across various industries[5], they are still engaging with our content at a rate higher than in social media, where the average engagement rate for a piece of content on Instagram, Facebook, and X (formerly Twitter) are all well below 1 percent[6]. Even just seeing our emails, seeing information in the subject line, communicates to potential clients about a new offer or expansion. This captures people's attention.

This final "S" covers paid and organic social media, paid ads, and customer advocacy efforts, and extends to influencer marketing as a powerful way to leverage other voices to augment your social media efforts. Some brands have transformed their organic social media marketing into influencer marketing, while also incorporating influencer-generated content into their paid social media efforts.

Social media can get your message and brand exposed, but you need the content. You need the other things first. Social media is not a magic solution to everything—it is part of your whole Digital First strategy. That is why I intentionally begin with search, follow with email, and will keep social third in the pecking order of the SES Framework.

There is a logical order to this that the framework is based on. It's a tightly woven strategy of different threads. Putting one piece in place is necessary for the next to work. We set the pillars of our bridge before grounding the cables and suspension. Without the proper foundation, the threads will come loose and your entire Digital First fabric will become frayed and weak.

For instance, you can't engage with external influencers if your own social media channels are a ghost town. Influencers will tag your social profile in their posts, only exposing and amplifying the fact that you don't "get" social media. Even if your social media house is in order, if you don't have a robust system to capture the emails of those who don't convert on your website, you have wasted your efforts. These are examples of why there is an order for things to be done to be most effective, with the strength of the system built in.

Key Takeaways:

- The six fundamental digital marketing containers help simplify the scope of your Digital First marketing activities.
- The strengths of digital marketing are in three threads—search, email, and social.
- Develop each thread, ensuring they build upon and complement one another in a specific order.

Companion Workbook Exercises:

- 2.1 | Google's Zero Moment of Truth
- 2.2 | Internalizing the AIDA Funnel
- 2.3 | Analyzing the 6 Marketing Containers
- 2.4 | Analyzing the SES Framework

Part Two

Rethinking It All

"One's destination is never a place, but a new way of seeing things."

— Henry Miller

The three key elements of the SES Framework are measures you're probably already doing for your marketing strategy. There's no need to preach the importance of undertaking search engine optimization, building an email database, or finding ways for your message to work on social media.

In a Digital First landscape, we need to look anew at these strategies, some of which have been around for decades. We need fresh eyes on these tools to see the way they work now in a world where digital is not an afterthought. It's not a *part* of your strategy. It *is* the strategy.

The SES Framework is a way to bring the Digital Threads of this new digital landscape together. Just as Alexander Fleming looked at mold growing on dishes differently and saw the potential for penicillin, and just as Willie Kizart used a broken amplifier to pioneer distortion in music production, we need to look at the tools we've been using and see how we can make them fulfill their potential from a different angle.

These elements are familiar to us. But the way we use them needs a fresh approach. We need to see them in a new light. And begin again.

Chapter 3
Rethink Search

"From east of the East-est to west of the West-est we've searched the whole world just to bring you the best-est."

— Dr. Seuss

Search engines exist for one purpose: to give you the best answer to what you are looking for accurately, so that you will return next time and hopefully click on advertisements along the way.

These days "search" means so much more than merely appearing in search engines. You want to be found in more than just Google or Bing. A search engine is anywhere people will find you. It's where people move from the first step of the funnel—noticing you—to the second, developing an interest in you. That means that YouTube is a search engine. Social media sites such as TikTok and Instagram are search engines. Even Amazon is a search engine. It's a digital environment where people can find what you put there and then guide themselves further along the funnel toward knowing and trusting you.

If marketing is about relationships, in a Digital First world that fundamental principle includes relationships with algorithms.

Long-Term Discoverability

If you can't be everywhere, and you don't want to waste more time than necessary in content creation, then you must be strategic and lean into content that is discoverable long-term.

Blog content, podcasts, and YouTube videos have a longer shelf life in search engines. That simply means that they are discoverable for a longer period than most other types of content.

The discoverability and longevity of content on those networks far outweighs social media content. It is said that the "half-life" of social media content, the time that it takes a post to receive half of its total engagement, ranges from an hour or two (X, Facebook) to a day or two (Instagram, LinkedIn). In contrast, the median age of the top-ranking URL in a search engine results page is somewhere between 3 and 5 years[1]. YouTube videos and podcasts will fall in between, making each of them an attractive option in terms of the value of longevity when compared to social media content.

When you stop focusing on long-term discoverable content and instead try to post to every social media site, you will find yourself on the dreaded hamster wheel of content. You'll keep creating content, trying to find what works, and that will take you away from your work. And, like a poor hamster on a wheel, you'll be chasing what's just ahead of you instead of what you really want.

That is why we begin content creation thinking of search engines first.

People need to find you, and to do so, find your content. That's why making your content discoverable where it has a long shelf life is your best chance to be found. Once they find your content through search engines, they will visit your website or your YouTube channel, or subscribe to your podcast. When the content is there and online, it stays there. When people come along and connect with you, then some will go back through your archives and catch up on content, "binge reading" the same way they might be binge watching on Netflix. For example, when I dive into a podcast, it's normal for me to listen to the very first episodes, even if they were from years ago, to catch up on what the podcast was covering and make sure I don't miss any nuggets.

When you create one piece of content focused on long-term discoverability that is unearthed via a search engine, it can open tens, hundreds, or even thousands of entry doors leading to your content and your business.

The Need for Evergreen

Evergreen trees are green and vibrant regardless of the season. Your content should be, too.

When thinking about creating content, we focus on those trends and happenings that are going on around us so we can connect. The question we should ask isn't what is trending now, but what might our potential customers be looking for in search engines we should appear for?

It's not about the latest wave we can ride. It's finding which wave has the best swell.

There is a time and a place to news-jack and talk about trends, and email and social media might be more appropriate for those transient subjects rather than targeting search.

Rethinking our approach to search means that we need to rethink our approach to creating content to cover our content bases in the search engines. We need to create content that will give search engines a reason to show our business in search results. We need to create content that is relevant after the latest wave has passed. And content that reaches deep. This is content for the long-term, content that is evergreen, and content that is aligned with the questions our intended audience is searching.

There is a term that helps us better understand this concept:

Search Demand

Anyone can publish any content they want online. That doesn't always mean that there's a demand for those who want to read it.

When I lived in Kyoto, I played drums in a Japanese pop-funk band named Jak-o'lan. No matter how great we thought our music was, if the managers of the various local live houses and clubs in Kyoto, and the nearby Osaka and Kobe, did not think that their audiences would be interested in our unique fusion of music, we simply could not play on their stage.

The role of the club manager is to sell more tickets. If we had some popularity—so that people were asking for us—and we could have filled the seats, our musical style might not have been as important.

Search engines are no different: You show your popularity through backlinks, a topic I will cover in Chapter 9, and this will help establish that your content will help satisfy the mission of the algorithm: a happy and satisfied reader.

These club managers were the gatekeepers between my band's music and our potential fans, just as search engines are the gatekeepers between your content and its intended audience.

There was another way to play those venues—pay for the tickets in advance that we would sell to our fans. In this way, the manager secured income from both a portion of the show's revenue and, presumably, a portion of the audience. That's analogous to Google Ads—paying to play, to be shown in front of people.

If my band wanted to build a larger following quickly, we might have to tweak our musical style to something that was trendier. Similarly, if we want to have our content found organically, we need to align our content with what people are searching for. We need to understand what the people are looking for when they should find our message. We need to align ourselves with Google's mission, because if we can't help Google serve their customers, they can't help us serve ours.

Once you have attracted your customers to your website and they have signed up to receive marketing communication from you, you can deliver more middle- and bottom-of-the-funnel content that might not have as large of a search demand. But at a minimum, your blog content should satisfy the broad content needs of your search engine audience.

When I work as a Fractional CMO, I trace the client's digital influence back to their blog. That content underscores their authority and drives other engagement. This isn't just a like on Facebook. It's engagement on your website that generates email signups, leads, and sales. Getting that content in front of the right reader is essential. When Google understands you know what you're talking about, that people come to you as an authority, then it boosts your other pages in the search engine algorithm. But the algorithm can't do it alone.

It is not a matter of "build it and they will come," as for every company I see successful with their SEO efforts, I see many others who are still playing baseball in their field of dreams.

To properly address the needs of search demand, we need to figure out what this demand is. And what topics we should create evergreen content around to get in front of our audience. This process is called keyword research.

Keyword Research

The problem that creators, entrepreneurs, and even larger companies often make is in keyword research, or lack thereof.

I have also fallen into this trap. I get excited about a blog post that could attract new clients, so I publish it, share it on social media, and even include it in my weekly newsletter. For those first few days, it might get some hits, and then...that's it. After a week, it gets little to no engagement. While there are many reasons this happens, the easiest way to explain it is that the content I wrote was simply not something people are searching for. It wasn't the algorithm's fault. There was no audience for it.

This is especially true in the advice that many "experts" give that "more is better." One that I commonly hear is that if we publish all our hundreds of podcast episodes as transcripts, we are feeding the search engine with more content and that will equal more traffic. What I have learned is the opposite: In terms of the relationship between content and search engines, more does not always equal more.

When people search, they're not searching for your blog headlines. They're not searching for the title of the podcast. No matter how well written your blog post is or how catchy your video title is, people are not searching for it.

People use search engines to do research or answer a question. The algorithm then does its best to show answers to that question that it thinks the searcher will appreciate. In a Digital First world, meeting your customers where they are doesn't just mean meeting them on social media. It means meeting them in the question that they want answered inside of search engines.

Your strategy is to tailor your content—and selection of keywords—to target to suit that question. What question do you want to be the answer to? Who do you want to bring to your blog, or video, or podcast?

The keywords that you use to get the algorithm's attention have to be the keywords that people are searching for. Do not simply begin creating a blog post without first confirming that there is an actual keyword search demand for the topic. Otherwise, from a search engine optimization perspective, we are shouting into a black hole.

If you post content for a question that you don't answer, then you will lose trust with people, and soon, with the algorithm. The key is to work with the algorithm, not try to trick it into giving you traffic. If you provide content that is just designed to fool the algorithm, then your credibility and trust will fade, and if your content comes up for those questions months down the line, then you'll be part of the bad and irrelevant content that you're already trying to get past. The algorithm knows who is naughty and nice.

If you want the odds in your favor and not rely on luck, you'll want to conduct research before even beginning to write that next blog post. Beyond keyword research, there is one other type of research that we need to do, and that is search intent.

Search Intent

One of my Digital First Mastermind members was struggling to rank for one of his blog posts. He did his keyword research. It was on a topic that he was an authority on, and there was a real demand for the keyword he was targeting. Similar topics had ranked well for his content.

When I looked at the results for that keyword in a Google search, I immediately knew exactly what the issue was: He had neglected to check search intent.

Before OpenAI, Google has long been creating AI technology to manage the algorithms that determine individual search results for each query and user. When you look at a result of a search engine query, the algorithm is making a prediction as to what content you want to see. The algorithm feeds that prediction with historical data coming from the actions and various digital signals of actual users. If you want to rank for that keyword, you should adapt your content to what is already ranking for the topic.

My mastermind member was a small business author and expert who sometimes writes about franchise opportunities. The phrase he was targeting, Google's AI had decided, held more intent for those looking to buy a franchise. Not marketing one. After he changed the phrasing and adapted his content to search intent, his post and site climbed the rankings.

This error was like one I experienced when a guest blogger wrote for my site. The blog was about brands that work with micro-influencers, and how to leverage influencers' user-generated content (influencer-generated content) to replace your own. If you were to search for the target keyword phrase "brands that work with micro-influencers," however, you see that the top results are all listicle posts of brands that are literally looking to work with micro-influencers. In other words, the algorithm determined that the searcher of this keyword is probably a micro-influencer looking for brands that they can pitch.

Keyword research without search intent is blogging in the blind.

Not only will the content fail to rank, but it might also attract a completely different audience than intended.

Google has spent many years trying to understand the intent that people have when conducting a search to look for information to provide them with the best results. There are context clues. If someone searches for "1960s film about pool" then they are more likely looking for Paul Newman's *The Hustler* about a pool shark rather than Burt Lancaster's *The Swimmer* about a man going through the neighborhood from one swimming pool to another.

Google is serving up answers based on what it thinks users are looking for—the "search intent"—backed by its data-driven AI algorithms. It is critical that we understand the search intent for each keyword that we want to rank for to see if it is something that we might be able to rank for, or if there is a mismatch with search intent type or plain-old search intent. The good news is this is as easy as searching for your target keyword on your target search engine, preferably in incognito mode, to remove any potential biases from your previous searches and browsing history, and then analyzing the results.

To help in analyzing the results, we can further classify search intent:

- **Informational search**—people want to learn ("benefits of influencer marketing," "how to make lemon zest," etc.).
- **Navigational search**—people want a shortcut to a website ("Google Docs login," "TikTok ads," etc.).
- **Commercial search**—people want to buy but are still researching ("which electric SUV should I buy," "best coffee makers 2024," etc.).
- **Transactional search**—people are ready to buy ("Los Angeles Lakers tickets," "Uniqlo HEATTECH underwear," etc.).

Understanding search intent classification is helpful in analyzing because language can be misleading. In the television show *Arrested Development*, a doctor who works in the hospital emergency room always tells the characters something accurate but unintentionally misleading. In one early episode, the doctor walks into the hospital waiting room and tells the characters, "We lost him," regarding their father. The news of the death devastates the family until the doctor reveals that they had actually misplaced the father, and he ran away.

If you search for influencer marketing-related keywords, you will find "influencer marketing hub" as a popular keyword. If you didn't know better or check search intent, you might not know that it is the name of a popular website for which it will be nearly impossible to rank high for.

Another example would be that of searching for "what is influencer marketing" and "influencer marketing definition." While they are two distinctly unique phrases, the search engine results are nearly identical. Since the search intent is similar, creating one post can expose it in both searches.

Word choice matters. Intent matters.

SEO tools will spit out many keywords with search demand that you can rank for. A simple Google search to confirm search intent will help you weed out branded search terms you will never rank for, multiple keywords that have a singular search intent to help you better optimize your efforts, as well as the complete flops that you can avoid simply by deciding to leave them off your radar.

Let me give you an example from my own blogging of the top 10 search phrases related to influencer marketing that currently have the most search demand, commenting on those that I deem to be irrelevant to my business objective:

1. influencer marketing: The search intent for this keyword is the same as for what is influencer marketing.
2. influencer marketing agency: I am not an agency and therefore do not target this keyword phrase.
3. influencer marketing platform
4. what is influencer marketing
5. influencer marketing agencies: The search intent for

influencer marketing agencies is very similar to that for influencer marketing agency.
6. influencer marketing hub: Branded keyword I cannot rank for.
7. influencer marketing jobs: I am not providing a job board service.
8. influencer marketing strategy
9. influence marketing: The search intent for this keyword is the same as for what is influencer marketing.
10. agence influence marketing: Although it is a French term, the search intent is almost identical to influencer marketing agency.

After confirming the search intent for the top 10 keywords, there were only three that made sense to target, each requiring a unique formula of content to best serve the needs of searchers.

The keywords you use must align with the intent with which people are searching. This is another example of meeting your customers where they are. This is even more important in a Digital First world where there are content mills—and now, AI content mills—that mass produce content to muddy the waters of the search engines. You must understand your customers, what they want, and how you can bring value to their questions in the language that they use when searching.

Beyond Traditional Search Engines

If we limit ourselves to traditional search engines in our quest to be found, we are leaving money on the table. Not every search engine works in the same way and thus requires distinct efforts to be seen.

On Amazon, because the platform can see actual sales conversion data, your product's conversion rate and sales history will help determine its visibility in search rankings. Reviews from other Amazon users also influence the algorithm.

YouTube stands out because recommendations on the platform generate 70 percent of its views[2]. These recommendations are visible on your home page upon logging in or in the "Up Next" panel. These are not searches, but videos pushed to you by the algorithm. This is how the TikTok For You Page works as well.

The YouTube algorithm has one job—to keep people watching. It's trying to give viewers the right video to keep them watching after the current one finishes. To get your video in front of people on YouTube, you cannot rely solely on SEO. Instead, the algorithm heavily favors customer satisfaction. Are people watching your content for longer than a few seconds? Are they engaging with it and watching the entire video through? Do they watch your other videos? If not, then that's a sign that the video doesn't answer the question people were searching for.

Search engines also favor customer satisfaction. When you click on a link, Google cannot continue to show you suggestions like YouTube can. Google monetizes from ads that appear within search results, but YouTube makes money from how long you stay on the platform to watch as many of their video ads as possible. To tap into that power of the algorithm, we must look at content not from a promotion and business perspective but from a viewer experience. Viewers already have to sit through an ad or two before the video starts. Looking at another video that looks just like an ad will not tick that box of viewer satisfaction.

Rethinking search requires you to reassess your approach from a technical, keyword-centric approach to a more holistic, audience-pleasing approach. Understanding the role that each search engine plays in the user's journey and aligning your content with it is your best chance for success in a Digital First landscape.

Key Takeaways:

- Search engines are no longer just Google or Bing. It's any platform where people look for information.

- Evergreen content has a longer shelf life than social media content. This leads to longer discoverability.
- Keyword research and understanding search intent are essential.

Companion Workbook Exercises:

- 3.1 | Content Discoverability Worksheet
- 3.2 | Timeless Treasure Hunt: The Evergreen Content Evaluation
- 3.3 | Keyword Quest: Intent Exploration

Chapter 4
Rethink Email

"The two words 'information' and 'communication' are often used interchangeably, but they signify quite different things. Information is giving out; communication is getting through."

— Sydney J. Harris

Email has been in popular use for close to three decades now. Despite many claims over the years that email marketing was dead, email is as powerful as ever. It's in use every day for booking confirmation, personal use, and multiple facets in the office. As a marketing tool, it has a reach that is unique. Some e-commerce brands like 100% Pure generate 20 percent of their revenue from their email marketing[1].

Influencer marketing and social media marketing have much more of a buzz around them. They're both newer forms of promotion and can return amazing results. Email is the reliable older brother. It's not as sexy, but it delivers: Many sources often cite email as having the highest ROI of any marketing channel, with a number often given between $36[2] and $44[3] of ROI for every dollar spent.

Part of that comes down to the low cost of email marketing software—some tools allowing you to message thousands of people for free or tens of thousands monthly for a few hundred dollars.

Another unique element of email is the intimate nature of the communication. When you email your customers, you send a message directly to them, and if you know their first name, you can personally address them. They have given you trust—moved further down the funnel—and accepted the conversation directly in their inbox.

A Direct Line to Your Customers

Think about it: Email marketing is the only channel you truly own outside of your own website. Everything else comes from rented land.

People may see us on social media, or they may not. They might find us in search engines, or they may not. The algorithmic sands are always shifting. But your email lists are yours. You own them, and all the invaluable CRM data that goes with it. When you're creating content, you're building assets. Building an email list means you are also building assets and continuing that conversation started by that content. You're more in control of the conversation and the relationship and guiding the contact down that customer's journey. You are not at the mercy of an algorithm or a cycle on social where a post dies after 24 hours or less.

That direct communication channel is so valuable. For one of my Fractional CMO clients, the sales they've generated from email marketing is comparable to the return they see on their Google Ad campaigns. They've invested around $100,000 in Google Ads annually. In comparison, email marketing costs you close to zero.

I've seen some similar results from my experience in building my Digital First Mastermind group (https://nealschaffer.com/member ship/). As part of the application of the initial intake, I asked on which channels the applicants consumed my content. Naturally, 100 percent of those who applied were already on my list—they had to apply to join the community and provide their email address as part of the process, but we do business with people that we know, like, and trust. Email is an important component in how we build that.

Many moons ago I saw Joe Pulizzi, whom I referred to earlier as the godfather of content marketing, speak at the Adobe Summit on the topic of email. He described how a prominent blogger generated 98 percent of his revenue not from his blog, but from his email list. To me, that was amazing. This is a blogger, not an email marketer. He sees people read his blog and opt into his email list. That means now the readers have moved down the funnel and into a journey he can control through other email communication.

Are Your Emails Providing Value?

People have opted into email lists. They want value from that interaction. If you want to deepen the relationship, you must give value in your messages.

The very nature of email and the direct, personal aspect of the communication means you have to make it human. If you simply send ads to people's inbox, they'll ignore them or, even worse, unsubscribe. Having earned someone's direct line of contact should not be squandered so easily.

Constant emails over a short period can lead more to unsubscribes or ignoring the emails than to engaging with you. Too many businesses have taken advantage of that direct communication to send aggressively promotional messages, both in their content and their frequency.

While there might be some short-term gains to such an approach, a burning of bridges occurs when prospective customers unsubscribe from your list, or, in a worst-case scenario, report your email as spam. When a prospect reports you as spam, they potentially negatively affect the ability of your other emails to reach their intended recipients.

It's All About the Segmentation

Some people might actually want to hear from your brand more frequently. Others only want to know when you have a sale. That's why it's important to understand what people want from your email list.

Most brands don't lump all their email subscribers into one group for this reason. You shouldn't either. And you don't have to make it overly complicated.

Here is how I tier my email list based on frequency. Some readers want daily emails; those come from the RSS feed of my new blog posts. Some want weekly communications, and others want monthly. Ideally, if they sign up to the monthly, I'd like to convert them to a weekly newsletter. For me, being able to keep in touch once a week is ideal. There are ways to understand what people want. There are trackers to see if someone is opening your emails. If someone hasn't interacted with the weekly emails for some time, then there are ways to automate that list and move them to the monthly list.

I am also tagging my subscribers based on what triggered them to subscribe to my list and their content preferences.

You can achieve the same by surveying your list and segmenting them into different buckets. Automations can also help you intelligently segment your email database. My example above was one of segmentation by communication frequency, but you can segment your own email list with any type of information that you can glean from your email subscriber. Usually, you can do that by combining their purchase history, asking them for additional information, and tracking their digital activity.

Segmented email campaigns not only produce 30 percent more opens and 50 percent more click-throughs, it is said that 30 percent of revenue generated from email marketing in its entirety comes from segmentation[4].

It's About the Journey

Not everyone is ready to buy at any time, and that is fine. If we remember the examples of funnels that were described earlier, we understand it is a process.

That means it also takes more than one email to help move prospects down the funnel. So how can you keep email subscribers' attention over time?

If you're a marketer, then your currency is storytelling. People love stories. When you're starting out, it's difficult to come up with what you're going to talk about. The key is to make it be human. It's to connect and communicate. Then you need to develop the trust factor. You develop some themes that are linked to you, your brand, or your personality. Communication is about engagement, not about converting every interaction to a sale. Marketing is going to be about converting some of the time, but communication is about engagement.

Emails help you with that. If someone has trusted you enough to give you their direct line of communication, then they are moving through the funnel. You have more control over that journey they take to being your customer. Now this relationship is about developing more trust through every email and guiding them down the path called the customer journey to the ideal location: the checkout page.

That means we need to be careful, even in emails, not to lose that trust through over-promotion. Television is a great example of this.

Network TV has a balance of entertainment and advertising. People understood there would be ads, but it was separate. If, in their network primes of the mid-'90s, Jerry Seinfeld, or Frasier, or any member of the *Friends* cast started talking to the viewer to sell a fashion or car brand, then people would tune out. They'd skip the show and change the channel. The viewer would feel betrayed. In email terms, they might unsubscribe.

In a flip of the script, there are now major events where ads are the centerpiece. The Super Bowl is famous for its ads. Many people who don't follow football in the regular season tune in to watch the Super Bowl. There are parties around watching it. Many of these more casual football fans are more engaged with the ads than the game. They'd happily talk through the game, but not during the ads. The Super Bowl ad has become a television event in itself, simply because the ads provide entertainment. The advertisers understand their audience.

Is it possible to create content that is as entertaining as a Super Bowl ad with every email? It's a high bar. There are some newsletters that are so entertaining that they then get passed around. In this way, there is more value that you give to people, and it comes back to you with further exposure. Your email list can become brand advocates for you. The like and trust factors are in place. In fact, some, like The Skimm, have been so successful with their newsletter that they have been able to grow it to over a million subscribers primarily through their passionate readership[5].

It shouldn't be perplexing why this is the case. By developing an email list, you have people who have given you permission, saying: "Yes, communicate to me." That's the medium that delivers the message. On social media, you have to make educated guesses (it's a shot in the dark) about what will generate interest and what people will engage with. You can try different video and pictures, or text, but an email is straightforward.

We now have a new generation of savvy entrepreneurs who are using newsletter communities such as Substack as their preferred choice for digital marketing, not search or social. In their social media handles, they don't link to their website but to their opt-in landing page to their email newsletter.

The List Isn't Just About Size

When we talk about growing a list, it's also important to note that a larger email list isn't necessarily better. You can buy an email list and make your database larger. This doesn't mean those people are actually interested in hearing from you. Sending a blast to people who aren't interested can lead to poor deliverability to the people with a genuine interest in your company, and in more extreme cases, your email marketing software vendor can ban you from using their software.

That is why you want to grow your list organically.

While counterintuitive, I would add that it sometimes makes sense to prune your list at regular intervals. By making sure that every person on your list still has a genuine interest in your company or product, you can ensure that you will maintain good deliverability while also reducing potential expenses tied to the size of your list. It's okay to remove people from your list. Don't feel embarrassed. People's needs change. If they no longer have an interest in doing business with you, it's best to devote those resources to people who seek your information.

My rule is that if someone has not opened one of my emails in the last six months, I will send them a little nudge asking if they are still interested in hearing from me. If they don't respond, I will remove them from the list one week later.

I used to have a larger list with 10 to 15 percent open rates. Now I have a smaller—yet still sizable—list with 40 to 50 percent open rates. If the whole point of email is to communicate directly with your customers, it serves no one if very few people read your emails.

Intelligently Automate

Reaching out to those who haven't opened one of your emails in a while can also lead to new engagement with your current list and even new business from those conversations. Sending out the "Still interested in hearing from us?" automated emails based on lack of activities is only one of many types of intelligent automations that you can easily program in most email marketing software solutions.

Email marketing is exciting and powerful because it allows you to automate the entire customer journey. When done correctly, you can send out valuable communications while you and your organization sleep. This means you don't have to always be managing the process.

In my personal experience, I have found very few smaller businesses that take full advantage of this functionality, although, once a feature of enterprise technology, it is now part of most inexpensive email software solutions.

The results, however, can be exceptional.

When I look at my email stats, I notice I am sending out nearly double the number of emails compared to how many receive my weekly and monthly newsletters. That delta is comprising the passive, automated communication that is being sent out regularly to deepen relationships with my audience. In doing so, I am building trust for when I want to make the sale.

Rethinking email begins with appreciating how this medium allows you to build the conversation without hoping that the algorithm will favor you. Harnessing the direct communication of email gives you the power to influence people on their perspective of your company and your products. You decide what information you will send them, and at which point, to solve the problem that they're facing. It gives you power to direct the customer's journey in your own way.

Email goes way beyond simply creating a newsletter and asking people to sign up for it. There is an art and science in encouraging and motivating our website visitors to join our email list, creatively thinking about all the different ways in which we can communicate with our prospects and customers to help them on their journey down the funnel. It is much more complex—and exponentially more powerful—than most businesses realize.

Key Takeaways:

- Email gives you a direct line to influence a potential client's decision-making process.
- Trust is the foundation of email interactions. It gives you the opportunity to build further trust and guide your customer through the funnel.
- Segmenting emails is part of the journey. People travel in different directions to get to completing a purchase.

Companion Workbook Exercises:

- 4.1 | Value-Driven Email Design
- 4.2 | Audience Segmentation Exercise
- 4.3 | Storytelling That Sells
- 4.4 | Clean List, Clear Strategy

Chapter 5
Rethink Social Media

"If you make customers unhappy in the physical world, they might each tell 6 friends. If you make customers unhappy on the Internet, they can each tell 6,000 friends."

— Jeff Bezos

As a Gen X-er hooked to television in the '70s and '80s, I vividly remember a commercial for a certain shampoo brand:

"I told two friends about Faberge Organics Shampoo, and they told two friends, and so on, and so on, and so on..."

The ad captures the original intent of social media marketing: viral word-of-mouth marketing.

It continues, decades later, as I repeat this commercial to you here in this book.

The reality of social media has led many marketers astray. They dive into it without properly defining what they want to achieve and charting a way to get there. They chase after vanity metrics like "likes." If there was any single component in the SES Framework for which it is critical to rid yourself of preconceptions and what you have learned and experienced, it would undoubtedly be social media.

The power of social media in marketing compels many entrepreneurs, small business owners, and companies to flock towards it like moths to a flame. There's no denying its power to connect with people. The hurdles rely on a core truth of the medium: social media was made for people, not for companies.

As my friend and fellow business author Jason McDonald said on my Your Digital Marketing Coach podcast: "Think of social media as a party." At the party, people are mingling, commenting on what other people are wearing or drinking, and sharing memories, jokes, or stories about their day. If you approach the party with a single-minded focus on promoting a product or your company, then the partygoers will shun you. People don't want to be advertised at. The party is there for people to enjoy themselves and share experiences.

There is a time and a place for promotion. When companies try to work on social media, then they're entering a human exchange without being human. I am reminded once again of that shampoo commercial, but this time for a different reason.

In the days of network television, long before streaming services, viewers understood that there would be breaks in the program for advertising. Similarly, in social media, the real reason people are there is for communication and engagement, not to be sold to. Whether on TikTok, Facebook, or Instagram, people seek visual entertainment. When companies deliver on this, then their content is far more likely to be engaged with. It's incredible common sense that is uncommon in many businesses.

Going back to the funnel of digital relationships, social media is the place to move through the funnel of being found, being heard of, and building trust. Constantly posting promotional content is the opposite of building trust. Instead, enjoy the party. Interact and engage with other people's posts. Connect as a member of the community, not imposing your will on the community.

My LinkedIn profile headline says that "Marketing is FUN" for many reasons, but if you can't have fun in social media, even as a business, then you might be missing the point of it.

The Algorithm

Many creators and growth hackers try to tap into the power of social media, hoping to make a hit. They want a viral post. They want that wave of engagement and encouragement, believing that will lead to sales. To do this, they try to create something that might trick or work with the almighty algorithm.

The truth is that people make things viral; algorithms don't.

Algorithms show you content it thinks you want to see. Social media sites thrive and grow when people are online. Their power wanes when people close the app or leave the site. The job for the algorithm is to find the right content for the right feed so that people stay and keep engaging within the website or app. On YouTube, the algorithm wants to find the perfect video for you to watch next, one that flows on from the one being watched now so that you don't leave. On Instagram, it's about finding the right post, or increasingly video, to continue the path the user is on.

It might feel like a struggle to get your content seen, but the essential truth is that the algorithm's purpose is to show your content. Just like it shows you content from other creators, it also wants to display your content in front of relevant people. That's why helping the algorithm place your content is crucial. The key is finding context clues. The key is treating the algorithm as your friend, not your enemy.

In an attempt to skew the algorithm in our favor, some believe that building a large follower base will make you look legit. It will tell the algorithm that people want to see your content. That's the common line of thinking, but it doesn't help the algorithm. We unfortunately get so caught up in the numbers game we don't think that far ahead.

An early consulting client of mine reached out to me after taking someone's advice to do an iPad giveaway on their Facebook page. Overnight, they gained a few thousand fans, but what next? They didn't have a posting strategy, and unfortunately, because they didn't target their ads properly, their new "fans" really weren't interested in the business, only the free iPad. Yes, the algorithm will see that they have more followers, but it will use the followers as a test base to see how their content performs. If their own followers don't engage with the content, why should the algorithm show it to others? Their predicament was that they had "sunk" their page with too many irrelevant followers, so none of their posts would perform well organically.

Buying followers is another way to muddy the results for the algorithm. Our content doesn't keep ~~a majority~~ any of these ~~followers'~~ bots on the page.

Fortunately, the algorithms have evolved on platforms like TikTok, YouTube, and Instagram where followers represent less and less of your content consumption. In this new era of recommended media, the niche and sheer quality of your actual content will decide who the algorithm feeds your content to.

Success on social media doesn't come down to follower count. It comes down to the fact that quality content counts more than ever.

This is the increasingly strong link between search and social algorithms.

The Importance of Consistency

Beyond the audience, the key point in working with the algorithm is consistency. When you're consistent in the type of content you are posting, the algorithm knows where to post it. Your track record will tell the algorithm which audience to put your content in front of. This extends to your audience. They know what you post, and they know what they will come back to.

Let's look at an example of a cloth diaper company. If we post about our personal life on our business account, perhaps daily posts about walking in the park with our new puppy, then either our audience will not engage with the posts because they're irrelevant or they will engage with them because we're posting pictures of a puppy in a park. Either of these outcomes muddies the water for the algorithm. In the first case, engagement will drop and that will affect the rest of our posts too. In the latter case, the algorithm might show our cloth diaper posts to people not interested in newborns or babies, but in puppies.

There are times to experiment with content. There are times to expand what we post about. But when we're looking to build clout with the algorithm, consistency is vitally important. It's so vital, in fact, that a conversation I had with a Meta specialist included advice on trying to post the same type of content on the same day of the week at the same time so that people—and the algorithm—can expect to see it regularly and build sustained engagement. Think of it like an old TV show that appeared on the same channel, same day of the week, same time. Or a magazine which readers would religiously buy for their regular features, such as a crossword puzzle or a humorous column. Reliable content draws a following. Consistency is key.

An often-repeated piece of advice to those cracking social media is to post three times a week or post every day. What does posting daily do for you? It's not one size fits all. It's about your individual schedule.

This is again about consistency. If you can consistently post every Tuesday, then do that. One time a week will be consistent for you. If you're posting for the sake of posting, just trying to make content so that you have something to post every week, then that will be random content that is not thought out. If you don't have time to make enough content to post each day but you're trying to do it, then your quality of content will also go down. Instead, focus on what works for you and be consistent in that. For example, if you want to provide information about deals to save your followers money, then #ThriftyThursday might be a good weekly post to aim for.

Define the key messages that you will deliver and focus on that. The increasingly intelligent algorithm will understand what audience interacts with your posts. Your consistent posting will best allow the algorithm to put your content in front of those who are like your audience, helping you expand your audience to people who have a high chance of being interested in your content.

Understanding What Works

It is essential to know how to communicate on each platform. Without this understanding, your message will not be heard or engaged with. This starts by understanding what the party is for. Each platform is different. Each set of users is different. You don't show up with balloon animals to a college graduation party—although the novelty may get you some attention initially.

When Dr. Brian Boxer Wachler, an eye surgeon who focuses on rare eye disorders such as keratoconus, looked into getting involved in TikTok, he saw one trend: there was the youth language "cap" or "no cap." In the parlance of these Gen Z times, "cap" means a lie. As a surgeon, he took this and applied it to different health advice he saw across the platform using TikTok's unique and popular duet feature. By engaging in the platform in a way that was already being used, he built a following in the millions.

Each social network communicates differently. TikTok is obviously through video, but there's a strong meme culture there as well. There's a lot of mixing videos and reacting to videos in the form of replicating dances, voiceovers, and even topics such as "Get Ready With Me." Instagram is about photos but has definitely shifted toward Reels. The influence of TikTok culture is bleeding through, but many of the users are millennials instead of Gen Z and, thus, although the medium is similar, the message often is not.

On Reddit, everything is anonymous, and users quickly shut promotional posts down. Engagement here requires an organic approach. On Pinterest, the users are more introverted. As explained in my Your Digital Marketing Coach podcast interview with Pinterest expert Kate Ahl, CEO of Simple Pin Media[1], users come to the platform with a question. They're not looking for a conversation but looking to research and find their own information. Pinterest users are not interested in influencers or brands in the way that Instagram users are, where they will actively search those posts and follow the content creators' lives. It is more of a search engine than a social network.

I bring up these somewhat niche platforms such as Reddit and

Pinterest to show that although we often lump social media into one concept, it actually represents many dissimilar communities. This is like how many who have never visited or interacted with its people might treat Asia as a singular entity when the cultures of the people in China, Korea, and Japan alone are vastly different. China alone serves as a home to over 50 official ethnic groups[2]. Using the same marketing approach in all three countries would fail, and companies must adapt to a good degree of localization, starting with the obvious language for communication.

Social Media as A Collaborative Community

No matter how hard we try as a business to break through on social media, it's difficult. Social media was created for people, not business. There is an easier way, though, when you think in terms of community. On any social network, your brand is one among hundreds of millions, if not billions, of other users. Why not team up for success? Or, in modern day social media vernacular, why not "collab?"

The power for businesses on social media lies in the ability to leverage the voices of customers, fans, employees, business partners—anyone who likes and trusts your brand. While you could attempt the daunting task of trying to convert your brand into becoming a person, why not instead lean into the people around you? This is my holistic definition of influencer marketing.

The term usually conjures ideas of a social media personality with millions of followers, but the true power lies with each user who can influence others, however few or many that might be. When you encourage or convert others to advocate for your brand, then that leverages the true power of social media. Now you have trusted entities talking about your brand at the party. It's getting others to pass on advice and opinion on your brand to their friends. This is the true meaning of word-of-mouth marketing at scale. And you can benefit from a lot of this without spending a dime.

This type of collaboration ranges from publishing the user-generated content of your customers on your profile to building a brand ambassador program which might include an affiliate marketing component to engaging with and motivating external influencers to talk about you.

With this in mind, just as you work to identify the core messages of your brand, you will want to identify those advocates and influencers who both share some of that same core value and reach the intended audience. It's not about throwing money at the person with the largest following. Those transactions come off to other users just like that—transactions. When you find someone who can benefit from your collaboration in a way beyond financially, then you're able to connect in a way that serves the message. Good content will connect with people. You just need to make sure there is an upside for both parties.

This leads us back to the topic of content, central to each component of the SES Framework, but created most frequently and in more content formats in social media.

Is there a method to the madness of the seemingly never-ending need to create all types of content for social media and avoiding that dreaded hamster wheel of content creation? I believe there is, but before going there, I want you to first understand two critical concepts about consuming content as well as experimenting.

First Become a Consumer

If you were going to write a book on traveling to Japan, wouldn't you want to read some of the popular books on the subject to understand what readers from your target audience typically consume? This same concept applies to social media.

It begins by treating the algorithm as your friend. There is no better way to do this than to set up a "dummy" account on the social network in which you want to strategically approach. The purpose of this account will not be to publish content to the public but to be a 100 percent consumer of the content that your target audience is seeing and engaging with.

The next step is to look at what's out there. What is there on the platform that your audience is already engaging with? Search for your keywords and see what was the most liked and engaged with content over the last few months. Find users who your audience would probably follow. Now, engage with the content that you think your target audience would engage with. Slowly follow those content creators, users, and even businesses you find creating content in your feed that your target audience would be following. Engage with the content that you find interesting and want to emulate. Then, let the algorithms do the rest. You'll discover more relevant content, and you'll develop a strong understanding of what your target audience is consuming on any platform. This process works extremely well on platforms that are pretty much 100 percent algorithmic driven, such as TikTok and YouTube.

The content that you will see is the content that the algorithm favors because it resonates with people. You might get some ideas for styles of videos, or how people present information that seems popular. Look for common threads. Find what works in their hook and the style —but don't copy it directly. Find what works and then do it in a way that works for you.

This research gives you insight into what works, instead of just hoping that you can make something and throw it into the middle of the party. The idea of "build it and they will come" does not exist in social media. Get to know people at the party before hosting your own to attract them.

Once you have become a true consumer of the content from the platform on which you want to engage on, you can begin to experiment.

Treat It Like an Experiment

Some of your content will do better than others. And that's okay. You can't expect every piece of content you create to go viral. What you can do is to try out many types of content, topics, and formats to see which resonate the most with your intended audience and the algorithm.

All these things are experiments you make. You will have content with very low engagement. When you're starting out, you need to be okay with having posts that don't hit their mark. You will test what works to build your foundation. There will be things that people don't engage with. It's essential to embrace this testing or development phase when you don't worry about how your posts do. It's an experiment. You want data points, not likes. These data points are about what is engaging with people. It is not about your brand or message. You note it and move on. Don't get hung up on it.

One approach often touted for beginners to engage with social media is to chart out your social media calendar for weeks in advance. On the one hand, that makes sense—you have your content mapped out, you know what kind of posts you'll make when, and you can do a handful of blog posts or videos or photos in one sitting to be prepared. What that approach doesn't consider is that social media moves quickly. If you plan out a month in advance, then you can't be nimble and change. Your last video might have hit something that worked. It might have raised questions or started a dialogue with users. But if you've planned out the next 10 videos, you can't adapt to that.

Keep going back to the research and seeing what resonates from other content creators. See what content you're posting gets more engagement. It only takes a few minutes to research what's happening. The algorithm changes daily, and so do people's tastes. What happened last year doesn't work now; what happened even just last week has a different effect now. The crucial thing is to listen to the conversation you want to be involved in and find your spot.

In such a way, social media should be only one part of your Digital First marketing strategy. It should not be the strategy in its entirety.

I want to leave you with one last thought for rethinking your approach to social media. In an eye-opening interview, Adam Mosseri, head of Instagram, explained how younger audiences post much less to social media these days. Instead of posting to an Instagram feed, many users prefer to use it primarily as a messaging platform or publishing Stories that do not remain part of your permanent record[3]. With that in mind, maybe businesses are simply focusing too much on doing the wrong things on social media.

By rethinking social media, we can better align our resources with expectations and make smarter investments of budget and time regarding the SES Framework that will be more effective for our business.

Key Takeaways:

- Social media is for people, not for businesses. Communicating as a business on social media takes a change in mindset.
- Social media is about communication, not sales. It's about conversations and collaboration.
- Treat your social media posts as an experiment and lean into what works.

Companion Workbook Exercises:

- 5.1 | How Much Time Do You Spend in Social Media?
- 5.2 | The Consistency Challenge
- 5.3 | Adapt & Expand Engagement
- 5.4 | Unlocking Social Media Content Success

Part Three
Begin (Again)

"Be willing to be a beginner every single morning."

— Meister Eckhart

Whether you already have an established infrastructure or are truly a startup, take Meister Eckhart's quote to mind and consider this an exercise in starting over. Start afresh and embrace the feeling of new beginnings. This will allow you to see things with a fresh perspective, enabling you to better implement the infrastructure of your Digital First approach.

Clearly understanding your goals and why you're using each channel in the SES Framework will give your strategy the focus necessary to be successful. It also allows you to pull back and look clearly: Why am I doing this? If it's because it's what you think should be done but for no other reason, or because that's how it's always been done, then the strategy needs another look. Maintaining the status quo is not a recipe for success in this ever-changing world of digital media.

I developed the Digital Threads process based on working with clients in a variety of industries. Each part of the process is the same, no matter what position your brand is in. Your company might be a startup or a mature company already doing these things, but I want you to continue reading to recalibrate your Digital Threads, which will exponentially impact your marketing efforts.

In the movie *Wall Street*, Gordon Gekko said that "money doesn't sleep." The Internet doesn't either, and having your digital infrastructure in place means you will take advantage of this, promoting constantly regardless of having a campaign or not. It is not about campaigns, although sometimes a campaign to pour some more fuel on the flames will help. When everything is in place, then your Digital First strategy will be a well-oiled machine that runs the whole time, even passively. However, it all begins with constructing on top of a solid foundation.

Chapter 6
Be Found

"Books constitute capital. A library book lasts as long as a house, for hundreds of years. It is not, then, an article of mere consumption but fairly of capital, and often in the case of professional men, setting out in life, it is their only capital."

— Thomas Jefferson

When I published my previous book, *The Age of Influence*, I faced the same problem as all of us—how do I get the word out? I realized it would be impactful if, when people searched for influencer marketing, they found my content as the answer. Thomas Jefferson's quote hints at the potential for knowledge, when packaged appropriately, to become the ultimate asset.

Being found in search engines doesn't happen automagically. Just because I am an author on the subject does not automatically lead to me being acknowledged by search engines as an expert. Traffic from search engines flows when we have content published for which we want to be found.

When I ran an audit of my digital marketing foundations, I found I was lacking rank. I had done little blogging about influencer marketing. My site and blog came up when people searched for content about

LinkedIn or other subjects. But for influencer marketing, I simply wasn't ranking.

Although I was an expert on the subject in the eyes of Amazon's search engines for books, that clearly wasn't the case with Google. The Google algorithm barely even glanced in my direction. I needed to show that I was an authority on the subject. How was I to do this? You can't rank unless you have content. Not a shocker, but it's something that businesses often forget.

I needed to create content about influencer marketing that, first, would find me when people were searching for those answers and, second, to show that I was an authority on the subject.

Digital marketing begins with a digital presence. That means creating your digital storefront—your website. In the past, having a physical store in the right location was extremely important. You wanted to make sure you were both visible and where your customers could find you. In a Digital First world, location is redundant. Your location is online. But you still want to be found, and you still want to be where your customers are. Now, Main Street is Google.

The problem that most companies run into is that they either: 1) set up their e-commerce store with a list of their products and services and call it a day, 2) they launch a simple corporate website heavy on branding but lacking depth in content, 3) or they launch a blog with the wrong content and for the wrong reasons.

In the first case, the content on those pages doesn't rank in search engines. It's static. There's not enough engagement with that content to lift it in the search engines. That's tantamount to setting up shop and hoping people wander in the store wanting your niche product. A blog can fix that. But only when done with a strategy for building your content.

The Role of a Blog in Search Engine Discoverability

A blog serves a very strategic purpose, allowing you to gain more visitors. With a blog you can build a content asset. In the same vein of "books constitute capital," over time it will contribute to your success throughout your SES channels. The first step is to build your expertise strategically in a way recognized by search engines.

Being seen in search engines is not just about appearing in Google. It is everywhere that people search for information—Amazon, TikTok, YouTube, Pinterest, Reddit, Apple Podcasts, and so on. If you execute your strategy correctly, some of these sites—the non-social media-focused ones—give more life to your content. Podcasts and video show up longer in search engines than in short video or image posts. They remain discoverable and relevant even years later.

Sometimes you can feed two birds with one scone. As part of my promotion plan for *The Age of Influence*, I made guest appearances on 100 different podcasts. That's 100 different ways people can now find my name and content. Considering how many podcasters not only publish their interviews on YouTube but also have websites where they include transcripts, show notes, and links back to their guests' websites, the impact from appearing on podcasts on discoverability is very high.

Search Engines are Always Looking for New Content

If you have been blogging long enough, you have seen your search engine rankings go up and down with every instance of Google implementing a major change to its algorithm. This is a natural part of the process of an algorithm that is in a state of never-ending kaizen mode.

Google's own advice is very revealing regarding this[1]:

> *There's nothing wrong with pages that may perform less well in a core update...the changes are about improving how our systems assess content overall. These changes may cause some pages that were previously under-rewarded to do better.*
>
> *One way to think of how a core update operates is to imagine you made a list of the top 100 movies in 2015. A few years later in 2019, you refresh the list. It's going to naturally change. Some new and wonderful movies that never existed before will now be candidates for inclusion. You might also*

reassess some films and realize they deserved a higher place on the list than they had before.

The list will change, and films previously higher on the list that move down aren't bad. There are simply more deserving films that are coming before them.

When you go to Google or YouTube and search for your expertise or for the product you sell, you'll find content that is often outdated. It could be old videos or just be plain old bad content. You might see a blog post from over 18 months ago as the top return on a Google search. Or a video created two years ago as the top hit on a YouTube search.

In my humble opinion, old content, irrelevant content, and bad content often dominate search engine results. This is the raison d'être for why search engines are forced to constantly update their algorithms. The emergence of generative AI has only complicated things. What this also intrinsically means is that search engines are always looking for new content. More than that, they are specifically looking for "helpful" content.

How Helpful Is Your Content?

Another important lesson I learned from blogging about influencer marketing is that truly helpful and good content always has a chance to rank.

It's no coincidence that one of Google's recent updates, as of this writing, is called the "Helpful Content Update." Here is how Google defines it[2]:

Google Search is always working to better connect people to helpful information. To this end, we're launching what we're calling the "helpful content update" that's part of a broader effort to ensure people see more original, helpful content written by people, for people, in search results.

One factor that Google looks for is:

Does your content clearly demonstrate first-hand expertise and a depth of knowledge (for example, expertise that comes from having actually used a product or service, or visiting a place)?

This means that content created showcasing your expertise for people to consume has an advantage. Assuming you or your business has expertise, you should be able to take advantage of this easily.

When I looked for the specific search terms that I wanted to be associated with, I found that companies that provided influencer or social media marketing tools created a lot of ranking content. However, their content focused more on driving sales rather than providing truly useful information. It wasn't as in-depth as my approach, and it was a lot more self-promotional. The content didn't offer what Google wants to give people who are searching.

In my search, I found marketing companies that blog about anything. Their software is not about influencer marketing at all, yet they were trying to rank for those same keywords. There were other sites who blogged about marketing trends that were currently hot and that included influencer marketing. A lot of this content is bad content. It's there just to be found briefly to get some attention.

When you look up your field, or a particular keyword, you'll find that there are often results from large content companies. They have big content teams. They generate TONS of content, sometimes publishing multiple posts on the same *day*. Sometimes they will even repurpose content they find that fits their needs while barely escaping plagiarism—I've even seen my content repurposed in this way. These large content mills have ways to find what is trending and churn out blog posts every day to fill up the search engines. Some of that will stick. Generative AI has only helped increase their ability to publish new blog posts literally in the blink of an eye.

It is not expensive, and it is, for lack of a better term, "factory-generated" content. The lack of quality shows. There are often spelling errors or factual errors. And the content is not engaging. The text simply repeats what has already been published online. AI is increasingly being used, creating emotionless content to dupe search engines. Because of this very fact, it will not stay high in the search engine rankings for long. People are not engaging with it. They realize the article doesn't answer their question despite being on the first page of search results, and they will leave.

Google's push to encourage helpful content, and further anti-spam algorithm changes, results from this.

When a blog post delivers value to the reader, then it can stay around for a long time. I have blog content from when I started way back in 2008 that is still often included on the first page of search results. This happens when you aim to create evergreen content. It's easy to revise when needed and republish. This approach to content brings a long shelf life.

Making engaging content is our goal. We aim to create valuable content. Our goal is, to paraphrase Google's advice, to give our readers a "satisfying experience." Our goal is to write for *people*, not for the algorithm.

We have positive intention with our content. Where a content mill will find what's trending and write as much as they can to scoop up traffic like a giant fishing net, our efforts are more focused. We create content to have an impact and a conversation, not a one-sided transaction. We will give value through our content, and that will translate to business in the future.

In parallel, we will send the search engines a powerful message that we are an expert in that field. Web visitors will send positive digital signals, such as spending more time consuming our content or digging deeper into our blog content by visiting multiple pages. These signals will help show search engines that our content satisfies the needs of searchers. While this might be a weak signal after publishing one or two posts, it gets stronger once you have published five, 10, 25, or more posts revolving around your expertise of a specific subject.

We do this through building what I call the Library of Content.

Planning Your Library of Content

I believe in drinking the same medicine that I'm selling, so I'd like to share the journey I went through with this concept.

Marketing has always been about relationships. Digital marketing is about relationships with both people and algorithms. Building trust is necessary for both customers and search engine algorithms. So that there are no potential misunderstandings, I repeat, we are writing for people and not algorithms, but we are also taking algorithms into consideration intelligently at every step.

To promote my book to search engine visitors, I needed to develop a Library of Content. This range of content had to showcase my expertise, and it had to build my authority in search engines and capture trust from potential readers and clients.

If I produced the content too quickly, and posted it all within a month, then the search algorithms would flag that content as potentially not being trustworthy. My strategy had to be consistent and tactical.

Since I wanted to be found for influencer marketing, I started by creating a spreadsheet of the relevant keywords surrounding influencer marketing that had actual keyword demand. To build this, I used a tool that told me what other keywords related to influencer marketing have actual search demand and other metrics to help you find keywords that will be easier to rank for based on the competition already ranking.

For influencer marketing, the SEO tool I used provided me with 14,172 keyword variations and 1,504 questions people often asked about the topic. That's a lot of resources to cover.

The keywords that you pick will carve out your path. You might be worried that everyone is picking the same words. They're not. That's why over 10,000 keywords came up for me in the first place—there are that many people talking about different aspects of the same niche. Everyone's focus is different enough that there is diversity. That diversity makes your content unique to your perspective and your journey.

From that list, I made my spreadsheet of the top 52 keywords. That would be one blog post a week for a year. If I blogged about that one topic steadily for a year, then my authority would grow. Perhaps you don't need 52. Maybe 26 would better suit your needs and consistency. But the process for refining the keywords would be the same. With influencer marketing, I discovered several topics that are relevant for me to respond to. This will help me showcase my expertise and generate demand for my book, as well as my Fractional CMO consulting services.

But not all of them are relevant, as I shared with you in the example of the top 10 keywords in terms of search demand back in Chapter Three, where I targeted only three results. Curating what is important about your topic is essential. It carves out your strategy for you. These are keywords for blog posts, not for product pages, to show the world—including algorithms—your expertise.

I considered each of these keywords as a writing prompt of sorts to help me better organize my thoughts and then share them with the world. How DO I define influencer marketing? What WOULD I recommend for an influencer marketing strategy? Thinking of my ideal reader, I could create content written for humans that would tap into both my expertise and my unique perspective.

As mentioned earlier, there was now the need to confirm search intent for each of these keywords to ensure that I would attempt to rank for 52 unique search queries, all with relevant search demand, aligning the search intent with my intent. I already discussed how the algorithm sometimes recognizes that different keyword phrases, such as "what is influencer marketing" and "influencer marketing definition," are looking for the same content. There's no need to write separate blog posts for these.

The second part of search intent is to go to your search engine of choice and, in incognito mode, search for your keywords. You might find that several search queries might at first seem unrelated, but they return the same results, just like the example above. In that case, you can target one keyword and write one blog post that might rank for multiple similar keyword search queries.

Another point to consider when collecting your keywords is to understand what people are looking for. They're not always looking for industry jargon. When you work deep in an industry or in a niche, sometimes it's easy to lose sight of the layperson's term for something. For example, people will not be looking for "dual action truss rod," but they will look for "broken guitar neck." It also pays to be specific. If you offer a service such as cooking, then that's too broad. Define what kind of cooking and claim your niche.

Remember that you also want your product and services pages to rank as well. One strategy is to align high-intent keywords—those keywords that people will use for a sale—with your product pages. You can use lower-intent keywords, aimed at building trust and familiarity, more in blogs.

Executing Your Library of Content

Once I whittled down the list to the essential 52 keywords that I could connect with, and confirmed relevant search intent, I ranked them in order of easiest to hardest to rank. This was based on the keyword difficulty metric that popular SEO tools provide you for each keyword. The metric shows you which keywords are harder to rank for, and which ones are less competitive based on the domain authorities of the websites that are already ranking in the top results for that search query.

Let me give you another example. I will introduce you to an actual macaron chef shortly, but if I was to open an online macaron shop, I would want to target these types of search phrases that have both significant search demand and confirmed search intent in the following order [number in brackets represents keyword difficulty, with 100 being most difficult]:

- macaron tower [8]
- macaron calories [23]
- macaron flavors [29]
- macaron pronunciation [41]
- macaron bar [52]
- macaron recipe [59]

- what is a macaron [63]

This is strategic. By prioritizing the easier-to-rank keywords, you can establish your authority more quickly. You're not competing as much to be the authority on those keywords. When the algorithm recognizes your authority, it boosts your content in the ranking, helping you stake your claim on the more competitive keywords. The algorithm recognizes the trust people have in your content, and that affects your other posts.

When I started blogging about influencer marketing, my numbers were low. On the first day of each month, I recorded my search engine rankings so that I could track my progress. The first month that I recorded the numbers was back in November 2020. I already had three posts in the top 10 for those keywords and 15 keywords total ranking in the top 100. By building the framework of my Library of Content and being consistent in my publication of insightful content on a weekly basis, a mere year later, I ranked in the top 100 search results for 47 of the 52 keywords, top 10 search results for 30 keywords, and five number one rankings.

Doing this research through tools gives you the insight into which keywords will connect. It shows you the roadmap to building your authority through your blog. When you're publishing 52 blog posts on one subject, you're showcasing your expertise to the algorithm—and to potential customers. Doing this research ahead of time makes sure that your expertise is not just thrown into the abyss of the web. With a focused direction, you can build a relationship simultaneously with the algorithm and those you want to attract, which amplifies your content in search.

Beyond Just One Post

Blog posts can be a fine source of evergreen content. Revisiting older posts, adding new information, or revising and reposting makes your Library of Content a living part of your site. Using the same research strategy, you can target and make old blogs relevant. You can also expand and create multiple Libraries of Content for related topics, as I have done for social media marketing, Instagram marketing, content marketing, AI marketing, and so on.

The algorithm sees people go to you consistently, and that amplifies the rest of your content. You have built authority in the relationship with the algorithm.

Part of this for me was to go through my blog and make sure everything I was doing was in the same direction. I had a large amount of guest bloggers on my blog. Having guest bloggers is great for many reasons, but their content didn't always align with mine. This broad range of published content confused the algorithm and detracted from the core Library of Content I was building. It took away from my authority. When I archived these guest blogs, my rank rose higher even with over three-quarters of my original content gone.

A great way to think of this concept is like this: If the algorithm were to look at all the page titles on your website, what would they see? If you are trying to sell pet food and 75 percent of your blog post titles revolve around cat food, all things being equal, the algorithm will probably assume that you are more of a specialist in cat food. You should regularly perform such an audit to see what the algorithm thinks your website is about.

Yes, Even a Macaron Shop Can Build a Library of Content

Anthony and Yami Rosemond moved to California from France to sell pastries and launched Pastreez (https://pastreez.com). They thoughtfully calculated their initial step as they discovered which French pastries would work well in California. Farmer's markets and other meet-ups were the first places to measure what pastries worked and get the instant feedback. The goal was always to move online to scale.

Using an SEO tool, Anthony looked at what his competitors were ranking for. He found a gap and made that the focus of their online content. "There were keywords they're ranking for, but also ones that they're not ranking for but were good keywords. There was a lot of buying intent for these good keywords."

The key phrase that wasn't being used was "macarons near me." It was rising in search demand, but their competition wasn't ranking for it. This was perfect since Anthony was looking for a strong keyword, but one that wasn't competitive.

Seeing SEO as a way to answer people's questions, Anthony set about building their new e-commerce website with a focus on answering potential customers' questions through a blog. Questions included things like: "why are macarons so expensive?" and "how do you make macarons?" and "are macarons gluten-free?" He made the blog posts to answer the questions. These questions came from the SEO tool, as well as what Google would autofill when searching topics about macarons. Differences they saw between themselves and the competition—such as shipping fresh macarons instead of frozen—sparked other ideas for blog topics. Commonly asked questions from customers at their store or farmer's markets filled out their editorial calendar.

This was Anthony's way of building up his Library of Content. When people looked for questions about macarons, they found the answers on the Pastreez site. He saw organic traffic to the site thriving.

As Anthony explained on my podcast: "Most of our traffic is organic. The good thing is you get more traffic, so people get to know you more. But when you go through informational keywords, even if people have their answer to their question, they'll leave your website without buying. That will drop your conversion rate. Our job is to hook them to an offer before they leave."

The Library of Content alone won't increase your sales, but it will increase the "foot traffic" you need to grow your business.

Building your authority in search engine results begins with building your Library of Content. That begins with strategy and intent to ensure the messaging and keywords build strength in the back end to do the work you want it to do. Failing to build content tactically is equivalent to throwing time and money into the abyss. The good news is that generating one piece—a single blog post or one video—is not the end of that content. The asset will take you further and connect with other Digital Threads.

Key Takeaways:

- Search engines are always looking for new and helpful content.
- Write content for people, but with algorithms in mind.
- By developing a strong Library of Content over time, you build trust in your content through consistency.

Companion Workbook Exercises:

- 6.1 | Rank Up with Blogs
- 6.2 | Timeless vs. Timely Content
- 6.3 | How Helpful is Your Content
- 6.4 | Planning Your Library of Content

Chapter 7
Be in Touch

"The meaning of life is to find your gift. The purpose of life is to give it away."

— Pablo Picasso

I have met many small business owners who have told me, "If only they would try our product, I *know* they would become lifetime customers." If you agree with this statement, you can begin doing exactly this without giving your product away.

In terms of your email, consider this: Would you limit your website visitors to only your current customers and avoid any potential prospects? Of course not. So, why are you limiting your email list to mainly your current or previous customers? This is a mistake I have seen many small businesses do. It is essential, as a business, to give away your "gift" to attract potential customers who actually have an interest in your product or service.

In 1888, Sears introduced the first catalog[1]. It was a time when there was a large migration westward, and an increasingly reliable mail route, so the time for mail order had arrived. How much was this catalog? It was free.

There were newspaper advertisements with an address where you could send a postcard, then the company would send you the large catalog. Interestingly, there in the bottom of the ad was a call to action that said, "Please show this catalogue to your friends and neighbors[2]." The company was savvy enough to be simultaneously tapping into mail order and word-of-mouth marketing in the 19th century. They introduced their club order program in 1897[3]. This was a company that knew its way around the marketing playbook at the turn of the last century.

The Sears catalog grew to become an icon of sorts in American culture. It was a company that could offer sewing machines, musical instruments, and even entire houses. The mailer was key to their success, and they knew it. The Sears catalog included things like paint and wallpaper swatches so people could understand the color and texture before ordering. Mass-printed handwritten notes that went in the mailers kept the customers feeling a personal connection to the company. This would have cost a lot to put together, but the company was happy to invest in the catalog because they knew the return it would bring.

In a Digital First world, being able to give away something that is of value continues to bring strong results.

The Problem That Our Library of Content Creates—and Its Solution

Since our Library of Content focuses on generating demand for our products and services, we should consider anybody who visits our site as a potential customer. How do we continue the conversation that our Library of Content began?

While the Library of Content aims to get people to know you in the first part of the funnel, email strategy is for those further down in the trust territory.

When people trust you and know you from your content, then we can move them along the funnel and begin directly communicating with them. When people come to your website from finding your content, we want to turn them into someone who trusts our brand.

Marketing is about relationships. Despite the bravado from many marketing "gurus," or the fiery and persuasive speech from Alec Baldwin, not everything is about closing a sale. Most marketing is about building the relationship, guiding the consumer through the customer journey. And that is based on trust.

If 99.9 percent of the traffic from our Library of Content does not convert into a lead or sale, we need a mechanism to invite those potential customers into our funnel of digital relationships somehow and communicate directly with them to build that trust.

When we can communicate directly with our customer, we can also control that customer journey. We have the flexibility to choose when and how we interact with the customer. But to do that, we need the client to trust us enough to give us their email address. We can do that by giving a gift through lead magnets.

Building Lead Magnets

A lead magnet captures the attention of your potential customers and gives them something of value in return for their contact details–usually an email address and a name—so that you can continue to communicate with them long after they have left your website.

There are three components to a lead magnet.

1. A Landing Page

This is clear information on what your offer is, and how to get it. All the focus is on the conversion. It's straightforward. Here is an example of the landing page for my weekly newsletter as an example: https://nealschaffer.com/newsletter/.

2. A Sign-Up Form

You can incorporate this sign-up form into the landing page itself or display it as a pop-up form on top of your website pages. On here you should ask for as little as possible. I find the most conversion comes from asking for just an email address, but I also often ask for a first name in order to personalize the communication. However, the more details you ask for, the more complicated the conversion becomes. If you want to ask for their phone number or birthday, consider doing so after you've developed a more trustworthy relationship with them.

3. An Offer

This is something your prospects would want from you. It is something of value, a gift, and most importantly something closely enough related to your business that everyone who signs up shows interest in becoming a customer. It easily answers their question of "What's in it for me?"

What you give away must give value to the transaction from their point of view. Free does not mean cheap. This must be an offer that keeps people moving through the funnel by giving them a quick win or taste of what it is like to do business with your company.

Since the giveaway component is something of value from you, it builds trust and authority. The engagement you receive shows you what customers want from you. If there's a disconnect between your offer and the foundation of knowledge in your Library of Content, then customers will not engage with your offer because they won't see any value in what you're offering.

You Attract What You Sow

The idea of a lead magnet isn't to attract anyone and everyone. We aren't trying to give away a free iPad to encourage as many sign-ups as possible. We are intentionally only attracting those to sign up who we feel we have a chance of converting to become a customer.

That is why, like everything else in marketing, lead magnet creation begins with the customer in mind.

Identifying your target customer is essential to understanding what is valuable to them. When we understand who they are, then we can make them an offer they can't refuse. Studying human psychology will work to your benefit if you want to be effective at manipulating the various Digital Threads to your benefit.

We put out an offer as a lead magnet to attract our audience and allowing us to keep in touch with them. We want to grow our email list, but it won't attract everyone.

Here's a great example of how to filter an audience through a simple lead magnet: a free pre-sales consulting call. The nature of the lead magnet will only attract those who at least have a need and might be interested in working with us. The offer will filter our audience and allow us to interact with those truly engaged with what we are doing.

Irrelevant subscribers are not helpful to your marketing needs. They will detract from your data analysis and possibly take your focus off those who are engaged with you. Not everyone is your audience—and that is okay.

Ideas for Lead Magnets

Deciding just what you can give you customers can be difficult. Knowing that it must be something that gives value, and something that is connected to the underlying themes and message of your Library of Content, makes creating lead magnets even more challenging.

I find marketing to be an incredibly creative (and FUN!) discipline, and lead magnets are one area where your creativity can carry you far. The rest of this chapter consists of a list of 25 potential lead magnets for you to consider in creating your own. Some of these will be more relevant than others based on your product or service, but having a variety of types of lead magnets will allow you to engage with more people based on what each person finds to hold value.

Each one of these lead magnets can be impactful in their own way. For instance, one direct-to-consumer (DTC) skincare brand called Primarily Pure used a third-party tool to create a deodorant quiz. The quiz allowed participants to "find out which deodorant scent is the best fit for your lifestyle and personality." If you had found deodorant-related content in search results and went to their website, wouldn't this quiz interest you? Obviously, before you see your results, you happily give up your email address. It ended up growing their email list by 30,000 leads—and generating over $100,000 in deodorant sales. Not bad for a lead magnet[4]!

1. In-Person Consultation

This is one of the oldest lead magnets out there. Sign up today to have one of our salespeople come to your house or give you a phone call for a consultation. Like every good lead magnet, it opens the door, literally, for the conversation to begin. On the flip side, having a free consultation at your business breaks that barrier for anyone who might think about taking the next step but still has that mental boundary, like someone needing that last push to join the gym. You guide that next conversation in person. This is a lead magnet that is more scalable through a phone call, but there is no better way to build "like, know, and trust" than in person.

2. Discounted Service

Everybody loves a discount. It can be the thing that converts someone just thinking about a purchase into reality. By offering it as a lead magnet, you get to communicate with them directly to turn them into a repeat customer. It can also be a free service added on—like free shipping. Often realtors offer free photography of their house when selling with you. The service changes for each industry and is something that makes it easier to slide down the buyer's funnel.

3. Coupon

Along that same line of thinking, a coupon can bring that person thinking about becoming a customer into your direct communication circle. Find me an e-commerce website that doesn't have a 10 percent coupon pop-up lead magnet and I'll buy you a sushi lunch—hey, another potential lead magnet idea!

4. Exclusive Access

Offering exclusive access to a service, or early access, is an ideal way to bring trust into the relationship from the start. This can be a sample chapter from an upcoming book, a beta version of a SaaS tool, first information about new properties on the market, or any other range of industries. People love things that are "exclusive" in nature.

5. Report or White Paper

These are common in B2B industries. Create downloadable PDFs containing more detailed or technical resources. These can range from the sector's current state to future trend predictions. You may even use your website, social media, or email blasts to entice prospects to move through your sales funnel to get these materials.

6. E-book

Repurposing one or multiple blog posts from your Library of Content into an e-book is an excellent way to entice customers. This promotes you or your company as an expert, showcases your expertise, and drives the relationship forward.

7. Guides

Your expertise is also on show here. There are so many options that cover different industries, such as beginner guides, guides to selling or buying, locality guides, a how-to guide, or a guide to the latest developments in the industry for that year. These are ideal and evergreen when you seasonally repurpose the content. One of my top performing lead magnets is an annual digital marketing tools guide, which helps guide my readers in finding the perfect technology for their marketing needs (https://nealschaffer.com/best-digital-marketing-tools-guide/).

8. Resource List

This is a simple type of guide that can just be a series of links that help navigate people to the resources that your business recommends. These could be products and services that complement your own or even reseller partners, system integrators, or contractors who are familiar with your product and whom you recommend. If you have special knowledge that you can put into a resource list, it might become a very attractive lead magnet.

9. Webinar

You can effortlessly repurpose a guide you've already created to share your knowledge and expertise in a webinar. Hosting a webinar brings your voice to the conversation and allows potential clients to ask you questions. It brings a personal touch and underscores your authority on the matter. Webinars are still extremely popular—perhaps benefiting from our shift further online during the pandemic—and can be powerful based on your topic and speakers.

10. Video Training

There are many platforms now where you can repurpose a webinar and break it into smaller video trainings. This can allow potential clients to take in your information without you always needing to be a live host. AI tools now allow you to create a human-looking avatar to deliver these recordings based on your script.

11. Virtual Summit

Similar to a webinar, hosting a virtual summit that comprises multiple webinar sessions over one or multiple days showcases your expertise and captures your knowledge of the sector. It allows new customers to join the conversation and be involved. You can also exert your influence and invite partners or other guest speakers and have them also promote the event to maximize the number of attendees and showcase your thought leadership as being the company behind the summit.

12. Email Course

Using email as the actual medium of your lead magnet is a terrific method to expand your subscriber base and get people to engage with your business. To deliver value over time, break down an e-learning course into smaller bits and send them out to your distribution list one by one for continued engagement. Or use it to educate your customer, as Bullet Journal does in sending out 12 emails to help you set up your notebook and introduce you to The Bullet Journal Method[5].

13. Online Challenges

This is a variation of the email course because it is a challenge that is delivered over a series of usually daily emails. While this type of lead magnet might be less scalable and require more effort, it is a great way to engage with people in a live setting and generate leads for your business. You are offering to assist someone in achieving a very precise aim ("learn how to code in Python") within a very specified time frame ("in 5 days"). We often run these programs over the course of a few days or at most a month to limit your time investment and make the result more achievable for your participants. It's large enough to be of value without taking much of an investment in time from them.

You can take this one step further by creating a Facebook group and inviting your participants there to engage with them daily while they are taking your challenge. Answer their questions every day in a Q&A session and build community. If you have people engaged there and show that your product is a natural solution to help them continue the challenge after you have stopped teaching, you have now sped up the funnel process.

Check out Morning Brew's Investing Challenge[6] for a real-life example of a four-week challenge to help you develop an investor's mindset that all begins with, you guessed it, entering your email address.

14. Free Online Course

Repurposing an e-book or a webinar to a free online course is a practical way to spread your expertise and knowledge. The value of a seasoned professional guiding someone taking their first steps is a valuable experience. And builds trust from the start. The content resembles other lead magnets, but it offers a different format for a distinct purpose.

15. Checklist or Cheat Sheet

For those starting out in the field that you're knowledgeable in, a checklist or cheat sheet to get their bearings or take the next step can be invaluable. You can easily put these together. Working with graphics allows you to start the conversation in the tone that suits you best. You don't have to make lead magnets overly complicated. You just want to give people an easy win in something that they are truly looking for information in.

16. Workbook

If you compile enough checklists and cheat sheets together and sprinkle in some exercises, assessments, and reflection prompts, you can create a workbook to help your prospective customers solve a problem and achieve desired results all centered on using your product or service. The companion workbook for this book is an example of what is possible: https://nealschaffer.com/digitalthreadsworkbook.

17. Quiz

A fun quiz where people enter their email to access the results is quite popular. It works because it's lighthearted, it's around a topic that creates a demand for your product or service, and it can be redeveloped seasonally.

18. Test

It's like a quiz, but more focused on a single subject. Testing someone's knowledge when they're new to an area of learning can be a very effective lead magnet. The answers can also guide their next steps with you to understand what to learn next.

19. Assessment

If someone is considering your service and they need an appraisal or assessment before going forward, then that's a perfect way to start the conversation. If you are selling a service and they are not sure if your services are necessary, an assessment can prove to them what they might be missing based on their own knowledge or experience.

20. Giveaway

Giveaways are a cornerstone of lead magnets. The lead magnet works as publicity when the offer is connected to your product, involves a local business, and is something the winner wants to share with their friends.

21. Contests

Like a giveaway, but with more skill involved, a contest can work wonders. It encourages engagement through the game at the heart of the contest. That leads to more conversations. A contest often gets attention on social media when people share it with their friends—sometimes with the incentive of another entry. Another aspect you can bring into the contest when it involves photographs or other content is that it can be a tremendous source for user-generated content.

22. Templates

Free digital templates are trendy and generate many leads. Make sure your template complements rather than replaces what you're offering. A free Facebook ad template or image generator for a Facebook profile page, for example, might be a good lead magnet if you offer social media consulting services.

23. Case Studies

A case study showcases your expertise in a way that shows how you can address a particular issue. Case studies, when done correctly, may disclose a lot about your company and sector, revealing vital information that your prospects will want to learn more about. Reaching out to your customers for testimonials strengthens your reputation in the lead magnet, giving more trust to your voice at the beginning of the conversation.

24. Infographic

Infographics are a simple and effective way to display and discuss data, statistics, and other information. They can be more engaging (and shareable) than written information, especially with attractive designs. As a result, in exchange for your prospects' contact information, provide them with a helpful infographic (one they can download and keep).

25. Free Trial

The free trial is a classic pillar lead magnet. This is an effective lead magnet for a SaaS company where it showcases your product and brings the users further down your funnel. They learn the benefits of your product, which they're already thinking of purchasing, and are further exposed to your company or brand. This allows you to guide them further down the funnel on your own terms.

Promoting Your Lead Magnets

Once you launch your lead magnet(s), you don't just want to wait for people to find it on your website. You will want to promote it actively. The first way most people approach is through promoting it on their site. There are different ways to do this—a dedicated landing page, exit intent pop-up, or fixed bar at the top or bottom of your site are popular options. Depending on your website design or the third-party tool you might use, there will be different options to incorporate the promotion of your lead magnet into your site.

There are avenues on social media beyond just posting about it, although that's worth doing to help make people aware. Additionally, you have the option to pin it as your top tweet or include it in your banner or profile cover image. You can place a lead magnet on the cover of a Facebook group you run. You can use your lead magnet as your main "link-in-bio" on your Instagram or TikTok profile. There are also the paid options of social media ads to have it appear in front of people. If you can calculate the revenue contribution that people who access the lead magnet end up generating as they become customers, this might be a prudent investment to make.

Although it's a digital connection, you can use lead magnets at in-person events, like conferences, trade shows, and so on. With the help of QR codes or automated text numbers, you can have people sign up and capture their details in a real-world interaction.

Don't just create one lead magnet and call it a day. You should be consistently creating them and comparing their performance, both in terms of conversions and the quality of the leads. Imagine the potential for creating a library of lead magnets, always engaging potential customers with different offers covering a variety of products and services that you sell.

As a rule of thumb, I always recommend my Fractional CMO clients to have multiple lead magnets and test them against each other. Which had the best email list conversion rate? What percent of those that came from a lead magnet ended up becoming a customer? How much did they end up buying from us on average in their first 90 days of becoming a customer?

Ultimately, the proof of the value of your lead magnets will be in the number of downloads and, more importantly, the business generated from those new contacts. When you truly align your messaging and keyword strategy from your Library of Content with your lead magnets, your audience will understand the value you provide with these downloads or free materials. Lead magnets are not things to be given away lightly—it is an investment in building a relationship and connecting the Digital Threads.

Key Takeaways:

- Lead magnets develop your list by taking the reader farther down the funnel into the trust territory.
- A lead magnet is a giveaway that has something of worth for your readers.
- Giving something of value, in line with your Library of Content, strengthens trust.

Companion Workbook Exercises:

- 7.1 | Creating Your Ideal Lead Magnet

Chapter 8
Be Seen

"We all want to be seen and heard. It's the human condition."

— Oprah Winfrey

The promise of going viral and becoming an overnight celebrity has intrigued every marketer since those early days of the Facebook Fan Page. The reality is that not only has social media changed so much over the last decade, but I would argue that since the pandemic, it has undergone its largest transformation.

Social media can play a much bigger role simply because so many people spend so much time there. But being successful in social media in today's digital landscape is as challenging as ever.

It also presents more opportunities.

Social Media Continues to Rise in Popularity

For each generation, the time spent on social media increases. Social media began as a place to spend spare time. But time spent there eats away at other activities, one being the most popular way of spending free time when I grew up: watching television.

We also have an increase in mobile connectivity, the speed of that connectivity, as well as the sheer number of smart devices that have social media apps on them. These factors come together to cause a significant increase in social media usage worldwide.

Marketing is about being where your customer is. It's a straightforward decision to have a presence in these networks. So, what presence do you have there, how much time and how many resources do you invest, and what outcome do you seek?

As Social Media Rises in Popularity, It Becomes More Challenging For Businesses

There is a supply and demand element to the governing algorithms on any given social network. No one knows this more than our friends over at Facebook. Years ago, I had the opportunity to tour their campus in Silicon Valley.

One of the most memorable things about that visit was not inside of that campus but what you see when you leave Facebook headquarters.

Figure 8.1

When entering Facebook headquarters, there is an image of the Facebook thumbs-up icon on a large panel. You don't realize it until you leave, but on the other side of that panel is the old Sun Microsystems logo from the previous occupant, still intact.

As I was told, that is a reminder to every Facebook employee to not become the dinosaur in their industry. The only way to avoid that is to make sure that they have an optimized news feed for every single Facebook user to keep them on the platform. There needs to be a delicate balance between ads for precious revenues to appease stockholders and pay for employee salaries, while also making sure that every user gets content that they would genuinely be interested in.

That is why social media companies spend so much money investing in their AI-infused algorithms. These algorithms are truly the blood, the lifeline, of their company's existence.

Over time, the supply of content being created by its users continues to increase faster than demand. That leads to the feeling that the reach of an average post on any given social network seems to have decreased. This is the same for people, but it just might be more pronounced for businesses.

Do algorithms rank content from businesses lower because they want them to pay to play? That is one possible and popular explanation.

I have a different opinion.

Businesses simply don't post like people do. Only when people have something interesting to say, do they post. People don't post according to an editorial calendar. People don't post content that was prepared a few days, if not weeks, ago.

The result is that visibility for businesses on social media has dwindled. The below example of Facebook's historic decline in organic search is only one such well-known and documented instance. It will continue to be this way so long as social media continues to be popular and the business model around it is based on revenues generated from advertising.

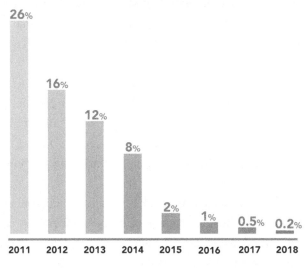

Figure 8.2

How Have Savvy Brands Pivoted Their Organic Social?

As the difficulty has increased in reaching users through organic content, every social network has stepped up their game by developing self-serve paid advertising platforms. Businesses can use hyper-targeting to reach their desired audience. To make sure their message gets across, they can employ different content formats.

A decade ago when I wrote *Maximize Your Social*, there were many purists who said that you shouldn't advertise on social media, that this defeats the purpose of its organic entity. They were right. After all, there's truly nothing social about a paid advert.

The reality is, though, that if you want to be seen where people spend more of their time online than anywhere else, you simply have to pay to play. That is why paid social is now an integral part of Digital First marketing, a digital thread with its own chapter.

Over the years, we as consumers have increasingly tuned out

advertisements. We drive past billboards without reading them. We tune out radio commercials and TV advertisements. And now we do the same in social media. Social media ads don't go viral. On the contrary, there are many younger marketers who feel that seeing an advertisement from a company "cheapens" the brand image and is a sign of desperation.

One of my early marketing consulting clients wanted to work with mommy bloggers because they wanted to see their product pop up in search results from a variety of sources that were talking about them. While this refers to search results, it really covers the same concept that gets to the core of what social media marketing is about: inciting word of mouth.

Many savvy brands have not only shifted to paid social, but now they're increasingly shifting from paid social to focus on user-generated content, brand ambassadors, and working with external influencers. We can consider these to be elements of influencer marketing.

Blatantly promotional content does not gather engagement and provides minimal visibility for companies. There is a time and a place for promotional content on social media, but it's more powerful to publish several other types of content before leaning into something promotional. To maintain a strong algorithm presence, consider using organic social only for non-promotional content and paid social for promotional purposes.

So, if you can't do promotional content, we need another way to lead people to our website.

Social Media Has Changed

Generating traffic back to our website from social media is truly an exercise in diminishing returns, as you can see from my example below.

PERCENTAGE OF TOTAL WEBSITE TRAFFIC FROM SOCIAL MEDIA TO NEALSCHAFFER.COM

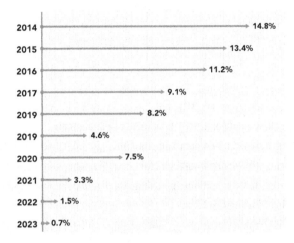

Figure 8.3

And this is despite having hundreds of thousands of followers and publishing consistently across multiple social media platforms.

Despite this decline, my website traffic has grown by 350 percent. The Library of Content strategy grew the search engine referral traffic, contributing to this growth. This is another reason I purposefully have the first S of the SES Framework to be that of search and NOT social.

Social media is for building relationships and to build conversations around your brand. It is not the place to drive traffic to your website.

Social media has gone from a place to generate link clicks to an algorithm that has become pay-to-play. It's changed even more post-pandemic in a Digital First world. To maximize visibility in today's social media algorithms, you need to befriend them, similar to our approach to search engine algorithms.

The algorithm, though, is half the story. The other half is the audience.

Seducing the Users

Part of the reason companies misunderstand how to use social media is because engaging in social media as a person is so easy. People like your vacation photos, or comment on images of food you've ordered at restaurants. Since they can do it on a personal level, many people think that engagement will translate into their business account. They hire younger interns or employees who are "savvy" in social media and expect them to deliver results for their business. Approaching social media as a person and as a brand is entirely different.

Beginning on social media means finding a way to join the conversation. Starting the conversation, or turning the conversation, to be about your product or service is the goal for every entrepreneur. And therein lies the challenge.

The key is first in engaging. We engage with other people's posts. We give to the community that we want to tap into. It's harder to do this as a brand than as a person. A person can like or comment on someone's post personally. A brand can't do that. Congratulating someone on their indoor soccer team's performance last night as a brand sounds hollow. But we can share content. We can comment on other content that is like ours or talks to the same audience as us.

To expand this concept to the users, you also need to understand what they want. They have come to the platform for a purpose, for what the platform delivers—TikTok for videos, Instagram for photos and videos, X for text posts. The creative digital agency We Are Social releases a detailed annual report on all things social media, and in their latest report, they showed the top five reasons people use social media to begin with[1]:

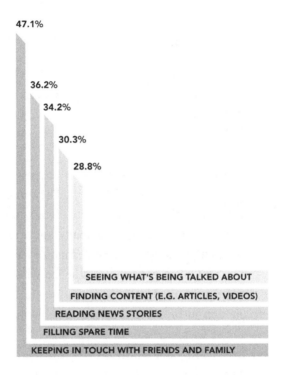

Figure 8.4

These are the things the user is expecting when logging in. It's hard to find someone walking along the street and convince them to go into your store. So how do you get them to click the link and go to your store in a Digital First world?

The answer in a Digital First world may seem counter-intuitive but, essentially, you don't.

Wait! Don't throw the book away—stick with me here.

It might seem counter-intuitive, but when put together with all the other Digital Threads, it becomes impactful over time. There is no better way of becoming friends with the algorithm and exposing your business to more social media users than by feeding the algorithm what it wants: Platform Authentic Content.

Embracing Social Media for What It Is

The solution is to embrace the platform. If people are there to watch entertaining videos, then give them entertaining videos. If people are on the platform for short text posts, then that's what you deliver. Don't publish content with the sole intent of asking them to leave the platform.

When GoPro started promoting their small but powerful camera, they didn't make content that looked like ads. They tapped into the network of extreme sports enthusiasts who were already producing this content and posting it on YouTube. The company knew their audience was watching this content already. The new technology would make it even more engaging. So GoPro gave their audience what they wanted —videos of extreme sports made by those in the field. The videos themselves were enough to promote the camera without a link to the store.

Today's popular social media platforms like TikTok and Instagram don't even allow you to link outside of the platform in each of your posts. You only have one link, and that is in the bio. If you can reimagine social media and your content's purpose to drive people to your bio and click on that link, regardless of the social media platform, you begin to see that social media is about selling your personality, not your product.

If your platform is X, then you communicate your message through X posts. You don't just make one post saying something with a link to your site. People will scroll past it. The users are there, on X, to read short posts and consume your content. They don't want to go elsewhere to read it. So why are you trying to always take them elsewhere?

In other words, social media is the ultimate place to build up your brand awareness and likability. There is no better way to do this than through Platform Authentic Content.

This content is not a call to leave the platform. If someone is on the train after work, tuning out and scrolling through Instagram, then that's where they want to be. You want to meet your audience and customers where they are. In that case, they're on a photo and video platform. Your content needs to speak to that format.

Platforms use unique content formats that their users engage with. This makes each platform, and the users of each platform, different.

A great example of this is X threads. When you break up your message into several posts, then they can consume it easily. It allows you to organize multiple thoughts into a series of tweets that then seem appealing to the X user. The result is that they end up consuming more of your content, making both the viewer and the algorithm happy. Some might just keep scrolling after that, but they have taken in your message. You have communicated with them, and you've continued to build awareness and trust around your brand.

YouTubers have always known it is in their best interest to keep people on YouTube as long as possible when a session starts with one of their videos. TikTok stars Duolingo also recognize that entertaining and gaining attention on TikTok is the most effective strategy for boosting sales to that demographic. It's time to equip ourselves with that same mindset for all of social media.

Platform Authentic Content is the concept of taking your message and making it to exist on the platform. We're not trying to get someone to click on it and go to our blog. We're not trying to send someone to our store. Our goal is to use the platform for meaningful conversations and create valuable content to build a presence and engage with others. The intent of the content is to engage or educate, not to drive visits to our website. We make our content work within the platform where we post it. Ultimately, once you have built "like, know, and trust," people WILL click on that link in your bio to find out more about you, so there is light at the end of the tunnel. But just like in real life, in social media it also takes time to develop relationships of value with others.

A similar concept, developed by Amanda Natividad at the audience research platform SparkToro, is the term Zero-Click Content. This emphasizes that the aim of social media content should be to add value with each social media post, not trying to provide that value elsewhere[2].

The other benefit to this lies again with our relationship with the algorithm. If you keep posting content that people see and then leave the platform, then that sends a message to the algorithm that your content makes people leave the app. This can affect how it will display your future content. Keeping the old ball and chain happy by showing that people engage with your content is a much better result for both you and the platform.

If you have been used to publishing promotional posts on your social media, old habits can be hard to stop. Start the transition to Platform Authentic Content gradually by reducing the amount of promotional content and increasing your Platform Authentic Content. Once you begin, you will slowly see a positive change in how many impressions your content receives and, in turn, the engagement it attracts.

Making It for the Platform

Perhaps you're active across several social media platforms. Making content specific for each of these platforms sounds like a lot of work. The good news is that you can repurpose much of it to engage with Platform Authentic Content.

If you already make a video, then you can break that into shorter videos to communicate on YouTube Shorts, TikTok, or Instagram. If you have a blog post, you can break that into smaller posts for Instagram, an X thread, or a LinkedIn carousel.

The intent of creating this content is to generate a conversation. It's not to talk *at* people. It is to create content that gives value to users through the platform that they're already on. Engagement is the goal here, not sales.

This value is authentic. You might have noticed the trend of someone on LinkedIn posting a selfie along with their thought for the day, or their "5 lessons from this week" type post. The key is authenticity. Other users see that and engage with that content differently. The selfie is not a perfectly groomed headshot. It's a personal glimpse. This is another holdover from the pandemic. When we all had to work at home, it became much more relatable to post in everyday clothes, not business suits. I received feedback that wearing a t-shirt for my YouTube videos made me feel more approachable than wearing a suit and blue shirt like in my publicity photos. It carried on the authenticity —after all, who wears a suit in their home office?

My first experiment with this approach of Platform Authentic Content was repurposing a blog post into an X thread. At the end, on the last post, I could have posted a link back to the blog, but my intent was to engage in conversation. I wasn't forcing X users to click the link to access the information; instead, I was providing them part of it in the preferred medium of the X thread so that they would receive value and, if interested in learning more, could go to my website.

This X thread ended up generating a lot more engagement than my usual posts. The flow on effect from that to my next posts was also remarkable. It wasn't like the original post—10 times my usual impressions—but it was about five times. The next post was about three times as many impressions as usual. The algorithm pays attention to previous engagement and passes that kudos to your next posts, albeit for a limited amount of time until your next highly engaging post.

The "Link in Bio" Approach

Naturally, we all want to use social media to promote things. We want to convert these followers and fans into sales. Where does the conversation come to the point of making a sale?

Our intent with Platform Authentic Content is to create content with value. Directly promoting our product doesn't translate into value.

We have to create the content with an intent of generosity, an intent of giving to the community. We build trust, familiarity, and brand awareness. It is not a matter of Always Be Closing. It is Always Be Connecting.

Another way of thinking about it is to conder the "link in bio" approach to social media.

Like many other marketers, I was confused when Instagram first appeared on social media. I was used to embedding links in posts on any social media platform, so Instagram seemed foreign. Instagram forced businesses to change their mindset. Instead of promoting links, you had to build relationships with users through your content. If they liked your content enough, at some point they would naturally go to your profile bio and click on your link to learn more about you or your business. In this way, every post should indirectly want people to click on your "link in bio" from the sheer value of your content.

When you're promoting on any social network, you want people to follow and engage with you on that network. The goal is to build the following on that platform. A percentage of those people will follow the links, but putting the links up front and in your face, whether it be in the caption or visual, makes the post about your off-platform content. It's an advertisement to go somewhere else. People will lose interest.

When you promote something that you want to lead people off of social media to, you want people to give it a chance. To do that, you need to create content that is just that—content. This is not an advertisement. It's something engaging. It gives value there on the platform. When people feel like they have seen enough value, they will eventually "check you out" by clicking that link in your bio.

While Instagram and TikTok do not allow you to embed links in your content, you should also take the same approach to Facebook, LinkedIn, and X. This will force you to win people over through your Platform Authentic Content instead of always trying to lead them elsewhere. Your followers will consume and engage with your content more frequently, and in turn, the algorithms will reward you.

When in Doubt, Reset and Reconnaissance

You might still be unsure of exactly what you should post as part of a Platform Authentic Content strategy. Consuming more content in social media exposes you to which formats and subjects perform better.

I hinted in Chapter Five about becoming a social media content consumer. YouTube expert Derral Eves, in his bestselling book *The*

YouTube Formula (the definitive book on YouTube marketing, by the way), provides a similar perspective, one he calls "reconnaissance." Here we aren't trying to locate the enemy before an invasion; We are doing research to better understand what and who is influencing our customers and prospects on the battleground that is social media.

The concept is to understand what the algorithm would feed you if you were acting like your ideal customer. You can't do this on your own profile because of all the signals you have previously sent the algorithm. That is why you need to "reset" and create a second new account for the sole purpose of reconnaissance.

While this is difficult to do on sites like Facebook and LinkedIn, which are more tied to your personal profile, it is very easy to do on Instagram, TikTok, X, Pinterest, and YouTube.

Create a second account with the intent of 100 percent content consumption. Like and view content that your ideal customer would search for. Then, let the algorithm do its work to introduce to you the content your ideal customer would see, based on the input you have already given it. Become a student of that content, analyze it, and ultimately emulate what you can authentically that's aligned with your brand message to maximize the chances of your Platform Authentic Content gaining visibility.

Output in social media does not equal results. If your content is not being consumed or noticed, you need to rethink your creation process. Leaning into this concept of Platform Authentic Content will help you recoup your losses and build a community that truly engages with your content—and follows through by clicking on that link in your bio.

Key Takeaways:

- Social media algorithms will continue to reward content that keeps users on the platform.

- Users of social media want to engage with content that is native to the platform—videos, images, text.
- Platform Authentic Content creates content specifically for a platform. The content aims to stimulate conversation, not promote sales. Make it *for* the platform. Make it *for* the people.

Companion Workbook Exercises:

- 8.1 | Analyze the Algorithm
- 8.2 | Adapting to Platform Authentic Content
- 8.3 | Reset and Reconnaissance

Part Four
Optimize

"You just stay here in this one corner of the Forest waiting for the others to come to you. Why don't you go to them sometimes?"

— Rabbit to Eeyore, in The House at Pooh Corner

In the past, when physical stores were more common, you would build your store on a popular street and attract customers by creating an appealing window display.

In Part Three, you built your digital window display to allow others to find and engage with you. The magic in Digital First marketing actually starts to happen when you proactively engage with others. Engagement with others is the first step in optimizing your digital process for future success.

In this new post-pandemic Digital First landscape, relationships go beyond those with customers, with competitors or collaborators, and with employees and partners. These relationships, as I've already mentioned, include that with algorithms.

Your Library of Content will establish your expertise in your field, but you cannot rely on the search engines alone to find it. You need to write your content for humans but build a relationship with the algorithm.

Similarly, building an email list alone is not enough. You need to turn these connections into conversations to truly leverage the most from such a direct form of communication.

And posting your own content on social media is not enough. Even from an idea perspective, you'll run out of things to say, and it will lack credibility because it is coming from a company and not a person. Instead, we turn to our fans and other content creators to help us.

Chapter 9
Build Connections

"We cannot live only for ourselves. A thousand fibers connect us with our fellow men; and among those fibers, as sympathetic threads, our actions run as causes, and they come back to us as effects."

— Herman Melville

Your Library of Content is a valuable resource that provides many advantages beyond search engine discoverability. However, to develop a relationship with the biggest digital influencer of them all in most countries worldwide, Google, it is now time to deepen that relationship with algorithms. Content alone is only one of many factors that go into search engine rankings—some sources say it's one of over 200 factors[1].

You are just one of many hoping to strike gold with your content. Prospectors needed to know where to find gold. You need to know how to get your websites ranked high in search results. Writing excellent content for humans is a good beginning, but it is simply not enough.

There are some prospecting clues to be found in the Google search results themselves.

Websites like Wikipedia—or HubSpot, with digital marketing—

always seem to have high rankings regardless of what content they publish. They have developed a fantastic, trustworthy relationship with search engine algorithms that has given them something we can call "domain authority." As Google tries to figure out which website to rank for similar content, this authority might tip the scales in favor of those who have it.

Let's flip the script here: If YOU were a search engine, how would YOU rank content?

While you would compare the quality of their on-page content, because of the interconnected nature of the Internet, you would also more than likely try to understand who might be connected to that website. In other words, websites that have many others linking to the content show a level of trust in that content. That website has an authority that is recognized by others—and search engines.

This link from another website to your own is something that we call a backlink.

Building your Library of Content strategically around a core topic builds your expertise. Having other websites link to your content builds trustworthiness. These backlinks send a powerful signal to the algorithms that you and your content are a trusted entity. This is where the concept of domain authority comes from. And it has become even more important with the emergence of AI-generated content as a way of filtering the authoritative from the automated.

Google—or any other search engine—wants to give the best search results to their users. That's their business. If they don't provide the best results for a search, then people won't return to their search engine. Of course, these search engines need to find ways to know which content is best in answering the user's query. The search engines want to give answers of authority and trustworthiness. We need to give that to them.

Building backlinks is possibly something that your company—or, sometimes, your SEO agency—might already be doing. Backlinks developed over years show a lot of trust, and with that comes more domain authority. You cannot build this in a day—that just looks suspicious and untrustworthy.

There was a time, back in the wild days of SEO, when link trading was very commonplace. You link to my site, and I'll link to yours. That's still relevant to a degree, but now the algorithm is more complex. Trading links won't deliver the same results.

I suggest we should think about backlinks not to game the system, but we should see them as a way of building relationships. Embracing that nature is a way to build relationships with webmasters, marketers, and content creators, such as bloggers and podcasters—as well as the algorithm. That will help speed up the visibility of your Library of Content to your potential customers.

One more important data point here: 95 percent of all web pages have zero backlinks[2]. By building backlinks, you are thrusting your website into the top 5 percent of all websites. You're already increasing your odds of finding gold!

Benefits of Backlinks

Backlinks show other people are talking about your content. They give credibility to your content to the eyes of the crawlers that search engines send out as they look tirelessly for new content and connections between websites.

To blog, I often need to research a topic to give validity to what I am saying. Naturally, I would perform a search in a search engine, go through the articles that show up on the search, find the perfect one, and link back to it as the source of the data that I am referencing. It's the standard practice in blogging, as it would be if you were writing a paper as a university student and backing up your sources. That means that when your site gets to that first page of search results, particularly the top entry, then you will naturally receive a lot of backlinks. Your content will become the go-to source for that topic. This explains why some outdated information stays at the top of the search results for a long time. So long as users stay on the site and don't leave or "bounce" right away, then the visit registers for the algorithm. The data also backs this up: The number one result in Google has an average of nearly four times more backlinks than the remaining results in the first 10 results[3].

The concept of linking to other websites is also important for your own content as well. Those who do that seem to rank higher in the algorithm[4]. There's an understanding that you're connected to the conversation, that you're referring to others and not just creating self-contained pieces focused on keywords. Search engines see your content as more relevant and trustworthy, and it shows your expertise through these linked references. If your content was all self-contained, then the algorithm would have trouble determining your domain authority and trustworthiness.

When you have the domain authority, people want your influence or authority. It's like they're borrowing it, or your presence is a signal to the algorithm that they know what they're talking about. Establishing that foothold on your keywords and the domain authority will attract more as others link to you for your expertise. The implied influence of your content can lead to greater promotional activities for your business altogether.

The data backs this up. According to Backlinko's definitive study of 11.8 million Google search results,

> *Getting backlinks from multiple different sites appears to be important for SEO. We found the number of domains linking to a page had a correlation with rankings*[5].

Begin With Gap Analysis

SEO tools give insights that guide us in building our backlink strategy. Just like the keyword research for the Library of Content, these insights target our efforts to build trustworthiness.

Use your preferred SEO tool to search for a domain analysis of your site and one of your competitors. Using the common feature that most of these tools have to analyze backlinks, you can see the domains linking to your site. You also can see the domains linking to your competitor's site or any other website on the Internet. You could do this for specific pages, but I recommend you do so for the entire website. Download this information into a spreadsheet, then sort the list by domain authority or whatever metric that your SEO tool provides you in descending order, comparing the backlinks that you have gained to those of your competitors. You will immediately find websites where your competitor has a backlink, but you do not. The list might become a long one: My SEO tool shows that I have over 10,000 websites linking to my own.

Using SEO tools, you can easily compare backlinks from up to five websites. This allows you to identify where your competitors have backlinks you don't.

What is important to find out is which websites that have a lot of authority are linking to your competitors' sites and not to your site. We begin with websites of authority because, once again, if you were a search engine, you would probably place more value on a link coming from a more established authority than a website that was just thrown up yesterday.

The purpose of this is to find opportunities where we might generate a similar backlink, seeing that there must have been a reason they linked to one of our competitor's sites.

Examining Authority

When I did this audit for my website, I chose a competitor who was getting more organic search traffic but had only a slightly higher domain authority than my site. I wanted to understand where they were getting backlinks from that might influence this greater organic traffic. One of the valuable insights SEO tools offer is the estimated search engine traffic for websites.

On the list I found, there were some high domain authority sites that I was getting traffic from, but mostly my competitor had more. These were the ones I was interested in. When I dug deeper into those sites, I found three places they were getting backlinks from consistently—guest podcasts, guest blogs, and other referring links from various blog posts. A closer look at the last one showed that several sites that were linking to my competitor were through articles written by the same author. There was the same writer who was guest-blogging on different sites and linking back, but this writer seemed to have no clear relationship with my competitor.

Here's my explanation of this phenomenon.

Many sites have content creation outsourced to SEO agencies or sourced from guest bloggers. There's an entire industry on writing blogs without clear credit or using a ghost profile. These freelancers can then link back to themselves or their clients. Some of these links might be unnatural. It still comes from relationships, and, in the world of backlinks, you need to build relationships with these freelance writers and webmasters.

Content marketing agencies aren't just about writing the content for you; they also get the links to make the content rank higher in search. That's part of the deal. To make this work, relationships are key.

Although appearing on podcasts and guest blogging are part of the relationship-building exercise to generate more backlinks, so was my competitor's relationship with other writers that allowed them to receive so many backlinks.

This idea of "trading" backlinks based on relationship is a gray zone of the Internet that search engines do not encourage. They want you to link to other content because of their authoritative nature. That being said, I often link to the content of my friends or tools that I enjoy using because I am an emotional human being. This is another aspect of the concept of "like, know, and trust." People or groups of people manage every website. So long as this is the case, there will always be a chance to persuade others to work with you.

That is why I like to call building backlinks an exercise in influencer marketing—but for SEO.

How to Build Backlinks

When you create relationships with other sites, bloggers, or brands, creating backlinks will come naturally. There are options for using organic approaches or paid approaches. Perhaps you have already received some of these pitches without realizing it.

Let me go through the most common and recommended ways to build backlinks organically.

1. Help a Reporter Out (HARO): connectively.us.

This continues to be a popular source of opportunities to generate backlinks while also giving you the opportunity to share your company's expertise. Journalists are looking for sources for news articles and will post queries here looking for input. You can sign up to HARO and receive daily emails and respond to those queries where there is a good match. Many of these journalists will link back to your website if they use your quote.

2. Directories.

Let's start with the easiest one, which any business could do: building backlinks by registering in relevant online directories. Being listed in respected directories for your specific industry or location comes with a solid amount of authority. You might need to join an industry or local association to be listed, but every directory listing usually includes a backlink back to your website. While these links, often called citations, won't link to your Library of Content, they are still important in building up sheer volumes of relevant backlinks. Usually, the competitive backlink gap analysis will uncover directories you can leverage that you might have never heard of.

3. Resource Pages.

In your backlink gap analysis, you might find that websites list your competitors on a dedicated page or blog post as resources. This might be a perfect opportunity to reach out to the website, explain why your product or service is a perfect fit for that resource page, and then ask them to link to it so that they can improve and have a more comprehensive resource.

4. Guest Blogging.

The traditional way of generating backlinks through outreach is through guest blogging on other websites. When you have more influence and domain authority, you'll have more opportunities to guest blog. There are many websites that accept guest blogging, but even if they don't, you can still pitch them on your ideas. You are tapping into a new audience and hoping to create a relationship between your blog and theirs with a link that might attract their readers back to your website. At a minimum, websites usually allow you to link back to your homepage in your author bio. Some websites, like my own, are generous enough to allow you to link back to your own Library of Content so long as it doesn't compete with the Library of Content on their blog. It costs money to create content, so some websites see guest blog posts as a way of sourcing content instead of outsourcing the creation of it. A Google search for "[industry name] blogs looking for guest posts" should help steer you in the right direction to start.

5. Infographic Outreach (also called Guestographic).

You can develop relationships with other content creators by simply reaching out to them and offering them something of value. Similar to a lead magnet, if you've developed a visual aid or infographic, then you can offer it to another blog or site to show with the agreement that they'll link back to you. You can also offer to write them a unique blog post to complement the infographic so that the host website doesn't need to do anything outside of hit the publish button. This approach was more popular a few years ago, but it all depends on your specific infographic and pitch, so you never know until you try.

6. Broken Link.

Often, people don't know that their links aren't working. When you find a broken link on a website that you have relevant content to link to, you can reach out to the blogger and suggest your link to replace it. If the site has a higher authority than yours, then that's a win for you.

7. Skyscraper Technique.

This is one of the most famous backlinking methods, and it is like the broken link approach in which you are looking for where your competitors are being linked from. Instead of telling the webmaster about a broken link, you are informing them that the information they are linking to is outdated, shallow, or just not of the best quality compared to the specific page of content in your Library of Content. Therefore, you are asking them to swap the link from your competitor to the superior content from your website.

8. Podcasting.

Being a guest on a podcast is an excellent way of getting backlinks as well as showcasing your expertise. Of course, you need to have some expertise and convince the podcast host you would be a worthy guest, but many podcasts like my own add links to their guest's websites so their listeners can reach out to them. Taking this approach one step further, while I'm not suggesting you should start a podcast just for backlinks, when you have your own podcast, other podcasters will pay more attention to your request because they just might want to appear on your podcast. Many podcasters understand the value of being a guest on other shows because they can more easily convert someone to subscribing to their own show when their voices are in the ears of people already listening to podcasts.

9. Link Reclamation (also called Unlinked Mentions).

Once you become a more well-known entity, you might generate mentions on other websites that don't link back to you. This is like a common occurrence in social media where people talk about you without properly tagging your company. You can find where you're being talked about through search engine searches or by using a more sophisticated social listening tool, and then asking the webmaster to link to you properly where they mentioned you.

Understand that websites are now receiving a LOT of these automated emails daily, so make sure you are authentic and to the point and offer some sort of incentive to encourage the other party to agree to your requests. Some of the common incentives I have seen are: publish the revised article with your link to your social media, give them a shoutout in social media, or sometimes agree to link to one of their relevant posts in exchange when and where it makes sense. There is much debate in the SEO world as to if creating mutual backlinks actually negates the value for both parties or not, but regardless, providing some incentive will ensure your efforts have a higher chance of succeeding.

The above methods are only some of the popular ways of generating backlinks. Once you reach out to other websites, only your imagination will limit you to the possibilities for collaboration.

It's Not Necessarily About the Total Amount

Do a Google search for "how many backlinks should a website have" and you'll see a common answer is between 50 and 100 backlinks to see the results of your activities raise your content higher in the search results. This depends on a lot of different factors, one being how many backlinks the content on the first page of search engine results already has and another being the quality of the source of those backlinks. I believe that backlinking is less of a numbers game and more of a relevancy one.

When the content of the site linking to you is irrelevant to your topic, then I'd suggest that the number of backlinks would not help you. This can muddy the algorithm and weaken your argument for authority. This whole exercise is about showing the algorithm our authority and trustworthiness. Why would an irrelevant website using irrelevant anchor text go out of their way to link to you? If it makes no sense to the average eye, it probably makes little sense to the algorithm either.

We build domain authority by showing our expertise through the volume in our Library of Content. The concept of the Library of Content is about targeting your blog to keywords and building authority on a topic. Collecting backlinks from random sources won't align with this authority. Just as my guest blogs on various topics were taking away my strength and focus on my keywords for my Library of Content, having multiple sites with unrelated content link to your content will detract from the strength you are building.

Let's look at it this way: I'm an authority on influencer marketing. Many influencers are involved with fashion. But if a fashion website asked me to guest blog on their site and then I linked to my site, the topics would be so out of sync that it would not be relevant to what I do. This data—their expertise—would be counter to mine. I don't have domain authority in that area so it wouldn't be relevant. There is so little overlap in our authority and keywords that the backlink from their website to mine might muddy my domain authority.

Finding Other Collaborators

When I search for places where I could guest blog, I use my SEO tool to see if their ranking keywords are relevant to what I do. For instance, do they rank for any of the keywords that I want to rank for? When there is a strong overlap in topics that we both rank for, it signals strong relevancy. When there's some overlap, then it's still a good fit. If the overlap is too low, then that site isn't relevant to me and won't be a relevant channel to show my expertise or send a positive signal to search engines.

Engaging in generating new backlinks to your website is like building expertise with your Library of Content. Just as you want to focus on keywords to build your pillars, you want to have targeted backlinks to send powerful signals to search engines that your content has value. With an entire network of content marketing and SEO agencies leveraging various freelance writers creating and ghostwriting blog content, it is becoming more common to see link swapping between sites and blogs as a complicated game of backlink Twister. While search engines do not condone this as it dilutes the meaning of the backlink to begin with, it is a reality.

Once your website builds domain authority, others will reach out to you. Decide whether you can develop a relationship of value with these entities. My advice is to keep an open mind and realize that while there are questionable people who might reach out to you, large businesses with high domain authority have also invited me to take part in the same effort, either directly or through various agencies. It takes some good prospecting—and an open mind—to find the relationships that will prove gold.

The Results Speak for Themselves

One of my Fractional CMO clients, SwagDrop (https://swagdrop.com), a B2B provider of branded swag and merchandise, followed the Library of Content advice and implemented a variety of the backlink methods mentioned here. In a published case study,[6] they were able to receive 86 new backlinks over a six-month period, helping to increase their domain rating (DR), one way of measuring website authority, from a 3 to nearly a 50 out of a maximum 100. Even Wikipedia "only" has an 86, so you can imagine how this higher authority will help all of their relevant content rank higher.

Publishing your blog does not guarantee being found. Optimizing your content through building backlinks is a sound way to speed up your content being found in search engines and thus increasing website traffic from potential customers. Begin with the Library of Content and then strategically build backlinks to your Library through the different methods discussed in this chapter to give it the best chance of reaching the most people in search engines. It adds an extra step in relationship-building, but those relationships pay dividends over time as a long-term investment in influencer marketing for SEO.

Key Takeaways:

- Building relationships with algorithms is about trustworthiness and authority.
- Backlinks create validity that your content is useful and trusted. This builds domain authority.
- Backlinks are relationships that show you're involved in the conversation.

Companion Workbook Exercises:

- 9.1 | Backlink Audit
- 9.2 | Directory Backlink Boost
- 9.3 | The Write for Us Lottery
- 9.4 | Pitch Perfect Blogging

Chapter 10
Build Paths

"A trail through the mountains, if used, becomes a path in a short time, but, if unused, becomes blocked by grass in an equally short time."

— Mencius

A common mistake that small businesses make is building a list without properly using it. Similar to muscles that turn to fat from lack of use, losing touch with your contacts leads to them losing interest in you.

Although lead magnets can help you grow your email list, you now need to build the paths to communicate with them. We need to find reasons to contact these people, without it coming off like trying to bump into someone who won't return your calls after a first date. You need something organic, something that engages, and something that delivers value to the relationship you are building.

Most experts say you want to communicate weekly to keep the contacts engaged. Some say as frequently as daily. This is to keep your brand fresh in their mind so they don't forget why they signed up in the first place—the value you would provide them. When emails go unopened, email clients like Gmail might relegate your communications to the promotions tab or, we shudder to think, the spam folder. The grass that Mencius warned us about has now blocked our paths.

Instead of pummeling our contact database with promotion after promotion, let's take a step back and focus on email not to send out communication but as a relationship builder. Through consistent communication, we build strong relationships. Through consistent communication, we enhance customer loyalty, and conversations open to drive advocacy.

Not only are returning customers cheaper to keep than finding new ones, but satisfied customers also become powerful advocates.

Mapping the Well-Trodden Path

The commonly accepted knowledge is that it takes between five to 20 touches to convert a prospect to a customer. The previously mentioned Google Zero Moment of Truth report suggests that it also requires time consumed for your content. In a Digital First world, when algorithms are the gatekeeper in both S elements of the SES Framework, the best way to do this is through email.

When someone has given you permission to contact them directly, without algorithms standing at the gate for your message, then it's a channel you simply must use.

The truth is, though, that you must have something to say, and your message has to bring value. Email as a communication tool gives you the power to direct the buyer's journey and control these interactions, but if you are not adding value, people will quickly unsubscribe or simply ignore your emails.

First impressions count. It is also at the very beginning of your email relationship when your customer has the greatest interest in you. Data suggests that your very first welcome email actually brings in more sales than any other type of email that you might send[1].

Weaving Your Story

Storytelling is not unique to email marketing, but this same concept can, and should, apply to wherever you publish content. It can be extremely powerful in the email medium because of the intimate feeling of direct communication.

Therefore, storytelling can expedite each step of the funnel. Storytelling is marketing. Email gives us the ability to tell our story over and over; add additional details, new perspectives, new angles, and new ways for the consumer to become part of the story. All audiences enjoy stories, and telling stories allows you to connect with the audience. This is why Sears had a handwritten, if still mass-printed, note. This is why the J. Peterman catalog, famously caricatured in *Seinfeld*, contained personal stories.

If the adage of "show, don't tell" works in writing, maybe marketing can tap into "show, don't sell." You're telling your brand's story, and you're telling the story of the consumer within the frame of your brand. You're telling them the possibilities that they can embrace by being part of your story. That story leads to the sale. You want to make them the hero of your story, a powerful concept developed by and fully explained in the book *Building a Story Brand* by Donald Miller.

Like blog content, developing stories over your emails comes back to knowing what you can write around. Through experimenting and brainstorming, discover what themes you revisit. In the way you gathered your keywords, pool the themes you can cover. Some might be new uses of your product. It might be innovations in your brand or industry. It might be different stories of the people at your company, or your customers. If you are at the heart of your brand identity, then the emails may be more personal stories. Everyone will develop their own ideas depending on their brand, their audience, and their own values.

A story can be a reason to open the email even when they're not looking at making a purchase. This keeps your brand in front of them.

A common technique used by a lot of public speakers is to create a database of your own stories that you can later use in your content. I use the Notion app, which I also use to take notes at meetings and conferences that I attend, but also use the text-to-voice feature of my smartphone to make a note of my thoughts and stories when I am on the go. All companies should create a similar "digital story vault" to collect and store stories from employees and customers for future content.

The 7 Primary Communication Pathways

To communicate with your list, you need a reason. There needs to be a purpose in contacting them without reminding them you want them to read your email. A regular newsletter is a common tool. It gives value to the reader and puts your brand in front of them. When there's no reason, just another email to say hi, then there is no value. And the unsubscribe button is just one click away.

You need a structure to base your email messaging around that you can easily implement through a combination of what I call the seven primary communication pathways. The goal is to organize your email marketing in a way that helps you engage and maintain the attention of your email subscribers.

You can use these individually or combine them based on what triggered the reader to sign up to your email list.

1. Welcome Emails.

I already hinted at the importance of making a good first impression with your emails. Email gives you power to control that first impression in a Digital First world. Customers might have come through that first part of the funnel to become aware of you, but this email is the first direct interaction. Besides the potential sales impact of that first email, welcome emails have an open rate of over 80 percent[2]. Beyond that, over 70 percent of people expect to receive a welcome email after signing up for a lead magnet[3].

It's easy to thank people in person. In a Digital First world, it's different but still important. This first email is essential to forging that relationship. It's the first step to tell the story of the values of your brand. It's the first chance to entice with offers, foster engagement, and lay the foundation for further communication.

While there is no one general rule how many emails need to be part of this welcome sequence, I like the published example of five emails over seven days that the help desk software company Help Scout has published on their blog[4]:

1. Welcome aboard: This email answered the question, "What happens now?" It includes an invitation to reply to begin a conversation with their team.
2. Curated list of five popular articles: They send out this email the next day, showing the articles as recommendations by various staff members—including their names, photos, and titles—to give it a personal touch.
3. Five more popular articles: Sent out two days later, this complements the second email and ensures that everyone can find an article that might interest them.
4. Customer success stories: Sent out another two days later, this email showcases customer stories to give social proof of the results that the email recipient can also receive.
5. Special offer: One day after the fourth email, a 45-day free trial offer is sent.

LandCafe, a Polish online retailer of coffee and tea, used a six-email welcome sequence, with one welcome email, four educational emails, and a final email with a discount coupon. They ended up generating sales from 54 percent of the recipients, with only 13 percent coming from the final discount coupon email[5].

2. Lead Nurture Sequences.

The above welcome emails are examples of a sequence of emails that are pre-scheduled to send at pre-determined intervals. There are different pathways in your email communication where you'll use a sequence. It's a designated feature of most email solutions. Since email is the only forum where you curate the messages in the order you want people to receive them, sequencing is a powerful "set it and forget it" tool.

The lead nurture sequence is a series of emails that build further trust and develops connection to your brand with the purpose of bringing the potential customer further down the pipeline and closer to becoming a customer. These sequences usually trigger when a specific lead shows interest in a specific product or service and registers through a specific lead magnet. The nurture sequence can push that conversion from the very start for someone who didn't have time to complete the transaction or needed some more enticement or information.

A great example of this is Plumb's Veterinary Drugs, the leading drug resource for veterinarians. They created a lead magnet, a free and downloadable veterinary medication guide. They created a three-email nurturing series designed to provide prospects who downloaded the guide with invaluable content, telling the story about why Plumb's Veterinary Drugs, and specifically the veterinary medication guides, were of value. The result is that this campaign converted 28 percent of its hundreds of leads that it generated[6].

3. The Newsletter.

This is the workhorse for email marketing. It provides valuable content while keeping the brand at the forefront of people's minds. The newsletter is a way of saying "we're here and we have something interesting to share." The frequency really depends on how often you've got something to share. Overdoing it increases the chance of losing a subscriber.

Deciding what to put in a newsletter is different for everyone. It should be consistent and provide value to the reader. Commonly, it's information about milestones for the brand, industry news, trends, blog content, curated pieces, FAQ, or a thought leadership column.

The goal is to develop brand connectivity. Customers spend more when they feel that connection. Newsletters are more common in B2B, but not exclusively. In the B2B sector, 83 percent of brands say they have a newsletter[7].

My emails to a customer after a lead magnet is downloaded is a welcome sequence tailored for the subject of the lead magnet. When that sequence runs out, I merge them into a weekly newsletter. I offer my own subscribers the ability to receive updates of new blog posts the day I publish them, combined with weekly newsletters; or a weekly newsletter on its own; or a monthly newsletter on its own. Each newsletter has its own format, which includes my personal updates, followed by a recent YouTube video, my latest podcast episode, and a host of news article summaries with links that might interest, keep top of mind and continuously add value.

Setting your own cadence and content will come down to your unique brand and your relationship with your list. It might take time to perfect your rhythm, so test different things and read the data in your email analytics to find the perfect combination of elements that work best for your audience.

4. Educational Content.

Educational content could be part of the welcome email, lead nurture sequence, or form the basis of your regular newsletter. It could also be totally separate.

If your brand offers products or services with a creative twist, such as beauty products or art supplies, providing content in different ways to use these products is a firm step for the relationship. An email series packed with tips, tricks, and tutorials delivered straight to your customer's inbox right after the welcome email or nurture sequence gives value. Another option could be to send out a handy educational guide whenever you're launching a new product. This is something practical to keep your audience engaged and informed.

5. Holidays and Seasonal Promotions.

Planning these emails far in advance is important because they revolve around holidays and seasons. Timeliness is important to these and can boost revenue. Some sources say that holiday sales make up over 25 percent of annual sales for half of small businesses in the United States[8]. Other special occasions like birthdays and anniversaries can also trigger an email if you have the data. Even if it's something more trivial, like an anniversary for being a loyal customer of the brand, you show the consumer that you value them. Acknowledging the customers' milestones gives value to the relationships.

6. Events.

People love being part of special events. If you're getting ready to take part in an in-person conference or virtual event, then tell people about it. By sending out event emails, you're giving more people the opportunity to benefit from your brand's offerings, and I'm not just talking about B2B events. If you're an ecommerce company, that livestream that you do together with an influencer might be something your audience wants to tune into. Pop-up shops are a perfect in-person event to promote via email as well. It's all about informing, engaging, and creating opportunities for your audience to experience what your brand offers, whether it is physically or virtually, and that is the power and value of event emails.

7. Promotional Broadcast.

I am intentionally putting this last here because, for some companies, this is the only communication pathway they know; however, it becomes most effective after you have built a relationship bridge.

Once you've laid down the other communication pathways, your prospects will be much more likely to open your promotional broadcasts. You've built rapport and added value to what they were looking for when they opted in to your email list.

Promotional emails are the easiest to understand of all the communication pathways simply because they are the type of email that we probably receive the most. Also, like social media promotional posts, these are the ones we've most likely sent early in building our strategy.

A promotional email is simply a communication pathway with a clear, direct call to action, an emissary in the inbox with the mission to drive sales. Promotional emails offer an effective way to engage your audience, showcase your latest offerings, and boost your revenue. But crafting an effective promotional email is an art. It requires a delicate balance of persuasive language, enticing offers, and a compelling call to action.

It can be tempting to always be sending a promotional email, but they are far more effective once you have developed a deeper relationship with your target audience. Your goal is not to make a sale. Your goal is to engage with your customer. The buyer's journey doesn't end with the sale. When your customer feels part of the brand culture, then you can leverage them as part of your promotional efforts.

If everything you send to people is a promotion, then many will tune it out. Is it really a sale if you offer 10 percent off every week? Some will sign up to the newsletters just for the promotions with the idea of only buying when you have a sale, but I wouldn't make that the core of your messaging.

The most common types of promotional emails are:

- Sales and discounts. Promoting awareness about deals is essential to let your customers know about the discounts. Email blasts can help here on occasions like Black Friday.
- Time-bound discounts. These drive visits to your site when there's a limited sale. You can't leave it up to hope people will know about it or find it on social media. This is especially true for "flash sales."
- New products. The release of a new product is always an exciting piece of news to share. You can amplify the email with social media when you mix them. If you're launching

a new product with an influencer, the emails can show the influencer showcasing the new product.

Email is a truly unique way to communicate. It remains the marketing strategy with the highest ROI. The benefits go beyond sales. Email's true potential lies in building relationships and establishing trust. That it's been around for decades at this point means that a lot of luster has worn off email marketing, but don't let that negatively influence your perspective on this critical digital thread.

Key Takeaways:

- Through consistent communication, we build strong relationships. Through consistent communication, we enhance customer loyalty, and conversations open to drive advocacy.
- Every email transaction presents a different way to continue the conversation.
- The unsubscribe button is always just one click away.

Companion Workbook Exercises:

- 10.1 | Weaving Your Story
- 10.2 | Evoke, Engage, Email
- 10.3 | Create (or Revise) Your Welcome Email Sequence
- 10.4 | Nurture with Knowledge

Chapter 11
Build Visibility

"Example is not the main thing in influencing others. It is the only thing."

— Albert Schweitzer

Where Platform Authentic Content is a way to be seen in a world of declining social media visibility, user-generated content—or UGC—provides an easier and more effective way of being seen in social media news feeds. When people see examples of your product or service being used by people like them, the business impact it can have is inherently larger.

The concept that companies and brands need to generate a full 100 percent of their own content for social media is not just wrong; it is a fundamental misunderstanding of how to operate on social media. The short lifespan of social media feeds beckons you to always be generating new material, which prevents you from leaving the never-ending hamster wheel of content creation. It takes away time from other parts of your business. One solution is to pay creators and influencers for content. The benefits are even greater when you can turn your customers and fans into organic content generators.

How can we so frequently publish without requiring much effort while also providing the credibility that we need for social media? More companies are turning to user-generated content to cover these bases. 86 percent of marketers claim they've attempted to incorporate UGC into their campaigns, but only 27 percent say they had a strategy for doing so[1].

My first experience with UGC was when I was helping a brand promote their baby health products to mommy bloggers—this was just before Instagram started emerging as a major consumer channel. While the output we requested was a blog post, some bloggers created blog post visuals of their babies using my client's products. These images were not just better visually than what the brand themselves had created, but also had the authenticity of knowing who was in the picture and who created the image.

While Platform Authentic Content is a first step in re-imagining your social media presence for today, UGC will speed up your visibility in the newsfeed of social media users.

Using user-generated content has become more popular because it is so effective. It has spawned a whole new industry that has emerged to satisfy the needs of brands to create it: a new type of content creator called the UGC creator. A quick people search on LinkedIn for "UGC creator" generated 175,000 results! These content creators might not influence the communities that you might want to target, but they are skilled at creating the visuals that replicate the "Instagrammable" look or type of viral TikTok video that brands are seeking to re-create.

Assuming that the UGC is of high quality, the authenticity helps tell the brand story equally or more often better than you can. The reach of UGC is powerful. It's not limited to just certain social media platforms—it relates to all of them and can be powerful in developing your brand awareness and interactions on social media. This power stems from the multiple benefits of publishing user-generated content.

The Many Benefits of User-Generated Content

To fully understand the power of UGC, let's review some of its most powerful benefits.

UGC Takes Authenticity to the Next Level

Nothing is more authentic than the voice of a customer. They have often invested considerable time in using your product or witnessing your company's capabilities in the case of services. People have always relied on word of mouth for purchasing decisions, and more often those same people are coming to social media looking for recommendations. Ask any teenager and they will tell you they first search for a company or product and see if it is being talked about by average users on social media. When it's talked about by the company itself, it just looks like an advertisement.

Consider this one data point: The average consumer is 2.4 times more likely to label UGC as being authentic compared to content created by the brand. Marketers are the exact opposite and are 2.1 times more likely to say content created by the brand is actually more authentic compared to UGC[2]. When in doubt about authenticity, let the social media users do the talking, not your marketing department!

UGC Acts as a Trust Signal and Provides Credibility and Social Proof

Besides the authenticity of user-generated content, that this content exists shows that other people use your products and that you have actual customers. This is especially important for startups and small businesses. And, while some people love trying the latest and greatest thing on the market, many others want to be certain that a product or service is something they can trust. This holds equally true for consumer goods as it does for B2B SaaS products. It should come as no surprise, then, that 79 percent of people say that UGC affects their purchasing decisions[3].

Increased Social Media Engagement

The average UGC post generates 6.9 times more engagement than a brand-created post[4]. Another interesting point related to this is that

UGC encourages more UGC because of this additional engagement with the original creator. This leads to 64 percent of customers saying that when brands repost their content, they are more likely to create and share similar UGC in the future[5]. If our raison d'être of social media is to incite word of mouth, it all starts with the engagement that UGC delivers.

UGC Is Cost-Effective

If you don't have to create the content yourself, then you aren't spending money on content creation. If you offer a small incentive, like a discount or free product, you might get a larger amount of UGC and even repeat business.

Even further ROI: Online data suggests that UGC-based ads get four times higher click-through rates and a 50 percent drop in cost-per-click than average[6]. The economics supporting UGC are solid.

UGC Diversifies Your Content with More Creativity

You should not limit diversity and creativity to your own internal content creation team. If anything, there's more creativity in your users. Staff, while creative, might not have the same depth of perspective. And their jobs depend on your company's overall performance. End-users don't view your products in the same way: it's one thing to tout the benefits of your products as defined by the company and something else to experience the benefits as a user. Users have different ideas than your internal team, if only because they're different people with unique experiences and have a different perspective on your product.

If you have ever used ChatGPT and found responses to your prompt that you had never thought of before, UGC is doing the same thing in showcasing the various use case scenarios for your products in social media.

Increased Sales

All the above benefits culminate in more sales for companies that leverage UGC. One data point suggests that companies that incorporate UGC on their website see an 18 percent increase in revenue[7]. This is because UGC leads 48 percent of customers to discover new products. And 84 percent of millennials say that UGC influences what they buy. We all know the value of product reviews coming from people like us, so these stats shouldn't come as a surprise.

All of this data shows the increased value and benefits that UGC content will deliver. But the content is more than just content. It's developing relationships with customers, fans, influencers, and content creators. Sourcing and publishing UGC will help you develop more relationships with more social media users that matter. If you reimagine social media not as another advertising channel but as the ultimate public square to develop relationships with people, you can begin to truly embrace a new Digital First approach in social media that the process of UGC embodies.

If Disney Does It, so Should You

Since this book focuses more on the small business that might not have the same resources as larger brands, I try to use smaller brands for my case studies to show you that if they can do it, you can, too. This example of a big brand using UGC is powerful because if there was one brand that already has a plethora of its own content and an extremely strong brand value that wouldn't seem to need UGC, it would be Disney. Even they saw the same value that you should.

In the early days of developing an Instagram strategy, Disney Resorts analyzed how its guests were engaging through the channel. They found that the quality of the photos, even from amateur photographers, was worthy of the Disney brand. To put it in Disney terms, it was nothing short of magical. The Disney social team crowdsourced the entire Disneyland Instagram feed from its guests—a 100 percent

UGC strategy comprising "re-gramming" or reposting of the best guest photos.

Disney Resorts also discovered that the sheer volume and creativity of its extremely passionate fan base was too much for them to match. It would take enormous resources to scale an original Instagram strategy that size, and it could never have the authenticity of its guests.

The initial challenge was legal. How could a brand so conscious of copyright issues use customer-generated content for its Instagram feed? The answer was simple, actually—they asked guests for permission. Disney implemented a clear and efficient approval process that takes place entirely within Instagram. Through the comments, Disney asks for permission to re-post a guest's photo. When the guest comments back with an explicit confirmation, Disney re-posts the photo with proper attribution.

The average engagement rate at the time for the UGC uploaded to Disneyland's Instagram account was over 10 times higher than other social media platforms and more than twice as high as other prominent businesses on the network[8].

It worked for Disney not because of their size but because they knew their customers and their audience.

How Instagrammable Is Your Customer Experience?

UGC worked for Disney because it is a naturally Instagrammable brand. To encourage UGC, try to make your customer journey as Instagrammable as possible.

I think just hearing the term "Instagrammable" should give you a feel for what I mean, but I believe the Japanese counterpart, "Insta-bae" (インスタ映え) explains the concept even better:

"Scenery, people, and things that look great in photos and are preferred by Instagram users[9]."

Once you have defined who you're communicating with, and understand how they communicate, you can pinpoint what you can offer them to communicate. What can you offer to see how people can post your content without you asking? With restaurants, it's asking what your clientele would share on social media. It might be a particular part of the interior design, or the dishes themselves. Making the experience more "Instagrammable" increases the possibility that they will share their experiences online. In some restaurants' cases, the food is not necessarily the best. It's about the experience, or the décor.

Let's look a little deeper into some potential UGC scenarios regardless of if you serve consumers (B2C) or other businesses (B2B). The same principles of UGC apply equally to B2Bs, but how to implement it and the content mediums you deploy might be different. You may offer a service and not a tangible product. Or your product may be so big and off-limits that it is impossible to get close to. For B2B, it is not as intuitive to have a UGC creator develop an Instagrammable image or TikTok video that reviews your product.

Even the simple act of having customers post a picture of your brand or some swag they received from you on their social media feed is user-generated content. When you think of the number of pictures every day posted online of Starbucks cups—regardless if the misspelling of names conspiracy is true—that's a lot of Starbucks branding online without the company doing anything.

5 Ways to Generate UGC for Your Business

All of this *sounds* good, but how do you actually *do* it?

UGC takes many forms, each of which you can leverage in more than one way beyond social media. To make it easier for you to implement, here is a list of five different activities, regardless of industry, that you can do to begin or speed up building your own user-generated content library.

1. Run Contests and Giveaways

One of the easiest and tried-and-true ways of generating user-generated content is through a contest or giveaway.

A simple way to do this is to create a hashtag contest to encourage the creation of user-generated content centered on a product or campaign. Usually, you'll have a campaign-based or product-specific hashtag you've already coined. For smaller brands, anything that's brand-specific can work well. Here, you'll give out some prizes, products, swag, or a combination thereof to a lucky winner. It's a nice way to give your fans some recognition.

Obviously, you don't need to be limited to hashtag contests, but they are one of the most effective ways to generate lots of UGC content in a short period. When you handle the contest as a lead magnet, by asking for the participant's email address, and as a source of content, then you can gain a strong foothold in two parts of your Digital First marketing framework at the same time—the email and the social.

2. Remind Customers Everywhere to Use Your Branded Hashtag

Create a hashtag for your brand and encourage your customers to use it when posting photos or videos of your products or services. Include this call-to-action in your social media profiles, website, email, and even physical packaging. A great way to launch your branded hashtag is through a contest or giveaway.

Fitness wear brand Lululemon ran the #thesweatlife campaign, encouraging people to post pictures of themselves authentically sweating in their activewear. In exchange, they would post the UGC on their social media profiles and eventually on their website. The campaign was massively successful, bringing in tens of thousands of entries[10], and it has generated over 1.5 million uses of the hashtag to date. The branded hashtag has even launched its own community. As a brand manager at Lululemon said, "We created the program as a way to connect with our guests and showcase how they are authentically sweating in our product line. We see it as a unique way to bring their offline experiences into our online community[11]." By tagging their distinct product with the hashtag, Lululemon got to show off their reach in authentic conversations—and create impact without saying a word.

If people like your stuff, they should know you'd love to include them in your social media. Publicize your branded hashtag and encourage people to use it. The more you share their content, the more they will share yours. Always ask for permission before posting someone else's UGC on your profile. This will make your legal team happy and further strengthen your relationship between brand and creator.

I interviewed UGC expert and Instagram Consultant Kathryn McCauley (@aguideto_socialmedia on Instagram) on my podcast. She guides companies through their social media and UGC journeys in Australia. She also promotes branded hashtags on her Instagram accounts related to tourism in her local Ocean Grove and Barwon Heads, two small seaside towns in Australia.

On my podcast, Kathryn explained that a direct call to action, such as "Tag us with your best shots, videos and shoutouts #aguidetooceangrove" or "Tag #aguidetooceangrove to share," works better than just putting the hashtag in your profile or caption. This guides people through posting. Kathryn actively goes through the hashtag mentions every few days to see what people have posted. After getting the approval from the creator, she reposts the UGC. She says from sourcing to publishing, the process takes a maximum of five minutes of her time.

By encouraging people to post their content with her branded hashtags, she's been able to generate approximately 17,000 pieces of UGC for her travel guides for the Ocean Grove and Barwon Heads Instagram accounts. These are small towns with a combined population of only 22,000, so you can imagine how impactful that can be in terms of promotion without the need to self-promote.

3. Partner with Content Creators

Content creators are good at—and love—creating the type of Instagrammable content that generates engagement. If you can find some in your niche, collaborating with them can help you reach a wider audience with your UGC should they also publish it. This content can drive sales by increasing brand exposure, building trust, and reaching new potential customers. For instance, many people might benefit from your products and services but simply not be aware of what you offer.

Content creators are not just on popular B2C social networks like Instagram. They are also bloggers, podcasters, and YouTubers. While not the most popular of marketing channels, the interview-centric modality of many podcasts is actually a great way to connect on a more personal level with content creators. Every podcast episode can become a piece of UGC content. While we see a lot of these types of branded UGC podcasts in the B2B space, an outstanding role model for this is an iconic consumer brand, Jack Daniel's, which hosts a podcast called Around the Barrel, which generates engaging UGC content with every episode.

Finding content creators in your niche is like looking for brand affinity collaborators and external influencers, a process I will describe in greater detail in Chapters 14 and 15. If you can't find content creators in your niche, you also have the option of working with UGC content creators here. There are literally thousands of UGC content creators you can engage with and hire; searching for "UGC creator" or "UGC content creator" on any given social network or freelancer marketplace that I will discuss in Chapter 18 will yield results.

Remember, if one benefit of UGC is saving money and time, even hiring a UGC creator will allow you to create content that is more effective and less expensive than you or an agency can do. This is why brands such as Disney[12], Nerf, and Olipop[13] have hired TikTok influencers to be their corporate social media content creators.

4. Ask Your Customers for Reviews and Leverage Testimonials.

There's no better way to leverage UGC than through actual reviews of your product or through customer testimonials. In addition, reviewers will often tell readers what problems the product helped them solve. You can post reviews in many places, from a link on your website to an excerpt in advertising. For maximum results, try to get product reviews from a variety of user types, if applicable. This includes everything from a simple review on Yelp or Google My Business all the way to prepared statements on your website.

Reviews provide valuable information, create social proof, and influence consumers' purchasing choices. That's because people often consider other end users to be more honest about the advantages and disadvantages of a particular product than the brand.

Depending on the forum, many people are quite happy to generate reviews, and often a simple reminder is sufficient. You can also offer a small incentive. The key is that most people won't create social media UGC from a review, as they often publish these reviews on third-party websites and not your own. So you will need to ask customers to cut and paste their third-party review into a social media post with a selfie and a tag to your brand for optimal effect. Even if very few people post to social media, you have already reaped a tremendous benefit of sourcing more reviews for your brand.

When I leased a new car at a local car dealership, they took a picture of me smiling from the driver's seat just before I drove home. I thought little about it, until a few minutes later I got an email from the dealer that not only had my photo attached for me to keep, but it also included convenient links so that I could easily post a review on Google, Yelp, or Facebook. This is a great example of including the ask for reviews as part of your sales and marketing process, especially at the moment your customer is happiest!

Customers in the B2B space often share their reviews on third-party sites such as G2, Capterra, and GetApp. Should they review you there, ask your customer to cut and paste and publish that same review on their social media. Even if they don't publish on their social media, you still have a public review on a third-party site, which you can repurpose and publish on your social media profile as UGC content.

While users publish reviews on third-party websites, a testimonial can be a simple reply to an email. You can also source testimonials on social media through a DM with someone using your branded hashtag or taking a picture together should you meet in person. Even a short testimonial can go a long way.

5. Ask Your Employees

A subset of UGC that can be especially useful for B2B brands is employee-generated content (also called EGC). This is the easiest way to engage with UGC for any company. Your employees are your biggest fans. Ask them to share photos or videos of themselves using your products or services or having fun at company events.

There is no accurate data as to the median number of connections that an average employee might have on LinkedIn, but let's say an average employee has about 250 connections. That means a company's brand can get in front of those connections through its employees. If a company has just 100 employees and only 10 percent are involved with employee-generated content, that is still 10 additional people creating and sharing on behalf of the company to their connections. That means different social connections can see EGC about the company, which can exponentially help brand visibility grow. The collective reach of a company's employees will often surpass that of its brand. Not to mention the added benefit of being able to share the EGC on your company socials.

EGC efforts frequently involve the creation of social media channels solely dedicated to employer branding, such as @MicrosoftLife or @WeAreCisco on Instagram. EGC efforts have become so mainstream at larger enterprises that LinkedIn has a new type of ad, called Thought Leader ads, which allows companies to boost posts from their employees and publish them in their own feed as EGC.

UGC Ties Together the Digital Threads

Incorporating user-generated content into your communication does not have to be limited to just your social media framework. When the content is quality content, then the authenticity of that creation can benefit every digital point of contact that your business might have. As a digital thread, you can use UGC everywhere, including your website, email marketing, and even your offline marketing materials.

Revel Nail is an example of a DTC brand that leverages UGC

throughout its website, including product pages, and in doing so has found an increase in site conversions of nearly four times. This has also led to a 2 percent decrease in abandoned shopping cart rate, which for one product page that gets 40,000 visits per month equates to $25,000 per month in revenue[14].

There are many brands who still want to maintain their brand story via their own content on their social media. Sometimes the UGC curated still cannot express certain things that the brand feels compelled to tell. On the other side of that coin, there are stories and angles that people can say about a brand that a company can't. That's the true power of leveraging UGC in your marketing.

By finding a blend of these messaging strategies, you can weave together your story and the story about you from the perspective of consumers. Together, they will both revolutionize and exponentially multiply your impact.

Key Takeaways:

- Generating all your content for social media is time-consuming and misses the point of social media.
- UGC shows trust and social proof.
- UGC provides ways to source content, as well as connect across the platforms.

Companion Workbook Exercises:

- 11.1 | How Instagrammable Is Your Customer Experience?
- 11.2 | Hashtag Hero
- 11.3 | Content Creator Collab Fest
- 11.4 | Review Rally

Part Five
Allow Growth

"The proper order of things is often a mystery to me."

— Cheshire Cat in Lewis Carroll's Alice's Adventures in Wonderland

The order of the Digital Threads is important. We weave these threads together in a way that builds on the previous ones.

You can appreciate how I felt when many companies reached out to me wanting to tap directly into the power of influencer marketing without having laid other foundations of their digital marketing in place. Companies wanted to connect with customers on Instagram without having searchable content in place. Others wanted to run a giveaway on social media without treating it as a lead magnet, meaning that their email thread was not in place. It is futile to start here without getting your Digital First foundation in place first. These are your assets in the form of content, email subscribers, and social media advocates generated from publishing user-generated content. There is so much else to do before then that true external influencer marketing doesn't get introduced in this book until Part Six!

Without the right order, you won't know if you're going this way, that way, or the wrong way, as our friend, the Cheshire Cat, might say.

You can only accomplish the recommendations for growth here after concluding your efforts on the previous pages. You can't automate a list without a list, develop brand ambassadors without customers, and repurpose content without having content. The Digital Threads are now beginning to be woven together. There is more work to do, and these next chapters will focus on leveraging the platform that we have for future growth.

Chapter 12
Grow Content

"To repurpose an old thought, idea or memory to a new purpose is the height of creativity."

— Steve Supple

Content is truly the currency of digital marketing. Like every other form of currency, its worth comes from ensuring you get the most out of spending it. Finding your keywords, understanding your audience, and developing the written word is a lot of work to just create one piece of content. The good news is that publishing your video or blog post is not the end of the line for the currency. In fact, it is just the beginning.

Content is an asset, a gift that keeps on giving. It pays dividends above and beyond all the benefits we have covered when we repurpose it for every type of digital marketing container in our arsenal. In order to grow, we don't need to be creating more content from scratch—we simply need to repurpose more of it in more formats.

Wanting to meet your customers across different platforms, even in different mediums as new social media platforms rise, is natural. As my friend and fellow marketing author of *Content 10X*, Amy Woods, reminds us, people consume content in different formats, like two diners at a restaurant, one who wants the buffet and the other who wants a set menu. Finding the time to create original pieces of content that work organically and natively on each platform is time-consuming. That's where your repurposing content strategy comes into play.

Your company might be swimming in content without realizing it. Every blog post, every email newsletter, every event that you host, every time one of your employees speaks, every webinar that you do—these are all different content. Once you record and develop these, they can become a powerful engine exponentially creating more pieces of content across different platforms. When you make content repurposing part of your marketing DNA, it becomes much easier to meet the needs of the digital economy of today.

Being active across different platforms doesn't have to equate to creating lots of content. On social media, the goal is to develop and maintain relationships. That means communicating your message in ways that work on each platform. You need to understand the language and ways to communicate across different networks. Reposting the same piece across platforms won't work. This lacks strategy and ignores the fact that different communities and different platforms require different approaches. It's throwing your message to the abyss and hoping for engagement.

Different platforms also engage different languages, different ways of communicating. To truly take advantage of a platform, you need to take this into consideration. Using the Gen Z meme-centric approach of TikTok on Facebook might misfire. Trying to push it on LinkedIn will discredit your message.

Sometimes, the algorithm can penalize reposting content from one platform to another. Instagram has clarified that videos that are clearly recycled from other apps will be less discoverable on the platform[1]. While it has yet to be proven, many marketers believe that even if you try to remove the TikTok watermark, it seems that there are ways that the algorithm recognizes that the video is not native to the platform. The algorithm is the data-centric gatekeeper, but the audience on different platforms won't engage with your content in the same way as on another platform. This difference needs to be dealt with to make it easy for the algorithm to put in front of your audience.

You should primarily focus the energy and time you spend on building content that lasts longer in search engines—blogs, YouTube videos, and podcasts. In building your Library of Content, almost every piece of content you created is evergreen in nature—the best content for repurposing. One way to begin is to look at your analytics for pieces with high engagement metrics, positive feedback, and long-term search engine traffic. These provide the strongest foundation for future iterations.

As with Platform Authentic Content, the content needs to work on the platform you post on without calling for the user to leave the platform and go to your site. At least you should not call for them to leave often. For most businesses, content creation will probably focus on text-first (such as blog posts, lead magnets, email newsletters, etc.) or video-first (like webinars, Zoom interviews, video recordings of podcast interviews, YouTube videos, etc.).

Repurposing Text as a Starting Point

Beyond efficiency, using what you already have and repurposing it is a neat way of ensuring your messaging is the same. You align and target your message and advice across different social media platforms.

Although you invest time in crafting your blog, it's not necessarily the piece that you'll want to be promoting. You primarily design the content for each platform to develop relationships on that platform, and specifically for search engine users with your blog. However, through the art of repurposing, we can transform that content into being anything we want it to be, including Platform Authentic Content.

Starting with your blog means you can repurpose it into shorter pieces. This shorter text doesn't need to cover all the content of the blog. It can cover pieces of the information with a link at the end: "Continue reading here:" How you use this shorter adaptation depends on the platform. By repurposing your blog points into small, bite-sized pieces of wisdom, you can engage your audience on X threads or Instagram Threads in a way they will connect with.

Repurposing your blog into a LinkedIn-style article, published in the LinkedIn newsletter format, presents your message to these readers. You can also make the blog into a series of visuals and use the Instagram or LinkedIn carousel feature, like turning the content into a "5 Key Points" type of presentation. The current data shows that the engagement of these visual carousels often outperforms the usual posts. Tips and quotes also work particularly well for visual engagement.

Repurposing textual content doesn't have to be restricted to social media either. Digital Threads are stronger when woven together. You can also adapt blog posts into an e-book and incorporate them into your lead magnet campaign. You can repurpose them into an email course or series. Repurposing blog content offers flexibility beyond keeping it as text. By harnessing the power of a graphics-editing software, such as Adobe Express, you can make a visual. Take it one step further and you can create an infographic, a collection of words and simple images that illustrate a point. A highly effective way to frame infographics is by taking the main points of your blog post and highlighting them in the graphic. Visualize your blog content by creating images about the main points and statistics that you can embed in your post or use as stand-alone visual posts on social media. When you expand your horizons, you can re-imagine visual posts as not just being singular images but also carousels, Reels, and even Stories.

You can even repurpose old blog content into new blog content. I regularly review my blog content, looking for older posts that need some revising to help the posts gain new traffic, a process that is part of proper maintenance of my Library of Content. No matter what kind of blog you're running, other content creators want to displace you on search engine results. The battle for SEO dominance is constant. By updating your content, you are not only able to refresh your content to make sure it is up-to-date and show that you're still at the forefront of your niche, but you'll also give followers an opportunity to revisit your website. Search engines also see that you took the time to revise your content to keep it fresh, which might lead to an increase in rankings like it has for others[2]. Both benefits result in additional impression and traffic opportunities.

You also have the option to adapt the blog into a video script that you can post on YouTube. New text-to-video AI tools now allow you to create videos with either a "human" AI avatar or stock video combined with on-screen captions that allow you to convey your message in a moving image form you can use for long-form or short-form video for social media. Or you can read the script yourself in a talking head video or audio podcast.

Repurposing Video as a Starting Point

While you can repurpose from text to video using avatars and stock video, the most powerful repurposing comes when you start with video content that features real people. If you have ever done a webinar, run an event where you video recorded the speeches, or done livestream interviews for your podcast or otherwise, you are sitting on a potential goldmine of content.

Professional videos have always been in landscape format. It copies what we're used to seeing in cinema and on television. Now that more and more people are used to mobile devices, vertical video has emerged as the new trend. It adapts itself so easily to platforms like Instagram, TikTok, and even YouTube, as many users engage with videos on their phone and not on a computer. Fortunately, there are a growing number of AI tools that will help us repurpose horizontal videos into vertical ones.

Shorter videos give your content a chance to connect with TikTok, Instagram Reels, and YouTube Shorts users. In a similar way to the X threads approach, you can cut a long video down to five key points and make each a short vertical video in a way that captures the different visual language that engages the audience across each platform. This opportunity doesn't just apply to videos of you talking to your camera. When you have videos of events, you can break down the content into smaller moments. You can also transform presentations about new releases or products into short vertical videos. It's even possible to break down a direct-to-camera FAQ presentation into shorter videos.

Repurposing archived webinar videos into shorter content, or shorter courses, is an ideal way to take content you have already developed. You can repurpose webinars into shorter videos, blog content, their own X threads, or even a podcast episode.

I take longer horizontal videos and repurpose them into shorter horizontal videos where it makes sense, allowing me to get the best ROI from my content.

As previously mentioned, reposting a video from one platform to another, especially when it features a watermark like it does on TikTok, triggers a flag in the algorithm. The algorithm will not treat the content as favorably as something uploaded natively. That is why most content pros will first create a platform-agnostic version of the video, then, upon uploading to a specific social network, will add special features like music or stickers that exist in that platform's edit features to make the video platform-specific.

It is possible to adapt any content, not just by taking something long and cutting it up into shorter pieces. I've taken blog posts and repurposed them for classes I've taught at UCLA Extension. In fact, many of these chapters began life as a podcast episode. I wrote some of them to adapt the podcast script into a chapter. After realizing their relevance, I adapted others. Once again, once Digital Threads like repurposing become part of your DNA, it all becomes much easier, just like muscle memory.

Repurposing in Action

There are no limits to what you can achieve with content repurposing. Your imagination is the only restriction. I want to share some case studies with you to inspire you to do more with your content:

- SEO expert Brian Dean of Backlinko created a blog post about on-page SEO and then repurposed it using over 75%

recycled content into a video which has now received over 240,000 views on YouTube[3].
- Brian also repurposed a YouTube video on how to get more views on YouTube by taking the best one minute and posting it on LinkedIn, where it got over 1,000 likes and comments[4].
- The social media management tool Hootsuite took a blog post on Instagram hashtags and repurposed it into a 6-minute YouTube video generating over 21,000 views and into an Instagram carousel receiving over 1,000 reactions[5].
- Hootsuite also repurposed a webinar into a 2-minute summary video that received over 12,000 views on YouTube[6].

Best-selling author Gary Vaynerchuk creates over 30 pieces of content from a single long-form piece[7]. Similarly, a marketing agency can take 4 video interviews of customer success stories and create 45 new video assets in various sizes and lengths, repurposing these assets across different organic and paid channels[8]. Content repurposing is an investment that treats your content as a valuable asset, resulting in long-term dividends.

Content repurposing can give your content a fresh start on various platforms and mediums. It also helps your business stay visible to potential clients for a longer time. A great example of this is the B2B SaaS marketing platform, Metadata. They repurposed the original 11 videos from their first virtual event, DEMAND. They created YouTube videos, social media videos, and blog posts which they drip fed to their audience over the course of six months to keep their event top of mind. This content, combined with the audience that they built doing this, helped them successfully launch a new 64-episode industry-leading podcast series[9].

Repurposing can have a powerful impact on your business regardless of your size. It's all about getting your message out and using your content to develop relationships with potential clients, however they consume your content.

The Content Chain

I realized the impact that content repurposing could have on my business when I was recording a podcast. Similar to recording my UCLA Extension classes, I used Zoom to record both my audio and video so that someday I could repurpose that video. Then I realized there was an option in Zoom to livestream the recording on YouTube with one touch of the button. I didn't announce that I was doing it; I just did it.

My original intent was to create a video that I could use later. The epiphany I had was now I had another way to connect with my audience—through livestream. If I could strategize everything properly, I now had a content-creating pathway that would guide my content repurposing from the same pool of topics that were relevant to my target audience.

I first write a script for my podcast, which I will later adapt into a blog post. I broadcast the livestream of the podcast on LinkedIn, Facebook, X, and YouTube. The livestream gets indexed on YouTube just like any other video, so YouTube archives it there for future viewing. My podcast channel is where the audio podcast is available. I can repurpose the video into a vertical format for YouTube Shorts, TikTok, and Instagram Reels. I can repurpose my blog for LinkedIn carousel posts and X threads in bite-sized pieces with the focus on asking for people's opinion and thoughts at the end. As a result, I now have a multi-platform message without having to start from scratch on each piece.

I now had both content that would be long-form and live longer in search engine results and shorter content for social media platforms, all with a focus on developing relationships. And all this content emanates from a single source.

Your sources of content are wider than you might realize. Whenever you want to develop a new range of content, an audit of the content you've already developed is the perfect place to start. The foundation work has already been done, and you'll be extending the worth of the content you've worked hard to create.

By internalizing these tips, you are ready to transform your existing content into a powerful multi-channel marketing force. This strategy maximizes the value of your hard work—it is not simply throwing scraps on different platforms. Done effectively, repurposing can fuel an expanded content engine that keeps your audience engaged and your marketing efforts efficient.

Key Takeaways:

- Content is an invaluable asset. Using and reusing content in various ways can provide ongoing benefits.
- You can repurpose your content across platforms in different formats, but with the needs of that audience and platform in mind.
- The most powerful repurposing potential starts with video content that features real people.

Companion Workbook Exercises:

- 12.1 | Blog to Textual Threads
- 12.2 | Blog to Image Carousel
- 12.3 | Blog to Video (Horizontal)
- 12.4 | Blog to Short-Form Video (Vertical)
- 12.5 | Reflections on Content Repurposing

Chapter 13
Grow Conversations

"Automation does not need to be our enemy. I think machines can make life easier for men, if men do not let the machines dominate them."

— John F. Kennedy

With an active list and engaging email community, we can orchestrate the customer journey on our terms. Email marketing automation—a common feature included in most email marketing software tools—gives us the power to design our ideal communication funnel with our community, increasing our communication without exerting additional effort.

In doing so, we can literally communicate—and build business—while we sleep based on an ideal, personalized, and (most importantly) automated communication path. These tools give you the potential to grow engagement—and business—with your list passively, through the proper design of a sophisticated marketing automation system. The Data & Marketing Association (DMA) reported that 75 percent of email-related revenue comes from these types of triggered campaigns[1]. This means that generic blanket promotions are far less effective than ones based on consumer interest, as shown by their actual purchase and other behaviors that they digitally show.

Automation might seem like something only done by large companies, but it's much more in reach. And it's powerful. In fact, much of the email marketing that your business might already do might have some aspect of marketing automation tied to it you might not have realized. These emails break down into two kinds of emails:

Transactional emails. We send these emails in reply whenever the customer has engaged in a purchase or other transactional activity that they started. This includes receipt emails, password reset emails, and many other small interactions.

Triggered emails. Here you can strategize the communication and design how your customer experiences the customer journey through various "triggered" automations based on the customer's interactions with you outside of actual transactions.

The Power of Transactional Emails

Transactional emails can apply to B2B businesses and the provision of services, but they will be especially fruitful for direct-to-consumer B2C brands. The additional details that a consumer transaction usually entails give further opportunity for engagement. For instance, when buying jewelry online, the website might ask you to input your birthday or anniversary, but a B2B transaction would never require such personal details.

A customer's specific action triggers transactional emails, such as making a purchase or signing up for a service. They are not your run-of-the-mill promotional messages. The messages are personalized, timely, highly relevant, and expected by the recipient. Transactional emails can be a secret weapon in digital marketing because of this personalization and relevance.

In a survey by Constant Contact, average emails across all industries recently managed a 36.5 percent open rate, with a click rate of 1.40 percent[2]. Note that there are other studies, like the one by

Campaign Monitor, that put the average open rate at a much lower 21.5 percent[3].

Transactional emails receive a staggering eight times more clicks and opens than average emails. And they generate six times more revenue[4]. These emails deliver valuable information that customers need or want, from purchase confirmations to password resets. This drives a high level of engagement, which leads to a click rate of 10 to 20 percent[5].

When you consider this difference with other emails, the mind-blowing thing is that we can pre-program these transactional emails to be sent out automatically. Someone sitting at a keyboard does not perform the personal interaction that drives more clicks and opens. Once you've set up the structure, it's an automated process that saves you time and significantly boosts your engagement rates and revenue. This helps to explain the high ROI that email marketing delivers: It is the only part of the SES Framework that companies can automate to a high degree.

While their primary purpose is informative, transactional emails present an outstanding opportunity to cross-sell and upsell. For instance, instead of just thanking someone for their purchase, you can inject recommendations for other related products or services that should interest them. This subtle promotion of your relevant offerings to a hungry audience is what can help lead to increased sales and contribute to the staggering six-times-higher revenue mentioned earlier.

I'll give you a personal example. My brother is a winemaker in California, and he offers a wine club subscription service (https://tercerowines.com if you were curious!). When new wine allotments are available, he sends a message out to all his members telling them they can view them online and place their order. This communication gives him great power to communicate with his members. From a business standpoint, having people order earlier means they'll order again sooner. To help this, he could include a link so customers could directly access their allotments. An extra link for "forgot password" could help customers who might not have ordered recently. Beyond this, he can take advantage of the transactional email by adding more information about the latest wines, including direct links to their product pages. He could focus on the new wine of the season, perhaps with a link to a behind-the-scenes video of the winemaker. He can use the information he's gleaned from earlier orders to tailor wine selections for each customer. Whatever it is, as you can see from this example, transactional emails are ripe for innovation.

Types of Transactional Emails

At its heart, these emails are about transforming a passive, automated email into an active way of deepening your relationship with the recipient. There are more transactional emails than just following a purchase or signing up for a service. Only your imagination—and the functionality that your email software provides you—can limit you here.

The common thread between all these emails is that they can be 100 percent automated, personalized, and injected with relevant information soon after a transactional event.

Many of the e-commerce CMS software platforms such as Shopify already have pre-made templates to facilitate the sending of these. Don't be lazy: Customize each of these templates. Or better yet, use a sophisticated email marketing software—like Klaviyo, Omnisend, or ActiveCampaign—that integrates with your CMS platform (Shopify, WordPress, etc.) to further personalize and customize these transactional emails.

Rather than thinking of each of these as "transactional," however, I want you to think about how, at every step of the communication cycle, you can work to deepen your relationship with your customer base to foster trust, loyalty, and—ultimately—advocacy.

The Abandoned Cart Email

The abandoned cart email is an example of a digital behavior-based automated message that can reap dividends for your business.

Data suggests that nearly 70 percent of online shoppers abandon their carts without finalizing the purchase[6]. There are different reasons for this—exploring other options, considering shipping costs too high, expected delivery was too slow, didn't want to create a user account, or even had payment issues. Without intervention, these abandoned carts often spell the end of a sale.

Abandoned cart emails can be a game changer. If you've already captured your customer's email as part of the purchasing process, you can reach out to them. The secret now lies in offering incentives to bring them back to their shopping cart that are too tempting to resist. Some brands offer generous discounts on a single item, while others opt for a smaller discount, say 10 percent, on the entire order. While you might hesitate at the thought of discounts, the technique proves successful. With an effective strategy like abandoned cart emails, you could see a conversion rate greater than 10 percent[7]. That's a significant portion of sales you would have otherwise missed, and it balances the discount you offer.

The email marketing software company Klaviyo did a data sampling of millions of abandoned cart emails sent out from its platform and found that the average open rate was 41 percent, click rate 9.5 percent, and, most importantly, the revenue per recipient was an average of $5.81[8]. This one small data set generated more than $60 million in sales over the three-month window of analysis. That speaks to the potential power that these emails can have for your business when properly architected.

Order Confirmation

This is the most prevalent type of transactional communication. And it offers a fantastic opportunity to drive further sales and enhance your customer relationship.

After a customer makes a purchase on your site, along with their order confirmation, you can send a tailored coupon or product recommendations that complement their recent purchase. Suddenly, a simple transactional email has transformed into a personalized shopping guide, offering you an ability to upsell your other products and services to them and boost order value.

By including shipping and tracking details in your order confirmation emails, your customers can follow their order's journey from warehouse to doorstep, knowing exactly when to expect its arrival. This builds trust. There are further follow-up emails you can send that can further extend this goodwill.

These thoughtful touches do more than just streamline the shopping process—they foster brand loyalty. Customers who feel engaged and informed are more likely to remain loyal to your brand for the long haul.

Account Activation and Confirmation

These emails are often the first point of contact after a customer makes a purchase or subscribes to your service. They provide you a chance to turn what seems like a formality into something more.

Instead of just a thank-you note, you can send a more comprehensive message that confirms their account, provides monetary details, and includes crucial company contact information.

You should also provide explicit instructions on how your customers can access their purchases or use new features. You can also use this transactional email to offer helpful tips or tutorials that enhance the user experience.

Shipping Confirmation

These communications are the second most common type of transactional email. They can offer more than just logistical information.

A shipping confirmation email not only provides them with a convenient link to track their package, but it can also include personalized product recommendations, or a tempting discount for their next order.

The potential of shipping confirmation emails goes beyond sales.

Believe it or not, this type of email was one reason CD Baby, one of the largest online distributors of music back in the day, became a success story. Their shipping confirmation emails would include lines like, *"Your CD has been gently taken from our CD Baby shelves with sterilized contamination-free gloves and placed onto a satin pillow,"* and *"...the entire town of Poland waved 'Bon Voyage!' to your package, on its way to you, in our private CD Baby jet..."* That email was so loved that if search for "private CD Baby jet" you will find thousands of results deriving from word of mouth—all from a transactional email!

"How Was Everything?" Email

Following up after their purchases with a separate email that contains a personalized thank you is one way to turn customers into advocates.

You can email a customer asking them how they feel about your product or service, what changes they'd like to see, and whether they appreciate your efforts. This shows your commitment to their satisfaction and the value you put on the relationship. Email is a perfect forum for this simply because emails are direct and offer scalability and automation like no other channel.

Also, these emails don't just have to be about thanking them and gathering feedback. Use this as an opportunity to have them provide their feedback, especially if it is positive, as a public review and offer incentives for participation. In doing so, you are now weaving a previous digital thread, user-generated content. Using transactional emails as a way of generating more word-of-mouth marketing through reviews provides additional pieces of UGC that you can use.

Only your imagination can limit how you can leverage these transactional emails.

Triggered Automated Communication

Although transactions in quantity might be fewer, marketing automation is valuable if you operate in an industry with a long sales cycle. There are a whole range of other opportunities in these industries. This automation approach sends targeted and triggered emails automatically based solely on customer activity or behavior, which doesn't require a commercial transaction.

To better understand the potential of these types of emails, it is important to consider what we can track and thus trigger. Email marketing automation software usually works off triggers such as

- a purchase was made (transactional emails)
- a website page was visited
- an email was opened and/or clicked
- a lead magnet or other asset from your website was downloaded

A more sophisticated email marketing solution can also add a "score" to each person on your email list. You can calculate this score using all the mentioned "trigger" actions and then send users into different email sequences when they reach different scoring levels.

As an example, a scoring system might be:

- 5 points every time a specific product page was visited
- 1 point every time another website page was visited
- 1 point every time an email was opened
- 3 points every time an email was clicked on

We can also attach expiration dates to the scoring so that we know that these actions have taken place; for instance, in the last 90 days.

Targeting by Customer Lifecycle

If we are going to automate the sending of emails based on trigger events, a convenient way of thinking about this is doing so at different points in the customer lifecycle, beginning with those who have yet to convert to becoming our customers.

Customer Acquisition, or List Retention, Emails

When engaging in lead magnets, you will increase the size of your list to include your prospects. You will do your best to win their business through your welcome email and nurture sequence, but over time, they still might not convert into becoming a customer. That is where customer acquisition emails come in, usually automated to deliver x days/weeks/months after email signup to those who have still yet to become a paying customer.

These emails are your golden ticket to winning the loyalty of new subscribers who are still on the fence. This type of email usually offers some sort of special deal and/or exclusive offer to win over these potential clients. You should also provide valuable information about the benefits of being a customer, increasing the perceived value of your brand.

The customer acquisition email is an example of automated emails that target email list members wherever they are in the customer lifecycle. Here that is the middle of the funnel, considering they have subscribed to your list.

The most popular triggered emails based on customer lifecycle are at the front end, like transactional abandoned cart emails, or back end, such as a re-engagement campaign to reignite interest among inactive customers or subscribers. With the proper design, companies can and should send them at strategic trigger points in between. This is because the benefits of these emails extend beyond just engagement, improving revenue, meeting customer expectations, and positively influencing retention.

Preference Targeting Emails

Every email address on your list represents an individual with unique preferences, habits, and behaviors. Understanding these nuances can be your ticket to success. That's where the power of preference-targeting emails comes into play.

Imagine this: you have two customers. One is a bargain hunter who always goes for the cheapest product on sale, while the other is a trendsetter who can't resist the latest and most expensive model. How can you engage with these vastly different customers effectively?

By leveraging data such as purchase history, link clicks, and survey responses, you can tailor your emails to suit each customer's preferences. For instance, you might recommend discounted items to your bargain hunter or showcase your new arrivals to your trendsetter. This way, you're not just sending emails—you're delivering personalized content that speaks directly to each customer's interests.

Preference-targeting emails work across industries. Whether you're selling fashion apparel, tech gadgets, or home decor, these emails can help you connect with your customers on a deeper level.

Location-Targeting Emails

We can also leverage what we know about the location of our email audience members. If they have a purchase history with us, we can easily glean this information from their shipping and/or billing address. Sometimes their email address or phone number reveals hints about their location. Some email marketing software tools can even record the IP address of where someone is accessing their email. If location-targeting emails are key to your strategy, consider asking for this information up front when people first download your lead magnet.

Let's consider an example: You're a global outerwear brand selling a variety of coats and jackets. While a heavy winter coat might be a must-have in Toronto, it might be unnecessary in tropical Singapore. Similarly, a lightweight summer jacket might be popular in San Francisco but irrelevant in frosty Berlin.

Location-based targeting goes beyond just climate and season. It also considers local tastes and preferences. For instance, a style that's trending in Paris might not resonate with customers in Tokyo.

Sending location-targeting emails is your way to cater effectively to these diverse needs and preferences. By using data about your customers' locations, you can tailor your emails to suit their specific needs and tastes. If you are doing in-person events or location-specific store openings or product rollouts, one can only imagine how much more boost to your campaigns these emails can add.

Re-Engagement Emails

Over time, some of your list will include those who stopped engaging with your content. Or, worse yet, were once a customer but haven't purchased from you in a while.

Studies reveal that brands typically experience an email list churn of around 25-30 percent per year[9]. While some churn is inevitable—like a children's clothing brand losing customers as kids grow—minimizing this churn is key to maintaining a healthy customer base.

Digital First marketing is about leveraging all the threads we have at our disposal and seeing how we can continue our conversations to grow our business. Re-engagement emails are a powerful tool for brands that have the potential for recurring purchases. These emails often contain special offers—discounts, gifts with purchase, or more—to entice customers back to your website. Engaging lapsed customers might require more than just one email—it might require a full-blown re-engagement campaign.

These emails can offer incentives or solicit feedback to understand the customer's experience better. And if these strategies don't work, it may be time to remove these customers from your list to optimize your resources, and often increase your email deliverability.

Re-engagement emails are not just about winning back customers —they're about understanding customer behavior, optimizing resources, and enhancing your overall email marketing strategy. In the world of digital marketing, re-engaging customers is as important as acquiring new ones.

Triggered Ecommerce Emails

Just as B2B companies can leverage transactional emails, B2C companies can make use of triggered emails. The price drop triggered email is a great example. You can send this email if you ever reduce the price on a product or service that a customer has recently purchased or shown interest in by visiting the relevant product page. Premier, a small Michigan-based shop dedicated to up-and-coming skateboarding products and brands, found that these automations were extremely simple to set up and had open rates of 73 percent and a click-through rate of 12 percent, generating thousands of dollars in revenue in a matter of weeks[10].

Don't Let the Complexity Limit Your Potential

Perhaps this chapter represents a challenge to those smaller businesses who might not have the technical resources to implement my advice. If that is you, I have you covered in Chapter 18 where I talk about how to scale your team and recruit those that are experienced at manipulating these Digital Threads.

Businesses do not adequately leverage the full potential of email marketing automation, despite its immense potential. While you don't need to include every single one of these types of emails as part of your automated infrastructure, you can see how just adding a few additional automated elements can have a significant impact on your relationship with your customers and prospects—and your bottom line.

Key Takeaways:

- Every contact with a customer or potential customer is a chance to build the relationship.
- Emails that the customer is expecting to provide more opportunities to inform, promote, and upsell.
- These automated emails can help guide the customer lifecycle.

Companion Workbook Exercises:

- 13.1 | Don't Abandon Me
- 13.2 | It Doesn't Have to Be a Transaction
- 13.3 | Score Your List
- 13.4 | Re-Engage!

Chapter 14
Grow Influence

"Every living being is an engine geared to the wheelwork of the universe. Though seemingly affected only by its immediate surrounding, the sphere of external influence extends to infinite distance."

— Nikola Tesla

Our goal on social media is to engage with our audience. It is to get our message across in a way that works on each platform. When it works, we will see engagement grow from our customers, and we'll be able to leverage these relationships to reach further than we could on our own.

The key to being seen on social media is Platform Authentic Content. Sourcing user-generated content makes our social media feed more authentic, engaging, and diverse than we could do ourselves and grows our visibility. Sourcing the UGC develops deeper relationships with creators of influence that have brand affinity for us: employees, customers, and other fans.

From UGC to... Where?

After you've done the work to identify the people who are talking about your brand and connect with customers already generating content about your product, you don't want to let that go. Just as you want to repurpose your content and make that currency go further, you want to develop those relationships with social media users and content creators.

Bringing these people together helps you keep in touch and engage with influential content creators all the time. Instead of managing multiple social media messages, you have your team in one place. You can guide and develop their skills in communicating and have access to their insights on the demographic and your products. The benefits are yours to tap into as regularly as you want.

Similar to how we can scale our Library of Content through repurposing and our communication pathways through automation, there is a way that we can scale these relationships that we have developed through sourcing UGC and funnel all our collaborators into a singular entity for maximum amplification, influence, and efficiency.

The solution is to create a brand ambassador program.

Defining the Brand Ambassador

A brand ambassador is a term that has been around since before influencer marketing. Brands would sign longer-term contracts with celebrities to have them "represent" and ultimately promote the brand. The company usually formally hires the brand ambassador, and they would often promote through traditional media such as TV, magazines, and newspapers. These brand ambassadors would become the public "face" of the brand. They're not a one-off promotion. Brand ambassadors want to grow their career along with your brand, and brands want a consistent representation in the market.

George Clooney is an example of a brand ambassador for his work with Nestle's coffee brand Nespresso. He has appeared in television commercials representing them since 2006, but in 2013 he signed an agreement reportedly worth $40 million that led to him becoming a brand ambassador for Nespresso and a member of the founding Nespresso Sustainability Advisory Board. Clooney has mentioned that he sees his collaboration with Nespresso as a way to merge his business and charitable pursuits. It's this ability for the brand to connect with the ambassador in another way beyond money that makes the relationship so strong. George Clooney actually turned down a more lucrative opportunity when the company didn't align with his personal values—a sure sign that money isn't everything in engaging with true influencers[1].

Brand ambassadors are loyal fans of the brand, and while there is often an incentive associated with their representation, they can't necessarily be "bought."

So Then, What Is a Social Media Brand Ambassador?

With the emergence and growing influence of social media and its creator user base, a new generation of brand ambassadors has been born: the social media brand ambassador. You do not need to hire a celebrity anymore. Instead, you can access everyday social media users to represent your brand, especially those who love your brand and products that you have engaged with to encourage the creation of user-generated content.

Social media brand ambassadors are an always online, approachable, and authentic representation and endorsement of your brand. They are social media users who really love your brand and aren't afraid to say so on social media. While regular influencers talk about brands that they find useful, or otherwise beneficial, true brand ambassadors go further.

These ambassadorships aren't a one-off influencer campaign. Rather, the brand ambassador becomes, at least to some extent, the face of your brand. The impact might not be as big as a traditional celebrity, but grouped together in a program as a single entity, they can drive massive results. At a minimum, they can provide you with all your UGC needs, which in itself has immense value.

You have no control over your brand, as people will formulate opinions based on seeing how others speak about you online. Having an army of brand ambassadors talking about your brand authentically provides the social proof that can help you build a positive reputation and ultimately convert more business.

Women's clothing line Princess Polly operates an ambassador program for college students. The brand gains benefits when their target demographic wears their brand, shares it online, and connects with their friends through social media. The brand ambassador receives discounts and earns a commission on their friends' purchases through the link they share online. It's a win-win. Their landing page for the program is a great example of what a brand ambassador program can look like: https://us.princesspolly.com/pages/college-ambassador.

An example of an impactful brand ambassador program comes from Caraway Home, a cookware and home goods brand. They launched their brand just before the pandemic began, and the stay-at-home environment meant there was a boon for the cooking industry. Caraway found that they were attracting the attention of influencers and social media users who were already organically posting about them.

Caraway created a program to not only promote Caraway's products but also to encourage content creation around broader food-related topics. They began in 2020 by inviting 35 influencers and fans who were already talking about them to join their brand ambassador program, which was providing them a promo link to buy a discounted product and an affiliate link to use when talking about that product in social media.

The long-term approach and continued expansion of the program has led to a four-person team that has managed to onboard 3,500 ambassadors in three years and paid out $350,000 in affiliate commissions in 2022. The ambassador program contributed to comprise 13 percent of the company's revenue; it is not far behind the 20 percent attributed to paid media[2].

Brands and people are unique, so there is no one-size-fits-all solution. Key to any program, therefore, is a way to reward brand ambassadors in such a way that they will participate. There is something you can offer, monetary and otherwise, that benefits them. You want to interest them in a collaboration and, ideally, inspire long-term loyalty.

Types of Brand Ambassadors

Seeing that a brand ambassador program has the potential to be much more than just an efficient way to source user-generated content, you might want to activate different ambassadors or manage them differently. You should also know these different types to help you find new brand ambassadors for your program. Part of the success of these programs comes from training and events.

Customer Ambassadors

Most of your brand ambassadors will probably come from the customers you reached out to in order to encourage the creation of user-generated content. These are customers who are already talking about you or those you can encourage to talk about you. They will become the heart and soul of your brand ambassador program because your brand is already a part of their life.

Employee Ambassadors

Employees as ambassadors are, as surprisingly obvious as it is, severely underutilized. Here, the idea is to encourage your employees to advocate for your company. It gives the company a human face, which can help edge out the competition. Employees know about your products and services like nobody else, and they don't hide their knowledge behind marketing mumbo-jumbo. In addition, using employees as ambassadors helps to recruit new employees. If your employees love you, it makes potential recruits think they would as well.

General Electric began their employee ambassador program to offset what they thought was a negative perception about them in the job market.

The program had a heavy training aspect, focusing on training HR managers to train employees on how to improve their social media profiles to better "humanize" the GE brand. The result is that not only did GE see an 800 percent increase in applicants, but organic engagement from employee ambassadors amounted to $3 million worth of advertisement value that helped them reduce the need for paid social to amplify their efforts[3].

Affiliate Ambassadors

An affiliate ambassador is someone who, as an affiliate for your brand, might already talk about your product or similar products online, but is not necessarily a customer. As the name suggests, these ambassadors usually run a website to feature your products using an affiliate link hoping to earn a sales commission.

In order to encourage your current affiliates to become affiliate ambassadors, it will often come down to how they get paid and how long they promote your products. You might already have a long-term business relationship with your affiliates, but understand that they invest more time and energy in the products they promote that generate the most revenue for them. That is another reason to include training or a community aspect in your program so that you can best convert these affiliates into becoming true brand ambassadors.

The example of Caraway shows how powerful it is to include an affiliate component in your brand ambassador program. If people are going to promote you, why not compensate them if their content generates actual sales? In this way, any brand ambassador can help your affiliate marketing.

Expert Ambassadors

An expert ambassador, who you might also call a Key Opinion Leader (KOL), is someone well known and listened to in their field. They'll become ambassadors for brands they use regularly, rather than just looking for a random opportunity within their niche. These are valuable ambassadors because they are so well respected. Their voice behind your brand amplifies your trustworthiness. If you are not lucky enough to have these experts as part of your customer ambassadors, these are the first external influencers you will want to reach out to, as I describe in the following chapter.

Building the Program

Like most things, the strength of your program will come from the foundation you put in place before putting it into play.

The first step is to determine the goals of your ambassador program. This includes understanding what you want out of it, the social media users you will approach, how you'll compensate ambassadors, and how you'll monitor success.

At the onset, email will suffice for communication with brand ambassadors. Like the Princess Polly example, you'll want to at least have a landing page linked on your website to allow potential brand ambassadors to apply to your program, complete with the incentives.

When you launch, your program will become an extension of your efforts to generate user-generated content, and those contributors should become the initial members of your program. After that, you will want to promote your program on your website, email, and socials to your customers and followers, inviting them to apply as well. This gives you a chance to see their content quality and social media following in advance, and then you can decide if you want to recruit them or not. Asking your current brand ambassadors for referrals to "closet fans" can be another way to expand your program.

Once your program is running, the mechanics will involve a combination of:

- What you will offer your brand ambassadors in terms of incentives and promotions.
- The education, training, and community aspects you will include as part of your program regularly.

- The expansion of membership and increased activities to make a broader impact.

These are deep relationships that you're creating with these brand ambassadors, and, like all relationships, it takes work. You need to let them do their magic, whether that involves your content or theirs, or a combination. And you'll need to let the ambassador know you value their loyalty. Nothing is worse for ambassadors than feeling like they're being taken advantage of or "used." At the extreme end, they might end the relationship under these circumstances. Money isn't everything. With employees, that could mean quitting; for others, it could cause them to go to the competition.

The Anatomy of a Successful Brand Ambassador Program

There is no better example of a successful brand ambassador program than Adobe Express, a program of which I am currently personally a member. This program shows surefire strategies that you should aim to implement in your own brand ambassador program.

While Adobe is a famous brand in the creative space, Adobe Express is a tool that is geared to a different audience than the powerful Adobe Photoshop. The last few years have seen the emergence of Canva, a tool that was targeting marketers, entrepreneurs, and business owners who weren't necessarily creative professionals but wanted to create their own graphics with ease for social media This is like the audience that Adobe Express is hoping to target.

To attract a new user base that would try Adobe Express and become part of the greater Adobe community, they launched their own brand ambassador program.

In the initial call for ambassadors, Adobe focused on describing the kinds of people they wanted:

We're looking for individual entrepreneurs, small business owners, chamber of commerce directors, online community group leaders, and more who like to help other people in their network learn new skills and tools to help them be successful in business to join the program.

They listed the benefits outside of any monetary reward, and they did not talk about the fact that they obviously wanted you to talk and promote Adobe Express on the socials. The emphasis was that they were looking for people who wanted to help others be successful in their business.

If you are building a program and want to create a community among its members, you want to make sure that you attract the right and similar-minded people so that the community grows on its own with your need to intervene.

The landing page to apply to the Adobe Express ambassador program expanded on this. You can view the current iteration here: https://www.adobe.com/express/community. This page makes it very clear as to the benefits of your joining but also the expectations that the program has for its members.

Once approved as a member, there is an online ambassador hub to bring everyone together. The Adobe Express team frequently updates this website and allows ambassadors to choose from activities that suit their style, ambitions, and availability. These include activities such as:

- Signing up to become an affiliate and promoting your affiliate link.
- Creating and publishing content in social media that focuses on new features.
- Sharing Adobe Express-published educational content with your community.
- Sharing experiences of using and promoting Adobe Express.
- Giving feedback to product managers.
- Hosting workshops and tutorials using Adobe Express.

While a certain tier of ambassadors might receive payment for some of these activities, most of the activities reward participants with points that they can exchange for various prizes, including Adobe swag, gift cards, and even products (such as books, hats, and tote bags) created by fellow Adobe Express ambassadors.

The highlight for me in being a member of this community is the opportunity to attend the annual Adobe MAX conference for creators. Not only do I get to meet my fellow ambassadors in person as well as attend the extremely educational, inspiring, and FUN conference, but there is also a day dedicated to the ambassadors. At the ambassador event, we can network, learn, get product updates, meet Adobe employees we have been interacting with virtually, and even see our fellow ambassadors on stage, educating our community.

It is not a trivial expense flying in dozens of people to Los Angeles and all the associated costs that go with it, but the result is the creation of a powerful community that is committed to both Adobe Express and to each other. The in-person aspect builds deep emotional ties that get participants like me genuinely excited about the product itself and the opportunities that come with representing it to our own networks.

It might sound like all the benefits go to the ambassadors and none to Adobe, but that is not the case. Many times, I heard from Adobe product managers how the feedback from the community of ambassadors allowed them to develop their product faster and to have features they didn't think of themselves but have proven to be popular in the market.

Above that, the content that the ambassadors have published over time has had immense reach. With 215 ambassadors today, the program reaches an audience of 34 million social media users. Adobe properly measures every activity that ambassadors do on behalf of Adobe Express, and at last count, the 200+ ambassadors had completed over 6,000 activities, which resulted in nearly 1.8 million unique engagements on social media in 2023 alone.

The proof of the value of the brand ambassador program is best shown in how community members get together and share their love for Adobe Express. These amplify the results that a single community manager can have over a group of a few hundred ambassadors. It is when the community members bond among themselves with your brand at the center of the conversation that you know that you have successfully scaled your efforts.

Your smaller business might not achieve the same scale in results that Adobe Express has, but by following the same principles, you can build something equally impactful for your own business and funnel your fans into a true brand ambassadorship.

Key Takeaways:

- Building advocacy is an extension of UGC. It provides more trust and social proof.
- There are different ways to interact with fans and advocates.
- Brand ambassadors are engaged with your brand because they like the brand. Create a program that revolves around them, providing support and encouragement for their advocacy efforts.

Companion Workbook Exercises:

- 14.1 | Defining Your Brand Ambassadors
- 14.2 | The Recruitment Game
- 14.3 | The Give and Take
- 14.4 | Fleshing Out the Complete Strategy

Part Six

Scale

"If you don't find a way to make money while you sleep, you will work until you die."

— Warren Buffet

At this point in the book, all the elements for your Digital First infrastructure are coming together. The Digital Threads are being developed and woven into a powerful digital marketing platform. In the order of things, you have satisfied the conditions necessary to scale your marketing operations.

In order to scale, let's begin with understanding the critical concept of "marketing mix."

This concept originated back in 1948 when Harvard University Professor James Culliton described a marketer as someone who was a "mixer of ingredients," sometimes following a recipe, other times adapting a recipe to the ingredients on hand, while other times experimenting and inventing ingredients. Culliton's colleague, Professor Neil Borden, further developed the concept and introduced the term "marketing mix" in 1964[1]. While the initial analogy of the "mix" in "marketing mix" was that of a chef, I have always thought of it to be that mixdown of elements you have in a recording studio.

Since writing *Maximize Your Social* back in 2013, I think of modern marketing similar to an audio mixing board. You plug in all your microphones and amplifier lines, and based on the data on how everything sounds, you adjust different mixes to get the best results to scale your budget.

Like every other part in this book, you can't scale without having all the other Digital Threads in place. You can't amplify what isn't already there. That is why I introduce these concepts here at the end, but they can truly help scale your business.

Chapter 15
Scale Influence

"You don't build a business. You build people, and people build the business."

— Zig Ziglar

Zig Ziglar might have been talking about "building" employees to help build the business, but in marketing terms, "building" influencers to become your advocates online is a powerful way to leverage word-of-mouth marketing to scale your business.

We have seen how encouraging the publishing of user-generated content has helped us build and sustain a brand ambassador program with all its benefits. You have done so successfully by tapping into and expanding your brand's sphere of influence. The problem is this: How can we increase our presence on social media to reach more people in our niche who have a dominant presence in our industry? The term "external influencers" that I introduce here refers to those content creators and social media users that speak to the community you want to influence but are outside of your sphere of brand affinity. They either don't know about you, know about you but have no need for you, or know about you but are currently using your competitor's products and services.

THE BRAND AFFINITY MODEL FOR INFLUENCER MARKETING

Figure 15.1

Many companies try to engage with external influencers before developing any of the other Digital Threads in this book. Fortunately for you, your work until now has helped you scale your brand's own influence. Scaling your own influence will not only make it easier to work with influencers, but it will generate more "inbound leads" from external influencers contacting you to collaborate.

Reintroducing Influencer Marketing

Influencer marketing has become something of a cliché and trend in recent years, but the concept is not new. I have already hinted at this throughout the book, but hopefully you have seen through the lens of brand affinity, user-generated content, and brand ambassadors that the term "influencer marketing" is also a lot broader of a concept than you might have thought. The attention that the term has received from the big players in the arena has distorted what the concept is about.

Influencer marketing is not about endorsements, although that can be part of it. The concept relies on using the voice of other social media users to promote your brand.

Marketing has always relied on word of mouth. Now word of mouth happens online. People trust people more than they trust an ad. People trust their friends and their families. When they want answers about a product they're considering, or they want to understand the difference between two brands that offer something similar, they ask someone who knows. That used to be a neighbor or coworker, an uncle, or a friend. It still is. But now it also includes strangers on the Internet, and people find the answers through authentic reviews on blogs, YouTube, Instagram, and increasingly TikTok.

Influencers are not just those with millions of followers on a platform. Influencers range from those with smaller but heavily engaged audiences to those who communicate daily with millions of people. Pre-pandemic algorithms favored delivering content according to your followers, but in the era of recommended media that TikTok has ushered in, it is not about your follower count but the strength of your content to engage others. Although it is one indicator of one's potential influence, follower count has become less important.

Below is an image of what a pre-pandemic Instagram-centric influencer marketing approach looked like to categorize influencers solely by follower size. You might have heard of some of these terms such as "micro-influencer" and "nano-influencer." Today, these classifications don't work because it is not about follower count. It is about brand affinity, and with external influencers, it is about niche relevance, cultural fit, an engaged community that is aligned with your target audience, and the actual performance of their published content.

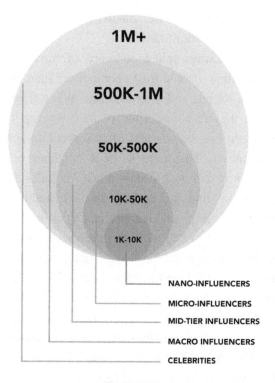

Figure 15.2

That said, they are still helpful in classifying types of influencers because the greater a following the influencer has, the more selective they will be in terms of who they work with as well as what they might request of you in exchange for a collaboration.

Your Community Is Always a Subset

Our efforts until now, especially working with brand ambassadors, broadened our brand awareness. Despite these efforts, no matter how many brand ambassadors we have, there are still more ideal potential customers who have never heard of us.

Those who know, like, and trust you will always be a subset of your potential customer base.

Consider a realtor who lives in a city with 50,000 adults who might be potential home buyers. Maybe the realtor has 500 friends in that niche community. That leaves 49,500 people whom the realtor should try to get to know. How to do that? By leveraging the city's "influencers," the realtor can reach a wider audience by tapping into their niche communities.

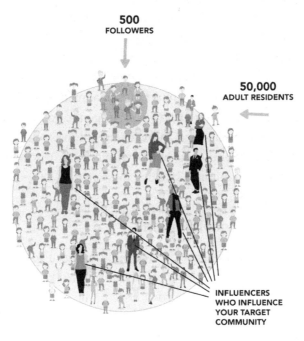

Figure 15.3

The collaboration between Dunkin' Donuts and the famous Gen Z TikToker Charli D'Amelio is a great example of a brand using an influencer to reach beyond their community. Dunkin' Donuts has been around for many years and has an established customer base, but perhaps they had few Gen Z customers. Charli D'Amelio has millions of social media followers, but maybe many of them were not Dunkin' Donuts customers. You put the two together—and you create a custom drink for Charli based on her preferences that her fans could order—and the results were magical.

After its premiere, the Charli sold hundreds of thousands of cups in just five days. There was a 57 percent surge in the number of downloads for the Dunkin' Donuts app. The day Dunkin' released the Charli saw a record for the number of daily app users. On that day, cold brew sales increased by 20 percent overall, and the next day they increased by 45 percent. Charli's fans were discovering other Dunkin' Donuts drinks they fancied[1].

Every business should take advantage of this.

In the previous chapter on user-generated content, we focused on those influencers who already have brand affinity for us. Funneling them into and expanding that program into a brand ambassador program allows your brand's impact on social media to grow exponentially. This is the beginning of how we bridge the gap in brand awareness. We can further scale this by reaching out to external influencers —those who have little to no brand affinity with us—and hopefully convert them into becoming a brand ambassador.

It's All About the Collaboration

To be successful in influencer marketing, you need to give up some control. This is an area where brands fail at working with external influencers: They impose their conditions on them to where they treat them like they are a programmable ad unit. Remember, these are individuals who 1) yield influence in the communities where our target audience hangs out BUT 2) have little to no brand affinity for you.

Many businesses misuse the term "collaborate," forgetting that it involves working together, not just pursuing their own goals.

That is why, while you are in full control of the activities of your brand ambassador program, working with external influencers is going to come down to a one-by-one personalized effort. No two content creators are the same. Some are in it only for the money, while for others it is a part-time side hustle fueled by a passion. Some are in exclusive contracts with brands and can't work with competitors, while others simply do not have enough spare capacity to collaborate with new clients. The way they produce their content, the format, and their size of audience are also different influencer to influencer.

Building a collaboration can be as diverse as the influencers who exist out there. Often, the best starting point is one of the following tried and tested methods.

Gift Product to Smaller Influencers to Incite UGC Creation

If you could get your product into the hands of an influencer who already speaks to the audience you cater to, wouldn't they fall in love with it?

This is the rationale for why brands are increasingly sending out product to launch collaborations with influencers. This works best with nano-influencers and others with smaller followings because larger influencers probably won't work just for a free product.

Passchier (https://passchier.co.nz.co.nz) needed to get their product in front of the people who would be interested in it. Their product is a high-end, handmade bicycle handlebar made of bamboo. The design and material provide benefits for those who spend a long time on their bike. Their concept was simple—get the product into the hands of those already speaking to their audience.

Passchier gifted the high-end handlebars to nano- and micro-influencers who created video content for their demographic. The subtle differences in the material and design make long hours on a bicycle more comfortable. They spread their message over videos and other social media content directly to their audience.

Getting people to talk about your product is difficult. Passchier found a direct way to those who they knew would be successful. It wasn't just gifting product—most of the work was in identifying the right influencer and curating the relationship.

As Passchier co-founder (and member of my Digital First Mastermind) Mike Baddeley describes it: "It was about homing in on the right people. They have a certain makeup, a certain audience, a certain tone. We've got a credible product. So we need a credible voice in the tone of the influencer."

Paid Collaboration with Nano- and Micro-Influencers for Sponsored Content

Finding the right influencer can truly grow your brand's reach. This isn't just true for those who speak to the audience you want to connect with, but also those who engage on a platform that you're less engaged with, or less adept at.

While gifting product is one way of starting a collaboration, motivating influencers through directly paying them is another.

Oliver Brocato started by considering what type of product would lend itself to viral content. He already understood social media marketing and TikTok before he conceived of Tabs Chocolate—dark chocolate aimed at heightening the sexual experience. In order to market the product, Tabs turned to TikTok and its community of content creators. The incentive was being paid per view. But Tab didn't want to collaborate with anyone. There was a strategy.

Once Tab had identified their ideal customer, they found micro- and nano-influencers who were already aligned with that customer. These influencers were in the same demographic, and they already had a following—meaning they already knew how to speak to that customer. The content was authentic and engaging. And they knew the platform. Tab used their own accounts to boost the user-generated content.

The strategy boosted visibility, authenticity, engagement, and sales. The partnership with Macia Wolf, a TikTok influencer with less than 100,000 followers, saw one TikTok video garner over 6.7 million views and generate $50,000 in sales. It's hard to argue with those numbers when the strategy worked out that Tab paid influencers around $100 for every 100,000 views[2].

Affiliate Marketing

I mentioned the potential for affiliates to become affiliate ambassadors in the previous chapter, but similar to how not every influencer is your customer, not every potential affiliate currently has a relationship with you.

Affiliate marketing, also called performance marketing, is one of the oldest types of influencer marketing. Many affiliates began with blogs before social media.

Affiliate marketing alone can be a lucrative form of influencer marketing. Case in point: The premium men's clothing brand Taylor Stitch. They have over 110 affiliates that generate 26 percent of all of their sales—at an ROI of 1,600 percent[3].

In modern influencer marketing, affiliate marketing is often also an option when gifting product as well as directly compensating content creators. It gives influencers a further incentive to perform, and it provides businesses a convenient way to measure the financial impact that each influencer can bring.

Product gifting, sponsored content, and affiliate marketing are the most popular ways to collaborate with influencers, but there are many others, including:

- Providing exclusive discounts to influencers, usually combined with the previous three types of collaborations.
- Incentivizing product reviews, usually combined with gifting product.
- Doing joint giveaways with influencers.
- Having influencers boost your promotional content.
- Co-creating content with influencers, like a livestream, blog post, or podcast interview (especially relevant for B2B companies).
- Hosting physical events, including inviting speakers or even organizing dedicated influencer trips.
- Product collaboration, where you name your product or service for that influencer—like what Dunkin' Donuts did.

How to Find External Influencers to Work With

If you yourself are active in the social media communities where your customers engage, you should already know who the big influencers in your niche are, especially if you did the reconnaissance exercise mentioned in Chapter Eight. To find additional potential external influencers, consider this question that I pose to my students:

If you wanted to be influenced by someone, how would you find them?

If you joined a social media platform and wanted to find more information about the topic of [fill in the blank], you would probably begin by searching for [fill in the blank] and note the creators whose content meets your needs. This is the barebones process that any business could do without buying software that is geared toward this exercise or trying to leverage an influencer marketplace.

Depending on the social network, you can search by keyword or relevant hashtag, but there are some other tricks:

- When you find an influencer, look at who they follow, as influencers usually follow other influencers who inspire them as well as those who they themselves collaborate with.
- Instagram allows you to see suggested lookalikes for every profile, indicated by an icon showing a person with a "plus" sign to the left of them. Take advantage of this.
- In Facebook (and LinkedIn) you can do a keyword search for Groups and then find the admins of these groups, who have undoubted influence over those communities.
- X has X lists, lists of people compiled by its users for which you can also use keywords to search and then see who others feel are influential in whatever they have an interest in.
- Listen Notes (https://listennotes.com/) is a fantastic podcast

search engine where you can enter a keyword and find influential podcasters.

How to Engage With Influencers

The first rule in engaging with influencers is figuring out where to contact them. Influencers get inundated with direct messages and emails daily, so you want to make sure they at least receive your message and have some sort of recognition of your brand when they do so that they will actually read your message.

That is why before you contact them, you first want to send them social signals, something that is surprisingly easy to do and which surprisingly few brands do: authentically engage with their content.

When you become the brand they recognize because of your thoughtful engagement, you will get a lot more responses to your communication.

This can be a labor-intensive exercise, but it takes time to get to know someone in social media just as it does in real life. This is the strategy that the now famous social media management tool Buffer used when they began as a WordPress plugin to help readers of bloggers easily share their blog posts in social media. By commenting on the blogs of these bloggers, they developed relationships with the bloggers (like me) who would embed their plugin on their blog, raising brand awareness for the company. This ultimately led to the bloggers becoming early brand ambassadors for their website tool and transformed their blog commenting into an $18 million annual revenue-generating company with over 57,000 customers[4].

I recommend you engage for a few weeks and then only—or at least initially—reach out to those influencers who have recognized your existence. The next rule is that you reach out to influencers in the ways they want to be contacted. Don't use some tool to find their email address; read their social media profile bio. This will often include instructions on how to contact them. When in doubt, first send them a DM on the platform(s) where they are active. Commenting on a post might also get their attention. If that fails, try to contact them through their website or a LinkedIn message, and then, only if that fails, try a cold email.

For the actual pitch, there are two different approaches you can take:

1. Present a specific opportunity: Provide enough details on deliverables, budget, and so on so that they can decide if it is attractive enough for them. This can risk not meeting their needs, but with a budget and a defined campaign, you present a clear, strong pitch.
2. Be more open-ended. This is what you consider doing if you are looking to collaborate long-term and want to understand better how the influencer works with brands. This puts the influencer in the driver's seat to suggest what they think would be the perfect collaboration.

The most important thing is to understand this: WIIFM.
What's In It For Me?
You should always have that in the back of your mind to see if you are offering them enough incentive or not.

If you haven't received a response from a potential influencer, it's a recommended practice to follow up. Not only does it show your interest in them, but some influencers make it a practice of only answering the second request. Many are also simply busy people who miss your first request or intend to respond and forget about it—so they appreciate your follow-up.

If the influencer doesn't respond after the second request, remember: Influencer marketing, like sales, is a numbers game. Therefore, make sure you are always reaching out to many more influencers than you intend to collaborate with knowing that not everyone will "convert."

Why You Should Try to Build Your Own Influence

An influencer media kit that a content creator might send you will often feature the logos of brands that they have collaborated with. The more influential the brand—think Nike or Starbucks—the more content creators would LOVE to put that logo in their kit.

Building your influence as a brand puts you in that attractive logo category.

Every step of the Digital Threads in this book grows influence. Platform Authentic Content gives your brand visibility in the algorithm; user-generated content builds social proof; and brand ambassadors amplify your presence throughout social media. Collaborating with external influencers can further scale the social word of mouth. More influencers are now talking about you in social media, and your followers have probably increased.

You can work with external influencers not just for social media, but also for SEO (gaining backlinks), podcast advertising (having them promote your show or appear on theirs), or even email newsletter advertising (appear in their email newsletter). While these are more niche types of paid media, they are all similar to the previous influencer marketing as you are paying or somehow motivating an individual to appear on their platform.

The more you do these activities, the more influencers will talk about you and provide social proof, and thus the more influencers will want to work with you when you reach out to them. In fact, more and more influencers will reach out to you because of your influence. In this fashion, your influencer marketing will also be more of an "inbound" approach, making all your communication even more effective.

Think of it this way: If you had a podcast interviewing entrepreneurs, would you rather interview Gary Vaynerchuk or Neal Schaffer? Don't worry, your answer won't offend me! After you have interviewed Gary Vee, you can add his name to the list of people you have interviewed, giving your podcast a tremendous boost in social proof and making it easier to convince Alex Hormozi to become your next guest. It's the same concept at play.

For most brands, it makes sense to wait until they have traction with their brand ambassador program *before* moving on to external influencers. It is part of the same order of doing things that can make your marketing the most effective. This is part of the experience that drove me to write this book: Too many companies immediately want to reach out to external influencers without following all the other steps, making their efforts extremely ineffective in comparison with what might have been possible. I am writing this book (and wrote *The Age of Influence*) so that you don't become one of them!

Key Takeaways:

- Your community is always a subset. Finding others to talk about you helps bridge that gap.
- Working with influencers is about collaborations. Their expertise is why you're engaging with them.
- Your own growing influence opens up more conversations and opportunity.

Companion Workbook Exercises:

- 15.1 | How Will You Collab with External Influencers?
- 15.2 | Mapping Your Influence Ecosystem
- 15.3 | Crafting Your Influencer Outreach Campaign

Chapter 16
Scale Budget

"You have to spend money to make money."

— Plautus

Scaling your digital media reach through paid media directly on each social media network and search engine is effective. The results speak for themselves. However, I've seen so many businesses bypass other Digital Threads to go directly to Google or Facebook Ads. People commonly believe that paid ads are the holy grail of digital marketing, and they often disregard the need for anything else. I have also seen businesses blindly invest money in paid social ads without measuring their impact or considering alternative ways to allocate that budget.

Paid media is an important digital thread that is always at your disposal whenever you have the budget available. But it needs to come after your other efforts. You want to strengthen the threads you've already woven. Undertaking the previous work to weave your search, email, and social media threads means that when injecting money into your digital strategy, it is to truly scale your voice instead of spending money hoping to find it.

Strategically placing your spend means considering where your organic reach is falling short. For instance, if we are already achieving the number one result on Google for each keyword in our Library of Content, it might not make sense to spend money to get the result on top of that. There are cases where even that may make sense, such as to fend off competitors appearing above our top organic spot. Outside of these cases, boosting what is already working could be a waste of spend and much more effective spent elsewhere.

For those of you who read *The Age of Influence*, you might remember the water spigot analogy: Whenever your organic efforts fall short, you always have the option to turn on the water to speed up your efforts with paid media. But your efforts will be even more successful when you first have all your digital bases covered.

Where and When Paid Media Makes Sense

With this in mind, there are three specific common scenarios to consider for strategically leveraging paid media to scale our Digital Threads.

Bridging the Visibility Gap

The modern consumer spends a lot of time researching across a multitude of channels and consuming content across platforms. Paid media can boost our visibility to have our content shown where the user is looking. Another strong benefit of paid media is that it allows us to have a presence in all areas of digital media, even in those areas where we might have less influence.

Retargeting

Bridging the visibility gap is all about promoting our business to cold audiences. Through retargeting, we can market ourselves to an audience that has shown interest in our brand before. They are further down in the funnel. Of course, retargeting is becoming harder to do with recent privacy updates from Big Tech, so my suggestion is to do as much of it now while you still can!

Time-Limited

Sometimes you need to do everything you can to push as many people as possible toward an event, a launch, or a time-limited sale. While this will not be the most effective way to spend budget—especially if an overwhelming majority of your target audience is cold—paid media does at least allow you to scale your visibility extremely quickly and get in front of your target audience.

It's All About the Targeting

The value of paid media is ensuring that you are getting in front of your target audience. Targeting options, based on all the data they have on their users, is the best guide that money can buy for this purpose. You can target by the basic demographics of age, gender, location, and many other demographic and psychographic filters. Within these, the three primary targeting groups you should consider for your paid media are:

Interest-Based

The more you understand about your ideal audience, the more you can use social media to target them. Every platform uses algorithms to define what interests its users have, and besides leveraging these suggestions, you can also target people based on other accounts they follow.

Custom Audiences

Custom audiences comprise a group of targeting options based on a warm audience that already has some "like, know, and trust" for your brand. You can target any of the following audiences, with options varying depending on the platform:

- website visitors
- engagers of your organic social media posts or followers
- those who engaged with your previous advertisements
- email list of customers or prospects, although the email address they use for the social network must match the email address you possess for this to be successful

Lookalike Audiences

Networks are excellent at leveraging their various AI technologies in finding lookalike audiences: The audience that is like yours based on the data that the platform possesses. The beauty is that you can create a lookalike audience for any custom audience, such as your current customer email database, website visitors, or followers of your social media account.

This is exactly what ChicMe, a female fashion e-commerce store, did to target lookalikes of its most loyal, high-spending customers. When compared to broad, interest-based targeting, they achieved a 271 percent higher return on ad spend[1].

How Campaign Objectives Will Influence Your Results

Whenever you want to create an advertisement, the first thing that any ad platform will ask you is how you would like to use their ad platform. This choice of campaign objectives will affect your results.

If your aim is to increase sales, the algorithms find who is likely to convert over click because they know the profile of those who will convert. When it's a cost-per-click arrangement, the networks will find those users who are more likely to click on ads regardless if they often convert or not. If you want to generate leads by asking users to fill in a native lead form on the platform, the algorithm will prioritize serving those ads to those that have previously filled in these types of lead forms.

The algorithm is what it is. That's why you need to experiment with your campaign objectives, in addition to your specific targeting. These situations change for every campaign, depending on the goals, network, and audience. By experimenting with targeting over three strategies, Kensington Market Sourdough in Toronto, Canada, boosted their sales. The campaign was to experiment with which mix of upper, middle, and lower funnel objectives was most effective. Experimenting with just these elements saw the bakery add 52 percent more sales and a 33 percent lower cost per purchase[2].

It is said that digital ad revenues from Google (including YouTube), Meta (Facebook + Instagram), and Amazon comprise over 70 percent of global digital ad spend[3]. Other networks like TikTok and LinkedIn are compelling in their own ways for their unique demographics and products, but your starting point should be to begin by investing where others have found positive ROI and build your benchmarks from there.

With this in mind, let's look at our options for paid media across the entire digital universe.

Paid Search Products

The easiest way to appear in search is simply to purchase your position through Google Ads. Target the relevant keywords and advertise. Obviously, there is more to Google Ads than just that—the Google Ads algorithm will try to convince you to broaden your keyword definitions. So, you will need to monitor ad spend and selectively add low-performing keywords to your negative keyword list.

The other distinguishing aspect of search ads is that people search with intent. Someone entered that keyword for a specific reason, and often they are looking for more information—potentially for your product or service. This differs from social media ads, which are disruptive in nature.

We can also reach people on the second largest search engine, YouTube, through Google Ads. These are video ads, but you can also target by keywords and/or interests.

If you are an e-commerce brand, we cannot forget the potential that Amazon Ads can have. Based on the same type of search campaign, Amazon Ads are a great way to expose your product when they are hidden in the organic feed. They can also be extremely successful: One of my Fractional CMO clients consistently makes $4 to $5 for every $1 spent on Amazon Ads. They simply cannot spend enough money on Amazon. There are several factors that go into this. If you consider search intent, people might research on Google, but they are definitely looking for something to buy when searching on Amazon. This purchase intent makes Amazon ads so valuable and potentially high performing.

What is interesting about Amazon search ads is that you can also target your competitors' specific products to increase your chances that you can appear on your competitor's product page as a suggested alternative.

Amazon offers its own collection of ad products. The type of product I mentioned above is the Sponsored Products ad, but you can also buy Sponsored Brands ads to feature your brand and multiple products prominently at the top of a search results page and drive people to your Amazon Brand Store.

Google also has its own Google Shopping ad product—which, at the time of writing this book, is being merged into its completely automated Performance Max product. Google takes the data feed of your product and matches it to its AI algorithm to display your products in a shopping widget when Google determines that someone has purchasing intent. While it may not have a direct relation to Amazon, considering it as part of an omni-channel strategy is worthwhile.

Paid Email Products

Google does offer products to allow your ads to be seen right on the top of Gmail, the closest thing to being able to appear in an inbox to people that are not on your list. Currently, Google manages these ads through its Discovery product. This allows you to target people with specific interests or purchase intentions based on keywords or people who searched for those specific keywords on Google.

The Discovery product is broad and allows you to get discovered across not only on Gmail but also YouTube Home, YouTube Watch Next, and Google Discover. This type of product is based on the AI and machine learning that has become the backbone of Google's Performance Max product. While you can retarget website visitors as well as upload other customer data, this type of product is relying on Google's AI to expose you in the best place at the best time with the best creative. For that reason, you are losing a bit of control compared to a traditional search campaign, and thus I would proceed with caution and carefully measure the ROI to determine its value.

The inbox is not just limited to Gmail. With the explosion of text messaging and using social media apps for direct communication, Facebook Messenger Ads are another way of getting into the "inbox" of your potential customer—that's covered below in paid social media.

LinkedIn also has a unique ad that allows your message to appear in the Inbox of LinkedIn users called Conversation Ads. It is an interesting option if your target audience is primarily on LinkedIn.

Paid Social Media Products

Where Google and Amazon ad products sit at the top of the search branch, the king of social media ads is truly Meta. While the Meta platform has become easier to use over the years, like Google's Performance Max, Meta is also trying to automate things to have you depend on their algorithm for the best results.

Success in social media advertising comes down to perfecting a combination of 1) ad creative and 2) targeting options.

Ad creatives on social media follow their organic counterparts:

- text—with or without link

- photo
- carousel
- horizontal video
- vertical video

Meta is actively promoting Advantage+ AI, which automates targeting and ad placement across Facebook, Instagram, Messenger, WhatsApp, and their partner network. You might have to switch a setting to have full control over all the targeting options.

Targeting options vary from platform to platform, but they give you these options:

- location
- language
- gender
- age
- device
- demographics, interests, and behaviors
- custom audiences, based on website visitors or email database
- lookalike audiences, often based on custom audiences

Here are some features that are unique to a few of the major platforms:

Meta

Meta, as well as Pinterest, allows you to integrate your product feed with your page. For this reason, they can also offer a product called Collection Ads, which helps facilitate interest and potential purchase of your products through your product catalog integrated with Facebook and Instagram. The look and feel is like the mosaic of a carousel post, with a large cover image or video accompanied by a group of smaller product images from your catalog. Each image is a purchasable product that, when clicked, can lead to a product page with a shopping cart.

Meta also has products that allow your ads to be seen and purchases started through Facebook Messenger and WhatsApp, in addition to Instagram DMs. Additionally, Meta has a click to call ad that gives you the potential to have your clients click to make a phone call to reserve time for an appointment or ask for additional information.

Another offering that both Facebook and LinkedIn offer are Lead Ads, which allow prospects to complete a pre-populated form that includes their email address, without leaving the social network. This is a perfect type of ad to experiment with for B2B companies or lead magnet promotion.

TikTok

TikTok is unique in that all their creatives occupy 100 percent of the real estate of a mobile screen, a feat that only Meta Stories/Reels or YouTube Shorts can achieve. On top of that, TikTok's TopView ads are unique because they guarantee it will be the first thing someone sees when logging into the app, and it will be full screen. TikTok also offers Spark Ads, which allows you to boost, with the approval of the content creator, organic UGC content. While you can do branded promotions on Meta as well, TikTok makes it super easy.

LinkedIn

What is unique about LinkedIn are the targeting options that LinkedIn offers called audience attributes. Because LinkedIn users include more professional information than any other social network, here you can target with many filters that no other platform has, such as company, education, and job experience.

Other Social Media

It is also important to note that, depending on your demographic, you might want also to experiment with ads on X, Pinterest, and even Reddit. But unless you are a heavy user of one of these platforms and truly understand how your audience uses them, I recommend you stick with the top social network ad platforms first.

The Funnel Approach to Paid Ads

With all these paid media options, it can be quite overwhelming for the smaller business to manage all of this. That is why many businesses will stick with a Google + Meta + Amazon (B2C), or Google + LinkedIn (B2B) strategy to rationally—and sanely—manage what can end up being a lot of budget and time spent.

We began this book talking about the funnel of digital relationships, and fortunately, almost every ad platform allows you the following groups of campaign objectives when creating an ad on their platform. If we consider this the framework for paid digital media, it is easy to see how we can create a strategy that leverages this.

Awareness: Our community is always a subset of its potential and therefore we always need to be reaching out to a new audience. Paid awareness ads allow us the ability to speed up that effort.

Consideration: It takes five to 20 touches to convert someone, so this is where we want to get additional touches, ideally from those that already know us, to bring them closer to conversion.

Conversion: Here is where we can specifically target those who engaged with us during the consideration stage and make them a special offer or generate a lead from them. We can also use this to target our current customers who have a higher chance of converting to encourage them to buy again or try a new product.

In such a way, we can build a strategy for paid media appropriately, which might look something like this:

Awareness Ads: (Top of Funnel)

- Google/Amazon/YouTube search
- social media ads (interest-based)
- target lookalike audiences

Consideration Ads: (Middle of Funnel)

- retarget awareness engagers (often through video ads)
- retarget website visitors
- retarget email database of non-customers (signed up through lead magnets but never converted, etc.)

Conversion Ads: (Bottom of Funnel)

- retarget customers campaign (loyalty campaign)
- retarget non-converters with lead magnets/lead gen forms (Meta and LinkedIn)
- retarget non-converters with product discounts

In this way, we can measure our ROI at each stage of the funnel to ensure that is efficient and truly scaling our efforts.

Paid media offers a lot of potential, and when combined with all the other Digital Threads, can truly scale your efforts. However, it comes at a cost that you need to monitor and analyze closely to get the biggest bang for your buck.

Key Takeaways:

- Flowing money into paid media is always an option, but it only amplifies what you've already woven with your previous threads.

- Paid media is especially effective at generating brand awareness, retargeting, and getting eyeballs on a time-limited offer.
- Understanding your objectives and targeting is essential before pouring in money.

Companion Workbook Exercises:

- 16.1 | The Spending Efficiency Audit
- 16.2 | Targeting Mastery Workshop
- 16.3 | Funnel Focus Group
- 16.4 | The ROI Revolution

Chapter 17
PDCA

"If you can't describe what you are doing as a process, you don't know what you're doing."

— W. Edwards Deming

Understanding Digital Threads shows the potential for your Digital First marketing in modern society. It can seem overwhelming quickly.

Many companies will simply outsource all this work to an external agency. There is value in doing this. But I assume, because you are reading this book, that you are looking to gain internal expertise. With that, even if you engage with an agency, you will do so more effectively because you can truly own your strategy and dictate where and how you need help.

If you can't measure what you are doing, you can neither manage nor improve it. The whole concept behind this book is that there is an order in which you should be engaging in the various Digital Threads. In scaling your marketing efforts, your marketing expenses can snowball. That's why now is the time to put a process in place to measure, manage, and optimize all our organic and paid channels.

The Struggle to Measure

In my early days as a Fractional CMO, I had a pre-sales conversation with a high-end landscaping company CEO. He hadn't bought into social media marketing at the time and was questioning how I could measure the effectiveness of their brand's engagement in social media.

This company was aggressively promoting their services and retail store in many local print magazines. When I asked how he measured the effectiveness of those ads, he didn't have an answer.

The beauty about Digital Threads is that they are digital and, to varying extents, trackable and measurable. The key to being able to do this is to understand what you want to measure and how you can measure it. Sometimes it requires a little creativity, just as those who have tried to measure marketing spend before the Internet.

The credit for the first coupon—in how we know it today—goes to Coca-Cola, who offered a coupon for a free glass of their drink in 1887. Coca-Cola aimed the campaign at generating awareness of the brand. By 1895, Coca-Cola was being served in every state of the Union. It's estimated that by the outbreak of the first World War, one in nine Americans had redeemed a coupon for a free Coca-Cola[1].

However, the credit for realizing that the coupon could do far more than simple brand awareness falls to Claude Hopkins. It was Hopkins who realized that if you had the information about where the customer received the coupon, then you could better guide your advertising dollar, energy, and focus.

Before Claude Hopkins pioneered the practice of tracking advertising spend, all companies could do was invest their money and hope for the best. Some companies still take that approach to digital marketing. Not only is that costly, but it is also so very misguided. There are so many ways to measure what works, but these ideas need to be planned from the start.

The Deming Circle

In postwar Japan, Professor W. Edwards Deming brought his ideas to a country rebuilding itself. His teachings formed a key part of the revolution Japan's industry experienced to become a high-quality, low-cost mass producer of goods. It was a key element of the success of manufacturing companies like Toyota and Panasonic. He was so revered in Japan that the Japanese government bestowed the Order of the Sacred Treasure in the second class upon Deming[2], making him one of approximately 100 people ever to receive the most prestigious first- or second-class order by the Japanese emperor[3].

I learned about Professor Deming not in my native United States but at the semiconductor manufacturer I worked at in Japan in the early days of my career.

Deming had originally adapted a concept from his mentor, Walter Shewhart, who had developed the Shewhart cycle. Where Shewhart developed the Shewhart cycle for scientific experiments, Deming brought the approach to quality control and experiments in production. Professor Deming's background as a physicist gave him the ideal insight into how a scientific approach could benefit business.

The circle works like this:

THE DEMING (PDCA) CIRCLE

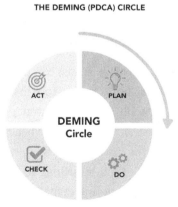

Figure 17.1

We start with planning to ensure a clear understanding of the goals of our work. We undertake the actual work in the second quadrant. From here, we check or study the results against the original hypothesis, which sparks the action to change the results. We then shift gears into a new planning stage, and then continue the cycle forever in a kaizen fashion.

Regardless of blog content or organic social media content or influencers or paid media, Digital Threads will only be as effective as how we have a defined process for our work and the amount of data that we can use to optimize those processes. You should try everything I discuss in this book as experiments; the data that you glean will provide you the single source of truth that you can then further optimize to get the best results for your business.

The Deming Circle has been an integral cornerstone to so many elements of my work, from when I was first exposed to it while working in Japan to working with social media platforms. In fact, I consider the core tenets of Professor Deming's teachings so essential to this type of work that I named my company PDCA Social.

The changes in online marketing, in Digital First approaches, in social media marketing, and all the modern world are never ending. Since the Deming Circle continues in the same way, I've found that they are a complementary fit for each other.

From Scientific Advertising to Digital First PDCA

At least as far back as Francis Bacon, we can trace the scientific use of a method similar to PDCA. For Claude Hopkins, it made sense to test the waters when working with advertising strategies, and he explained this in his book, *Scientific Advertising*, published in 1923. The man was ahead of his time for marketing. Some sources attribute the creation of the modern idea of toothbrushing to him, intending to boost toothpaste sales rather than promoting dental hygiene.

In *Scientific Advertising*, Hopkins explains the idea of testing different methods of advertising and measuring them to know which one works. He would test different headlines and different copy for campaigns. He would try different marketing letters on a small scale, measure the success of each style, then launch the larger campaign with the one that proved the most successful. Over 100 years later, we are still doing these same things.

In a Digital First landscape, we have that power to test these elements easily. The power of the Internet and the ability to connect directly with our audience or consumers gives us an urge, like a call of the abyss, to jump right in. Rather than testing the best bait from the pier, there's a strong call from the open waters to sail out to where we know the fish are waiting without knowing what will work.

Don't.

Working through the PDCA cycle on a Digital First landscape means plotting out how to use these Digital Threads to make your fishing net strong. It will direct your spend, your energy, and your focus toward the success that you plan for.

- We make a plan, which is our marketing strategy.
- We create some assumptions based on the data we have how our marketing will perform.
- We then "do" or implement according to plan.
- We then check and see how we did compared to plan—this is where a concept of a regular report comes in.
- We then analyze and act upon our findings and go through the same cycle again in a never-ending circle of kaizen.

This PDCA cycle can apply to any single chapter that we have discussed. Are you looking to improve your Library of Content? Experiment with new topics or republish selected older items. Trying to improve your lead magnet's contribution to email list growth? Try different types or topics. Do you need a boost in your brand ambassador program? Use the 80/20 rule to experiment with greater incentives for the top 20 percent of your ambassadors who are generating 80 percent of your results. The same applies to external influencers. And every other digital thread.

Once you internalize PDCA and it becomes part of your team's core DNA, all of this comes naturally. Your business will always be in a state of experimenting and driving for higher and higher ROI. The beauty of PDCA is that it can apply to anywhere in your business—and even your personal life.

Applying PDCA Begins With Data

The PDCA approach is only as good as your data. With no data, we can't plan out what we are trying to do and what we hope to achieve. We need a process to collect all our data from all the efforts emanating from our Digital Threads in a report that will make it easy for us to decide how to plan where to shift resources to generate the greatest ROI.

Each business has its own needs across the SES Framework, but I have found that taking a funnel approach to the data can lead to the best results. Here is one example of how you can compile this data to best understand the results of your activities and where you need to invest more or less.

Top of Funnel

At this end of the funnel, we always need to ensure that we are reaching outside of our current community subset and continually bringing new eyeballs to our presence. We primarily achieve this through the search and social containers, so here are some important relevant metrics to measure:

Search

- Achieve x% visibility in search engine rankings.
- Generate x website sessions from organic search.

Social (for each platform)

- Increase followers on x social media to x followers.

- Increase profile visits on x social media to x.
- Generate x impressions on x social media content.
- Receive x engagements on x social media content.
- Achieve an average x% engagement rate on x social media platform.
- Generate x website sessions from x social media.

Middle of Funnel

While every part of the SES Framework can apply to the middle of the funnel, email and paid media will probably have the biggest impact here.

Email

- Increase email list size to x.
- Increase email open rate to x%.
- Increase email click-through rate to x%.

Paid Media (for each platform)

- total spend
- total impressions
- paid visits
- cost per impressions
- cost per click
- cost per lead magnet conversion (if applicable)

Bottom of Funnel

Here is where we want to put everything together and find out where our conversions are coming from and which channels contributed to our success.

Conversions

- How much converted from each marketing channel?
- How much did it cost for us to achieve these conversions per channel?

Advocacy

Don't forget to include some advocacy component in your report, especially if you are creating a brand ambassador program.

Brand Ambassador Program

- # of ambassadors
- # of brand mentions
- # of pieces of user-generated content published
- engagements generated
- website views generated
- leads generated (email signups)
- sales generated

In preparing a report like the one above based on the impact that each of our Digital Threads has and at what cost for how many conversions, you are creating a strategic dashboard that, like the mixing board at a live concert, gives you the ability to adjust things up or down for both maximum clarity of your message and optimal efficiency of your budget spend.

The Never-Ending Experiment

Taking advantage of this PDCA approach is also working under the assumption that your marketing is one never-ending experiment. While there might be product launches, the traditional concept of a "campaign" merely becomes one focused type of experiment.

A campaign is a method of spending lots of money focused on a product or service that serves to disrupt. This is necessary when launching a new company or a new product. But after that initial launch to get attention, what comes next?

The key to longevity and relevance is the PDCA circle. Through this, you understand where the money is going. You understand the ROI. When the algorithm changes, you'll see it and you'll be able to react. When you engage the PDCA circle, you'll understand what connects and what brings results. This will save you time, money, and other resources.

When you're measuring the returns and seeing what works, you can put the money where it needs to be amplified. And that brings us to another key element of the PDCA cycle—budget.

So many companies look at their budget from last year and extend it into the next. There are some companies I've worked with who found some success with certain paid media channels, then never changed how they spent their budget in the next years. Even as the returns changed, as the audience changed, as other avenues came up, they were not in touch with what worked and what changed.

The budget, too, should go through a continual experiment. There are new platforms. There are new algorithms. I urge you to rethink how you commit your spend.

With all this information in hand, similar to that mixing board analogy, we can now raise the levers by devoting more budget to those containers or activities that have greater impact at each stage of the funnel and reduce those that have less impact. This is how we scale our Digital First marketing.

When we reduce the spend on certain activities, we also might want to do dedicated experiments to see if we can optimize them for improvement. We sometimes see less effective results when there are algorithmic changes, so perhaps optimizing our activities on one channel can bring the numbers back up. But once again, the key is to really invest where you are doing well with a data-driven approach and not to spend too many resources on trying to optimize activities that aren't working unless there is some similar data to back up that there is too huge of a potential to pass up.

A Real-Life Case Study

Ikecho (https://ikecho.com.au) is an Australian provider of contemporary jewelry featuring pearls that are carefully sourced. Primarily a B2B wholesale company, Ikecho pivoted and launched a DTC e-commerce brand shortly after the start of the pandemic.

Like many companies, Ikecho was operating in the blind with a limited and disconnected view of business performance. Their paid media spend was greater than their ad-generated income. Then they created their own comprehensive report using the platform provided by the company Digivizer (disclaimer: I am a Digivizer Certified Expert Partner: https://digivizer.com/partnerships/neal-schaffer/)

In the words of Ikecho founder Erica Miller:

"We had been experiencing negative ROAS for a while, although it had gone unnoticed, largely because of our inability to compare and combine different metrics with efficiency. Especially across the separate channels used for direct and wholesale customers. It was clear that traffic was declining, and that there were chunks of content that just weren't performing."

"I focused on increasing the accessibility, searchability and discoverability of our products, driving growth in overall brand awareness and building a stronger conversion funnel. We achieved this by using data-driven insights from Digivizer to build out our social and content strategy and optimizing our paid media campaigns. We could use these same insights to optimize our creative branding, ad assets and website, focusing constantly on insight-driven tweaks to promote growth."

"Transforming a business is an ongoing process. You don't hit a certain mark and then just stop. You've got to keep a close eye on your real-time results. And, of course, use the insights they provide to keep on refining your next step."

The results provided by the visibility of the data together with the PDCA and kaizen approach to improve and optimize are impressive[4]:

- From an above-the-funnel perspective, social engagement rates increased by 176 percent on Instagram and 873 percent on Facebook within 12 months. New website visitor numbers grew by 25 percent.
- Paid media has also shown significant improvement with ROAS moved from being in negative territory to hitting over 12 on Facebook and 7 across all channels.
- The result of all this growth has had a hefty impact on Ikecho's bottom line. Overall revenue growth in retail has more than doubled.

Digital Threads can be a complex undertaking and it is easy to lose visibility how all our efforts are working. Only when we bring all our data together and see where we can move the volume slider up or down can we hear the results in our mixing board.

Key Takeaways:

- The PDCA circle is the optimal framework to manage an ever-growing cycle of threads
- Digital Threads are experiments to see what works with different audiences.
- Measuring what works is essential. Then you understand what to develop.

Companion Workbook Exercises:

- 17.1 | The PDCA Cycle in Action: A Social Media Experiment
- 17.2 | Create PDCA KPIs
- 17.3 | Create Your Digital Threads Report

Chapter 18
Scale People

"Growth is never by mere chance. It is the result of forces working together."

— James Cash Penney

Many years ago, after I launched my consultancy, my father's accountant told me:

"If you want to grow your business, you need to hire people."

You cannot do everything. And the truth of running a business, of being an entrepreneur, is that you shouldn't try to do everything. There are other people who are better at that skill than you are. When you work with them, it frees you to do what you do best.

When we return to the formula for scaling, people become an important thread that we can't ignore. Marketing, like any other work, is all about the efficient use of people, process, and tools. For larger companies with a sizeable workforce and agency budgets, finding the right resource may be a lot easier than it is for the small business owner, startup, or entrepreneur.

The Four-Hour Work Week by Tim Ferriss introduced a new way of thinking about outsourcing our own work. Through the efforts of people and businesses working as contractors in their expertise over the last decade or two, there are a growing number of freelancers around the world who have the experience and desire to help you.

An Introduction to Freelance Marketplaces

Expanding your company without breaking your budget takes some creativity. The Digital First landscape allows you to look for help in different places.

Agencies are certainly an option, as are sourcing interns from local universities or placing ads online in places such as LinkedIn or even Craigslist. If you want to tap into a global marketplace of talent, there are more options than ever before with freelancer and gig marketplaces such as Upwork and Fiverr.

The outsourcing revolution has been going on for longer than a decade, and the beauty is that now there are experienced professionals waiting to serve you. Though levels of aptitude and experiences will differ according to the freelancer you find, there are so many out there that you should be able to find someone for whatever Digital First marketing task you have on hand. Laid before you, there are about 1.57 billion people worldwide who call themselves freelancers[1]. These freelancers have expertise at working for similar companies in your industry and doing similar digital marketing tasks. Some might be happily self-employed, while others might look for a side hustle or are launching their own company.

A source estimates that the top four specialties of freelancers include creative (33 percent), consulting (21 percent), writing/content creation (17 percent), and technical or web development (15 percent)[2]. These are all necessary for a modern Digital First marketing program. And you can harness their knowledge on a per-project or per-hour basis to scale your business.

The two largest global talent marketplaces that I will cover in this chapter are Fiverr (800,000 "sellers" serving four million businesses) and Upwork (18 million freelancers).

Depending on your location, there are other networks that can be worth exploring. In the UK, there are networks such as Freelancer (60 million freelancers), PeoplePerHour (with 1.4 million freelancers), and other niche sites. I find, at least in the United States, that Fiverr and Upwork are the most popular in marketing, and they are both truly global in coverage regarding the freelancers who are in their database.

These networks that I'm outlining here are the primary ones that I have used for more than a decade with much success. Although I am an affiliate for both companies, I am not being compensated to write about them and only want to serve you by just sharing my experience with the platforms. Every platform offers slightly distinct features, but many of them, such as freelancer reviews, are common, so even if you do not end up using these two platforms, you can apply the knowledge elsewhere.

Fiverr

In my experience, Fiverr is best for one-off, pre-packaged projects. The freelancers here offer you their skills applied to a specific task, which is called a "gig." For instance, if you know you need a certain task done, say create LinkedIn carousel posts, you can search for LinkedIn carousel. When I did this search, I found 177 different services offered.

Each of these services is further defined differently by what specific things they will deliver, lead time, and how many revisions are possible, among other things. You will also need to confirm how directly their skills and experiences can contribute to what exactly you need done. The more defined your project is, the better results you'll find.

There is a skill to finding the right collaborator, but there are filters to help you.

Filtering Your Fiverr Options

The key in selecting the right service provider and offering is through analyzing the data that is provided. These are the areas that I always focus on to find the best person:

- Gig title and description: This should go without saying. The Fiverr search engine will feed you a result which might only be slightly relevant to what you are looking for. Always make sure that the gig title and description match the exact work you are looking for.
- Level of experience: Top Rated Sellers are the most experienced but also the most expensive. Personally, I opt for a Level 2 seller whenever an attractive option is available.
- Number of reviews: While pricing is a factor, more importantly, I pay attention to the review numbers that appear above the price. These reviews are not for the provider, but for the specific job.
- Orders in the queue: How many orders they have in the queue, which if they have any, will appear to the right of the number of star ratings they have. The greater the number of orders in the queue, the more confident you can be that you're working with a trusted individual.
- Revisions: There are many reasons the provider might not get the job done right the first time. That is why I always choose providers who offer as many revisions as possible.

The best approach is to send a message to the seller first, and you can do it for free with no obligations. Let them know what your project is, confirm the details, and use this as a chance to ask questions. From their replies, you will learn even more about each seller and how responsive they are, so that you can find who is the best fit.

Always be sure to get the source file for creative projects. This gives you the options to work with these assets in the future. In this early stage of communicating with the freelancer, you can understand what format the file will come in.

It can truly pay off to invest time in showing the freelancer exactly what you want from them and teach them so that you can create a repeatable process. Returning to someone who knows what you expect, and that you can trust to deliver good work, makes your work so much easier. With that in mind, I usually tell my clients that Fiverr is good for specific projects with specific outcomes, not paying per hour. Its strength is in finding collaborators for a single one-off gig, but it could blossom into something more regular where you know upfront what your costs will be and the quality provided with each iteration.

Upwork

For longer-term work, and for more collaboration over time, I turn to the other major talent marketplace—Upwork. Just as different social media networks offer different ways to engage, a unique experience for their users, and a different culture around it, each network of freelancers has a similar difference in culture. The presentation of their services and the listed collaborators vary.

How to Find Talent on Upwork

The first step in working with Upwork as a search engine is to think laterally. Instead of searching for the job or product you want, you need to think of the specific title of someone who would do that work. So, whereas on Fiverr we would search for the direct task—like "LinkedIn carousel"—on Upwork we would search for a "social media content creator" or "LinkedIn content creator."

The variety of titles next to the people who appear in search results gives you a feel for who might be the perfect collaborator. However, I would focus on and work through the following filters so that you get better quality candidates from the get-go:

- Talent badge: By selecting "Top Rated," the platform will only show you the top 10 percent of all Upwork freelancers. I will sometimes add "Rising Talent" if I don't see enough "Top Rated" profiles as you might find some diamond

freelancers who are still new to the platform in the rough here.
- Talent type: I always choose Freelancers, and not Agencies, as that is the entire purpose of using Upwork.
- Job success: I would only choose 90 percent & up to ensure quality.
- Earned amount: I would always choose $10K+ earned, and if there aren't enough profiles to search through, lower it to $1K+. This ensures you are getting truly experienced freelancers.

From here, I will review each individual's profile. What is telling here is their "Work history." You can see the titles of the exact jobs they have worked on, how much they earned for that job, and their employer's review of them (for public jobs). You can also see their jobs "In progress." Reviewing this is critical because you will find some freelancers advertising themselves as being everything to everybody, but finding someone who has done the exact work that you will ask them to do should raise your confidence that they are the right person for the job.

You can easily and efficiently engage with these candidates by creating a job posting. While you can message people on Fiverr once you've narrowed down the gig provider, the approach I would take on Upwork is first posting a job—which is free to do—and then sending out an invitation to all of those on your shortlist. Upwork allows you to send out 30 invites for free. I would take advantage of this because not every freelancer is available and some, for whatever reason, won't want to work with you.

The aim of using Upwork is to hire someone, so you should make a list of questions that applicants must answer, much like an interview when you invite someone to apply for a job. These can give you a neat way to see inside the way they will approach working with you. It also allows you to gauge how well they can follow instructions. I usually end these questions with one covering what I need to provide them to get the best work done. They're the expert so it's always good to let them tell you what they need to do the project. These are all steps to mitigate risk and find the most appropriate person.

Upwork is a little more complicated than Fiverr, but when hiring for a long-term collaboration, it can give a better option, in my experience.

Experiment and Then Scale

You will end up using these freelance marketplaces when you have a need but lack the resource.

I always try to hire multiple people for a project and give them some test work. Rather than putting all my eggs into one basket, give the same task and instructions to three different freelancers and the results will show you who to work with.

How far can you scale through outsourcing? C9 Staff, a staffing solutions company, offers a case study of how they helped a 100- to 200-employee digital marketing agency hire the following freelancers[3]:

- 7 senior Shopify developers
- 6 senior WordPress developers
- 3 senior email graphics designers
- 2 senior web designers
- 1 senior copywriter
- 1 senior social media designer
- 1 senior email developer
- 1 motion graphics designer
- 1 media buyer
- 1 technical project manager
- 3 strategy project managers

In the United States, this would come at a cost of approximately $145,000 in monthly salaries. With benefits, bonuses, and office space and equipment, this estimation would come out to $220,000 monthly.

Through outsourcing through this agency, they are paying $70,000.

If you hired these freelancers directly, I imagine this would become even less expensive.

The idea here isn't to save money but to find the right resource that can help you scale. Outsource the work that others can do so you can focus on the work you do best. Being able to do so to help make your marketing spend even more efficient is icing on the cake.

Key Takeaways:

- The worldwide network of freelancers can help you scale your business.
- Finding regular collaborators can keep your workflow rolling and productive.
- It is not essential to be an expert in everything. Finding others with expertise allows you to focus on what you do best.

Companion Workbook Exercises:

- 18.1 | What Should I Outsource
- 18.2 | Crafting a Compelling Project Brief
- 18.3 | Find Your Freelancer
- 18.4 | Evaluating Freelancer Proposals
- 18.5 | Building Long-term Freelancer Relationships

Chapter 19
AI & Marketing

"If a machine can think, it might think more intelligently than we do, and then where should we be? Even if we could keep the machines in a subservient position, for instance, by turning off the power at strategic moments, we should, as a species, feel greatly humbled."

— Alan Turing, the father of modern computing, in 1951

The placement of this chapter on artificial intelligence and marketing between the previous chapter on scaling people and the following chapter on scaling technology is not a coincidence.

AI plays a unique role in potentially helping you do more with less, a concept that should excite every reader who represents a smaller business that doesn't have unlimited resources. It also represents a unique blend of "human" and "technology" that might help you more efficiently weave together most, if not all, of the Digital Threads mentioned in this book.

While there have been other trends that have come and gone (whatever happened to Google+?), AI is clearly being mass adopted as we speak. In fact, the research and advisory firm Gartner has projected that by 2025, generative AI will create 30 percent of outbound marketing messages from large organizations[1].

Examining AI's past, present, and future is vital for gaining a comprehensive understanding of its role and impact.

Why ChatGPT Changed Everything

Comparing the terms "AI" and "marketing" in Google Trends shows that search demand for "AI" spiked during the week of December 4, 2022, shortly after the release of ChatGPT. It spiked again on the week of April 16, 2023, during a time when AI finally "crossed the chasm" and became entrenched in our media.

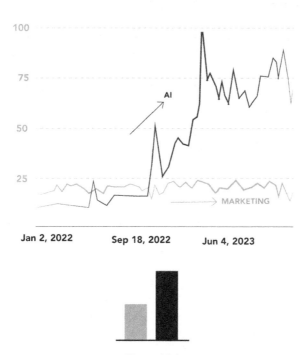

Figure 19.1

This spike comes from the developments surrounding artificial intelligence at OpenAI. Microsoft invested a billion dollars in the small tech startup in 2019. In 2020, OpenAI began to beta test a deep learning-based model called GPT-3 that could produce code, poetry, and other kinds of language. Despite not being the first of its sort, it is the first to produce content that is essentially indistinguishable from that produced by humans.

In 2021, OpenAI released DALL-E, making further steps with artificial intelligence in the visual world by processing and comprehending images well enough to provide accurate captions. ChatGPT was first announced on November 30, 2022. GPT-4, released on March 14, 2023, showed significant advancements. These two developments meant that anybody could register for a free account and harness the power of decades of AI development by merely having a conversation with a chatbot and giving it instructions, or "prompts."

As a result, ChatGPT surpassed every other social network in history in terms of its speed in acquiring users.

Figure 19.2

Due to allowing other tools to access its APIs, there was a boom in various companies creating specialized applications that could specifically help marketers with a variety of content creation needs.

The AI that I will focus on here is generative AI, which IBM defines as "deep-learning models that can generate high-quality text, images, and other content based on the data they were trained on^2." In other words, AI for content creation.

The most spoken-about generative AI tools are ChatGPT and Google ~~Bard~~ Gemini. These are far from the only two. In fact, an appropriately named site called THERE'S AN AI FOR THAT (https://theresanaiforthat.com/) tracks over 12,000 AI tools.

This industry and technology continue to develop quickly, and the leading companies will change, but this provides a specific starting point to envision where this technology will make the most sense for your specific needs. This technology will see massive leaps quickly, similar to the early use of computer-generated imagery (CGI) in movies. AI's limitations compared to humans will soon decrease in tasks it struggles with.

What Is Possible With Generative AI Today

If we can understand the containers for generative AI technology, we can visualize how we can use this technology in our Digital First marketing. Understanding how to leverage these tools begins with understanding what is possible with them. Only then can we decide how to strategize on using them as part of our Digital Threads efforts.

Textual AI

Text generation is where generative AI has progressed fastest. AI-generated content is so good that it is getting increasingly difficult to detect. While AI does "hallucinate" by sometimes providing false information to fulfill its task, it can also follow instructions, assuming you are giving it the right prompt or series of prompts.

A look at what is possible using just one tool, Jasper, gives you an idea of what is possible in creating textual content that you can immediately use for your marketing based on the "recipes" that the tool has provided that don't require you to provide a prompt:

- Amazon: product features (bullet points), product description (paragraph)
- blog: topic ideas, outline, intro paragraph, concluding paragraph, a "one-shot" complete blog post, SEO titles, SEO meta descriptions
- email: subject lines, personalized cold emails
- Facebook Ads: headlines, primary text
- Google Ads: headlines, description
- Google My Business: event post, offer post, product description, what's new post
- image prompts: use AI to create a prompt to help you create an AI-generated image
- Instagram: threads post, photo post captions
- LinkedIn: single image ads text, text ads, personal post
- Pinterest: pin title, pin description
- TikTok: video captions
- X: "viral" posts
- YouTube: video description, video script hook and introduction, video script outline, video titles, video topic ideas

Static Image AI

The term "deepfake," which was first used back in 2017[3], hints at how good AI imagery has become. While sometimes AI-generated images do not look as realistic as a photograph, it is probably only a matter of time before it gets close to the real thing.

There are use case scenarios where you don't need a realistic stock photo but just an image to make a point as part of a blog post or even an advert. In these areas, AI-generated static images can save you time and money.

One use case scenario in marketing where AI usage has become popular is in creating product images. There are a growing number of software tools that will help mix your real product photo with an AI-generated background to create a product photo. You can use this on your web or Amazon store, and it looks very close to being real. It's a great option when you simply don't have the budget for a photo shoot yet want to create a variety of creatives.

Just as there are AI-based textual editing tools such as Grammarly, these same tools exist for images. These tools can boost the resolution of your pictures from regular to high definition while also tackling various issues, such as helping to clear blurriness, update your old photos, and enhance compressed images.

Video AI

AI can help you with your video in a variety of ways today, but it shines in creating text-to-video assets. All you need is to input a few simple prompts, and voilà! AI tools can help you go from text directly to video and easily customize the output without being an experienced video editor.

These tools operate under two different mechanisms:

- A content library of human-like avatars is used to create videos. These avatars move and read scripts in the same way as we do, but although they visually appear to be lifelike, their voices still sound a little robotic, although it is only a matter of time until their voice cloning capabilities improve. Many of these AI tools allow you to create these videos in over 100 languages, which is nifty for international audiences. This makes it easy to create explainers, educational videos for training, and other marketing material. Enter your text, select a background

and an avatar, and observe as the robot spreads your message.
- The other common type of tool can take a text that you input (or even import full blog posts) and create videos based on a mixture of stock footage combined with transitions and animations.

There is more that you can do with AI in video that, while not being pure creation, can help improve your video content, or turn your longer videos into shorter excerpts for social media. Other tools include pre-made voices in various languages to help create a custom voice-over for the videos you are creating.

Video editors are also incorporating AI functionality, which not only allows you to repurpose longer videos into shorter ones, but also finds and removes pauses and filler words. Some use motion tracking to eliminate fillers in your content, resulting in better, more condensed videos. The jump cuts can have a major impact on user experience, thus helping your social media posts go viral. These tools often feature audio-to-text AI to help autogenerate subtitles and prepare your videos for digital publication.

Audio AI

Generative AI has impacted audio as much as it has video, and in fact some of the video features mentioned beforehand, such as finding blank spaces in a recording or creating subtitles from a recorded video, are audio-related functionality applied to video.

How far can generative AI take audio? My podcast host, Buzzsprout, has an optional podcasting AI option called Cohost AI. The process is simple: You simply upload your raw podcast audio file in .mp3, and you receive the following outputs in five to 10 minutes based solely on your audio file:

- five proposed podcast titles

- a pre-written podcast description
- chapter markers
- transcript
- blog post (approximately 400 words in my experience)
- three short social media posts

The beauty is that this is all based on your raw audio, which is then transcribed and then, using text AI, produces outputs that are specific to what a podcast needs to publish.

Descript is a noteworthy tool that serves as both a video and audio editing tool. Not only can it find and autodelete blank areas of your recording, but it also includes AI features specifically for audio, such as removing noise, enhancing speech, canceling acoustic echo, and enhancing audio quality.

Descript also can instantly purge recordings of "um" and "uh" and "you know" and all those repeat words podcasters prefer to remove to sound more professional. Its most interesting functionality called Overdub can create a shockingly realistic clone of your voice, then record new words that sound like you by simply typing them into your podcast transcript and then exporting the revised audio file.

Finally, there are an increasing number of audio AI tools that will allow you to clone your voice, and even some that allow you to upload all your podcast recordings, videos, and written content to create a talking avatar that looks like you, sounds like you, and actually says the things that you would say. Yes, that is correct: you can soon create your own virtual doppelgänger!

With the help of generative AI, content creation in any medium has become exponentially more accessible, and it will continue to become increasingly more so. Some of the most useful of these tools have immense value because they can help simplify your workflow. That is the key to finding exponential value with AI technology.

How to Best Leverage AI for Your Marketing Today

When social media first emerged and every business was trying to figure it out, I said that *"social media replaces nothing yet complements everything."* I believe the same is true for AI: You are not creating a new workflow for AI, but seeing how it best integrates and complements what you are already doing.

Let me first say that AI is unnecessary to be successful with your Digital Threads strategy. Just because we have the technology doesn't mean we have to use it. Or use it all the time. Just like in movies where some filmmakers blend CGI with practical effects, the best results I've found involve using AI as a tool to complement what you do. Relying solely on AI to complete the work can leave mixed results. Should you decide to deploy any of these technologies I will refer to, remember this: It is okay to be AI on the inside, but always be as human as possible on the outside. Digital Threads are all about making human connection so be careful how you end up deploying AI. Efficiency and convenience are one thing, but you should not lose the soul of how you appear to your customers and prospects and how they can engage with you on a human level.

Effective content creation needs to have a system, a process, or a workflow to help manage everything. As with any tool, you need to find where AI either makes your workflow more efficient and/or improves the quality.

With this in mind, let me propose a standard content creation workflow template and show where I believe AI is most suitable.

Figure 19.3

Plan

If there is any one area where generative AI will become your best friend, it is here. AI content creation tools can help you at every stage. Have writer's block? No problem! Don't have time to research? Let AI do it for you! Run out of ideas? Explore the vast database of human thought, the Internet, and witness the incredible output AI can generate for you!

If you are using AI for research or an outline, you will not only want to make sure that the content makes sense, but you will also want to make sure and check the sources for the data to ensure that it is real and not a "hallucination." Also, understand that there are debates over how biased the current state of Internet content is.

Planning incorporates the following activities:

- **Brainstorm/Ideation**—What are you going to create content around? You might already have a content strategy, but at some point, there was some brainstorming done to create that plan and pool the topics.
- **Research Topic**—Even if you are an expert on the topic, your writer might not be. You also want to make sure you have all your bases covered and are sourcing the right statistics.
- **Create Outline**—It is common practice to develop and approve an outline before proceeding. This will define the content containers but also make it much easier to produce the content.

Produce

This is where opinions on leveraging AI will diverge, especially when talking about content creation. I would never 100 percent rely on AI for content creation, as you always need to ensure the accuracy and brand relevance of the text. On the other hand, you could ALWAYS use AI as part of your content creation process to help you expand your content or provide you with a boost of creativity as part of your writing process. This could apply to video and podcast scripts as well.

Content production includes the following tasks:

- **Create Content** (including a script for audio/video)—This is the actual creation of the content, which is the writing (in terms of text and/or script) and/or filming or recording your video or audio content.

- **Optimize for SEO**—This is an extra step that some companies who are serious about SEO might have. Before moving on to the editing stage, it's important to make some adjustments to optimize the content for SEO. This could also apply to the creation of SEO-optimized YouTube/podcast titles and descriptions to complement the content you are creating.
- **Edit and Proofread Content**—The last step of content production is the editing and proofreading stage. The editing applies universally to text, video, and audio, where proofreading would primarily be for textual content or textual components of video and audio content including video subtitles, audio transcripts, and so on.

Manage

This is an area where you can once again lean heavily on AI for both creating supporting media and the repurposing of content, like the Buzzsprout Cohost AI example. This is also where you could use AI-generated art to create blog post images that are embedded in the blog post or shared as the featured image for the blog post.

From a repurposing perspective, there are tools that can create a video from a blog post. You can also use generative AI tools to generate a series of short-form videos automatically from a long-form one. AI can also help you summarize YouTube videos, podcasts, or blog posts for sharing on social media.

Managing content includes:

- **Create Supporting Media**—Whether it is a blog post (visuals, tables, graphs, social media image), video (thumbnail, short-form video excerpts), or audio (episode image to share in social media, short-form video excerpts), there is often supporting media needed before publishing that will either become part of the content itself or will be crucial in the content's promotion.

- **Repurpose for Multiple Platforms**—Developing the original content through this workflow simplifies the process, but we still need to figure out where to repurpose each piece of content. Consider creating a separate workflow for repurposed content if you always repurpose for the same distribution channels.

Publish

Although it is possible to integrate certain AI tools with your CMS, such as WordPress, it's always advisable to publish content directly or through a trusted social media dashboard that you're already using to ensure the highest level of quality. From a scheduling perspective, there are some tools that might recommend when you should publish your content. However, it is a best practice to use the analytics provided by your social media dashboard to create the perfect time to schedule your posts and then optimize according to your own unique analytics.

Publishing content involves:

- **Schedule/Publish Content** (main platform)—The scheduling/publishing of your content usually happens natively in your CMS (WordPress, Shopify, etc.) for blog content, YouTube for video content, as well as a podcast host for audio content.
- **Distribute/Promote Content** (social media, email, ads, repurposing, etc.)—You want to make sure that you distribute/promote your content to your main promotion channels, which usually include social media and email, once you publish and have a live URL. This is also where you want to distribute your repurposed content to social media.

Measure

Analytics is an area where I believe AI has been far behind generative AI from an impact perspective. There might be some AI tools that can offer you more specific advice based on your analytics, but this is still an area where humans rule until AI, or the marketing technology companies, gets smarter.

Tasks related to measurement include:

- **Review Analytics**—In PDCA fashion, it is important to monitor the results of your efforts and determine which topics/channels to lean into more (or less) to achieve better results.

Optimize

Once your analytics identify the content that needs revision or optimization, you can use the same AI content creation tools to rewrite or optimize your current content. The current AI SEO tool I use, for example, Frase, asks you at first if you are creating new content or optimizing old content. Following the instructions for optimizing old content will allow you to re-optimize your content for SEO as if you were writing it for the first time.

- **Revise/Republish**—This is an important step for blog content but equally important for YouTube videos. You can revise and republish a blog post with new publishing content and reap the benefits of having "new" content from an SEO perspective. Currently, 25 percent of my blog posts are being republished. You can't do this on YouTube, but you can revise your thumbnails, titles, descriptions, and tags, all of which might help you gain better results for the same content you produced.

- **Archive**—From all the time you spent creating content, you might think you would never want to "archive" content. I used to say the same thing. Then came the closing of StumbleUpon, Ello, Tsu, and Google Plus, all of which I had blogged about. Your brand might also pivot into new products and industries. At some point, you might find it necessary to archive your now unrelated blog posts and YouTube videos.

How Others Have Found Success With Generative AI

Even though generative AI is a recent phenomenon, we are already seeing companies save time and have more impactful results from their marketing through utilizing AI as a co-pilot. A look at some of Jasper's published case studies gives us a feel for what is possible.

Goosehead Insurance found that AI could help them increase content creation (to a record five blog posts a week), create more engaging email copy (with a 22 percent increase in click-through rate), and strategically revise web content. All of this helped contribute to an 87 percent increase in web traffic[4].

Mongoose Media, a digital marketing agency, found that with AI they could create content 400 percent faster, and they have benefited from a 166 percent increase in organic traffic as a result[5].

Amplitude, a digital analytics platform, was looking to build a new Glossary section of their website for which they extensively used AI. They ended up quickly creating 15,000+ words of content, which led to an 88 percent cost reduction and appearing on page 1 of Google search results in three weeks[6].

There is no doubt of the power that AI can have for your business. At a minimum, it is time to experiment with these tools, understanding how they work and help your workflow, and finally doing your own PDCA experimentation.

AI Ethics and Your AI Policy

While there are certainly many benefits of using AI, the fact of the matter is that there are still ethical and legal issues remaining to be figured out. It is crucial to be aware of the potential ethical pitfalls and how to navigate them effectively.

Without proper oversight, generative AI might amplify the spread of misinformation or disinformation. The ability to infringe on intellectual property rights is another thorny issue. Furthermore, consider the implications for data privacy. Generative AI models can train on personally identifiable information (PII), potentially misusing it and violating privacy norms. The same is true for bias. If we train the AI models on biased data, the resulting content will reflect that bias, possibly perpetuating discrimination and inequality.

Generative AI might also create plagiarized work. AI pulls from existing content to understand how to create, and there are times this runs close to plagiarism, and in doing so, both borrows ideas from other writers without giving them credit and generate content that closely resembles existing content. The same applies to AI-generated visual content.

Therefore, it's imperative to mitigate these risks. Here are some recommended actions to consider:

- Always be aware of the latest news and regulations regarding the use of AI.
- Do not share confidential information, including personal identifiable information with public AI tools, unless safeguards are in place.
- Make sure to always fact-check and check for plagiarism any AI-generated content that you might use.
- When possible, confirm the sources of AI-generated images to avoid any non-open-source content.
- Strive to achieve authenticity and originality in AI-generated content because of the absence of copyright protection.

- Respect others' intellectual property rights and give credit if AI-generated content is clearly coming from an identifiable source.
- Properly label and attribute AI-generated content.
- Strive to ensure unbiased data training.

Restricting the use of AI to certain areas and always having a human fact-checking and bias-checking the results will help mitigate some of these risks with textual content. Visual AI leveraging images and other visual art from the Internet, where copyrights are clearly held and defined, is an area that is still developing and still has some inherent risk that you might want to stay away from if possible. AI-generated works, like those that are 100% created by AI, are not eligible for copyright protection.

There are companies like Adobe who, with their Adobe Firefly product, have created a generative AI product cognizant of these issues. Adobe has made Firefly suitable for commercial usage and trained it on Adobe Stock pictures, publicly licensed content, and public domain content. They have created a compensation approach for Adobe Stock contributors to retrain Firefly models to make sure that creators may profit from their contributions to generative AI. It will be interesting to see if similar safe for commercial use generative AI solutions will appear in the market.

Key Takeaways:

- Generative AI can cover a lot of content and help scale your operation.
- AI content must still have a human touch if you want to connect with humans.
- To be most efficient with AI, first document your content

creation workflow and see where it makes the most sense to leverage this technology.

Companion Workbook Exercises:

- 19.1 | Let the AI Experiment Begin
- 19.2 | Textual AI for Social Media
- 19.3 | Visual AI for Marketing
- 19.4 | The AI Workflow

Chapter 20
Scale Technology

"Do not wait; the time will never be 'just right.' Start where you stand, and work with whatever tools you may have at your command, and better tools will be found as you go along."

— George Herbert

Since founding the first conference dedicated to social media marketing technology, the Social Tools Summit (2014-15), I've seen the impact that having the right technology can have on your digital marketing. Digital First marketing has not changed that need. In fact, the innovative solutions emerging from generative AI technology mean that there are more choices than ever before.

For an entrepreneur or small business, leveraging technology is one smart way to scale. And even if you're a large organization, technology will allow you to scale even more. These tools that I'm going to introduce here will be relevant to you, whether you are a small business like my own or a large enterprise, since you can leverage most of these tools either way.

The biggest takeaway, however, is not a specific type of tool or vendor name but understanding what is possible with the technology.

Since technology innovation happens rapidly, this chapter will include very few specific tool names so that the content can be as evergreen as possible. To get my most recent tools recommendations, please make sure you download my free companion workbook, which will include these recommendations and over 70 exercises I created for you. As a reminder, you can find the workbook here:

https://nealschaffer.com/digitalthreadsworkbook

Search Tools

SEO Dashboard

An SEO dashboard is a general SEO tool you will use very often and can provide you with the ability to:

- Perform keyword research to understand the search demand for different keywords.
- Manage keywords through a dedicated keyword manager that can help you manage your content creation workflow priority for targeted keywords.
- Visualize your rankings through a rank tracker to assess how your Library of Content is performing from a search engine rankings aspect.
- Conduct a backlink analysis of any web domain.
- Analyze keywords any web domain is getting a lot of traffic from or determine which of their content has generated a lot of backlinks.

SEO-Optimized Content Creation Tools

There are many tools that promise to optimize your content for SEO, beginning with the basic Yoast SEO plugin for WordPress. SEO has come a long way from simply keyword stuffing to writing content. You want to find a tool that leverages the top search results and, using natural language processing, provides you advice on what topics and keywords to cover from a semantic search perspective.

YouTube SEO

TubeBuddy and VidIQ are currently the definitive two tools for YouTube SEO. They are very similar but offer different functionality, especially for AI. Many YouTubers I know, as well as yours truly, subscribe to both tools to get the best of both worlds. These two tools offer you a myriad of options to help you ideate, create, and ultimately optimize each video to rank higher on YouTube.

Video Creation and Editing

Using a software platform that records both your video and audio regardless of whether you are conducting an interview or doing a solo podcast recording puts you ahead of the curve for repurposing. Once you have the audio, you can easily transcribe it into text. With that in mind, you want to use a platform that not only records in the highest possible video resolution (4K, if possible) and best audio (uncompressed crystal-clear audio in 48kHz WAV), but also records the video and audio in separate channels locally to allow you more flexibility in repurposing later.

Another important component of these tools is the ability to livestream that content to popular platforms such as YouTube, LinkedIn, Facebook, X, Instagram, and TikTok. While not every platform will livestream everywhere, you will want to take advantage of this functionality to get the most juice out of your content.

There is a plethora of choices here for video creation and editing, all the way from recording yourself and editing using your smartphone or whatever pre-installed software your computer has.

Audio Content

If you are creating audio content to improve discoverability in audio search engines, you will probably upload your audio as a podcast to major podcast apps like Apple Podcasts, Spotify, or YouTube Music. To do so, you will need to subscribe to a podcast hosting service.

Audio Editing

Editing an audio for a podcast is like editing a video for YouTube: You either have an internal resource to help you do it or you end up outsourcing the task, which is what I do.

Content Repurposing

Video creation tools will normally provide you with raw audio and video files. You can then import these into content repurposing tools and easily repurpose them for blog posts, social media posts, e-books and lead magnets, email newsletters, or short-form video for social media.

For any text purposes, you will first need to use a tool to transcribe the audio file as accurately as possible.

There is no one killer app that will do all this repurposing for us across blog posts, social media posts, and longer content, so I would recommend a combination of the following two types of apps, both infused with AI features.

The first would be what are now referred to as AI podcast content generator tools, which also generate transcripts. Even if you do not plan on running a podcast, you can still use these tools to upload your audio and take advantage of the assets that they will automagically repurpose for you.

The other option for converting your podcast transcript into a marketing asset is simply to use an AI content tool, free or paid, and prompt it to "create a xx-word social media post for xx network" or "create a xx-word summary of this for my email newsletter," etc. For social media specifically, you could use a social media dashboard that already has this functionality embedded, but there are a growing number of AI content creation tools that you can use as well.

There are AI-powered software tools that can help you both find and repurpose your content to make short vertical videos that you can edit and then upload to the social media platform of your choice. This is one type of AI tool that is absolutely exploding in terms of the number of companies offering this technology.

Email Tools

Lead Magnet Creation Tools

There are a variety of lead magnets you can create, so there is no one tool that will help you create any and every lead magnet. What is important is that there are tools that can help you create different lead magnets, facilitate promoting that lead magnet, and help integrate it with your email marketing software.

Lead Magnet Distribution Tools

Marketers usually display lead magnets for access in one of the following places:

- overlaid on top of the website (modal pop-up, slide in, or sticky bar)
- displayed inside web content (inline)
- on a dedicated landing page

There are many email marketing software solutions that support the creation of these elements as part of your monthly fees. In case you prefer a distinct aesthetic and advanced analytics, you will need to use a third-party tool that integrates with your email marketing software.

Email Marketing Software

Many email marketing software solutions can integrate with

existing lead magnet distribution tools and provide their own solutions. Some of these solutions feature more marketing automation than others, AI features, and CRM functionality.

Marketing Automation Software

Marketing automation started off as an expensive piece of software, equally complex to manage, that larger enterprises, especially in the B2B space, initially purchased. Larger enterprise software companies hoping to create a full suite of products acquired these marketing automation companies. This severely limited the availability of robust marketing automation software for smaller businesses.

At the same time, we've seen an explosion of small businesses using email marketing software, and a boom in lower-end platforms. ActiveCampaign is one example of an email marketing tool that might have enough marketing automation capabilities to do the things that I talked about in the chapter on marketing automation. Other marketing automation software solutions provide:

- Salesforce CRM integration
- WhatsApp integration
- logged in visitor identification
- omni-channel marketing automation
- contact scoring
- A/B testing
- deal and company scoring

Marketing automation software differs from email marketing software in that its focus is on lead generation, nurturing, and conversion over a longer sales cycle. When you are ready to invest in a high-end solution that focuses on marketing automation features, which are often tied to more of a CRM-based sales and marketing approach, then you should invest in marketing automation software.

With marketing automation, you can transform your email marketing into a true customer engagement platform.

Social Media Tools

As good as your tools are, the engagement you get on social media will only be as strong as the effort you put into your content and engaging on the platform. In social settings, people can understand who is just there for self-interest. Social media is the same. Although there are some great tools here, the best tools for social media are literally the platforms themselves.

Over-reliance on social media dashboards can lead to your social media content simply being out of tune. Tools amplify your existing work. If you weave the thread poorly, then there's little that tools can do to strengthen it.

Social Media AI Content Creation Tools

These tools work as an extension of a ChatGPT prompt by asking you the following questions you input into a form to generate a text output you would then revise and post to social media. While the inputs may differ across tools, it's important to choose an AI tool that covers these options:

- prompt (what you want the post to be about)
- main points, or keywords to cover
- length
- writing style and tone
- include hashtags and/or emojis
- number of variations to produce to choose from

Some tools, after you receive a response, provide additional prompts to adjust tone, shorten, lengthen, and further refine.

Most general AI tools support this, and you could even instruct ChatGPT and Google Gemini to do the same thing.

Social Media Dashboards with Integrated AI Content Creation Tools

Optimize your workflow with AI tools that both help you create social media posts *and* schedule them. An increasing number of social media dashboards have built integrated AI writers to make your time spent there even more efficient.

Social Network-Specific AI Content Creation Tools

If you truly want to create Platform Authentic Content, there are a few tools that use AI to analyze what types of posts are already doing well and then introduce similar types of content or templates to help you generate engaging content for that platform.

Once you see how these tools work, you will see how a lot of the content you have been engaging with and even comments you have seen might be the work of one of these types of tools.

User-Generated Content

These platforms allow you to manage the entire lifecycle of user-generated content, which is to find, curate, manage, publish, and analyze its effectiveness. These tools also include an email component, which allows you to ask for reviews from your customers to encourage UGC submission, rights management for the UGC, and analytics to measure their ROI.

Another type of platform does not help you source UGC from your fans but facilitates the creation of UGC on your behalf from their pool of content creators. You could consider them a UGC creator marketplace of sorts, each having a database of creators to choose from. This will cost you more than merely sending free product, but it is a type of influencer marketing that provides you tangible results in terms of content.

Another option to increase the creation of user-generated content around your brand is through a user-generated content giveaway that encourages people to submit photos and videos with branded hashtags. Many contest or giveaway tools support contests that can generate user-generated content.

Brand Ambassador

It's not necessary to run your program through a brand ambassador platform, but at least for the analytics, it pays to use a program that will track your ROI at a deep level. When looking at brand ambassador software, it is important that you find a solution that helps you manage the entire lifecycle:

- landing page to facilitate applications
- dashboard to manage applicants
- the ability to individually or group message your members
- facilitation of product to your ambassadors
- facilitation of affiliate marketing and discount codes to your ambassadors

External Influencer Search and Discovery

There are a host of influencer marketing tools that are available, but all you need here is an influencer search tool, and then you can ask these external influencers to opt-in to the same brand ambassador tool so that you can manage all of your content creators from one place.

Some influencer search tools also include overlapping functionality with some brand ambassador tools.

These tools allow you to apply the following filters to help you create a shortlist of influencers:

- location
- language
- followers
- followers growth rate
- number of engagements per post

- average engagement rate
- authenticity/fake follower analysis
- previous brand collaborations track record
- estimated cost

Paid Media Tools

AI Tools to Generate Ad Copy

Many generative AI content creation tools have specific functionality that helps you easily create ad copy for the major social networks.

AI Tools to Generate Ad Creatives

Ads for social media often require visuals, both static and video, so we can use AI to create compelling ad creatives in a fraction of the time it used to take.

General Ads Platform Tools

Although you can manage ads directly on the ads managers of each platform, there are a plethora of tools that allow you to manage your ads more efficiently across multiple networks on one platform. Some of these tools also include automation and AI technology for optimization.

Amazon Ads Platforms

To focus on Amazon Ads, you'll need a tool that covers the analytics specific to this platform. These include:

- product research
- keyword research
- keyword tracker

- listing optimization
- advanced analytics
- manage Amazon-approved communication with buyers

Technology Is Only as Good as Your Strategy and Process

The idea here isn't to use all the technology. It is to find those pieces that help you best weave your Digital Threads for an efficient and cost-effective way to help scale your business.

Key Takeaways:

- Tools can help you in almost every aspect of the SES Framework.
- Your productivity and platform, your workflow, and your analytics can all benefit from tools that refine what you do.
- Don't use a tool to create a new workflow. Always see how and where tools can help improve your current marketing operations before investing in them.

Companion Workbook Exercises:

- 20.1 | SEO Tool Audit
- 20.2 | Email Marketing Tool Audit
- 20.3 | Social Media Dashboard Tool Audit

Conclusion

Facing an unfamiliar landscape, one that's constantly in motion, can be intimidating. The uncertainty of the process, of where the footholds are, and of what to hold on to can be paralyzing.

This is not a new state of affairs. New technology, shifting cultural movements, and politics have always created uncertainty. Embracing Digital Threads is, as I said before, not throwing away all the marketing advice you've learned over the years. It's finding new ways to put it into play.

While this book never concisely defined Digital Threads as a concrete concept, I hope it's now clear why: There is no formula or one thing that can help you become successful long-term in today's digital environment. Digital Threads represents a culmination of these synergistic concepts and strategies woven together with our relationships with people that truly tie all the Digital Threads together and bring them to life.

Marketing is about mindset. Digital Threads brings human connection back into focus and puts this through the lens of our times. It refocuses interactions from making a sale to making a connection and continuing a conversation.

Connecting with people earnestly and honestly, in a way that is personal, will always be effective marketing. People now spend as much time each day online as they did watching television in the decades I grew up. Socializing takes place in a digital realm. And that's where we take the core of our message.

It's a Digital First world.

Digital Threads, I hope, shows you how to weave these tools, platforms, and other online strategies in a way that puts the human first.

CLAIM YOUR FREE DIGITAL THREADS COMPANION WORKBOOK!

As a special bonus to help you apply what you learn in Digital Threads, I have created a separate companion workbook with dozens of exercises to help you use the concepts in the book to build and grow your business.

Relevant exercises to work on in the companion workbook are indicated in the summary at the end of each chapter in this book.

This companion workbook contains:

> Actionable exercises based on the concepts taught in Digital Threads

> A glossary of recommended tools for most of the essential threads covered

> Appendix on common legal issues

Please download your free copy of the electronic version of the companion workbook to help you internalize all my advice here:

nealschaffer.com/digitalthreadsworkbook

THANK YOU FOR READING DIGITAL THREADS!

I appreciate any feedback and would love to hear
what you thought about Digital Threads.
Your input is essential to help make this book,
the accompanying workbook and make my future books
even better to serve more people.

Please take a minute now to leave a review on Amazon
letting me know what you thought of the book:

nealschaffer.com/digitalthreadsreview

I cannot thank you enough! If you used a non-recognizable name,
please send me a screenshot to neal@nealschaffer.com so that I can
personally thank you!

- Neal Schaffer

IF YOU LIKED DIGITAL THREADS, YOU'LL LIKE MY OTHER BOOKS:

nealschaffer.com/maximizinglinkedinforgrowth
A practical guide to building your brand and driving results on LinkedIn.

nealschaffer.com/ageofinfluence
The definitive guide to influencer marketing.

nealschaffer.com/maximizeyoursocial
The definitive guide to creating and implementing a social media marketing strategy.

nealschaffer.com/maximizinglinkedin
The definitive guide to using LinkedIn for social selling, employee advocacy, and social media marketing.

Visit **nealschaffer.com/books/** for more information.

WORK WITH ME

I work with businesses in a variety of ways, from strategy creation to audit, implementation to training. Please find more information below and contact me below if I can be of any help to you or your organization.

GROUP COACHING — My Digital First Mastermind Community includes four monthly Zoom calls, one quarterly 30-minute private coaching call, and a private Facebook Group.

PRIVATE COACHING — When you need one-on-one help. Provided in one-hour increments.

FRACTIONAL CMO — My signature marketing consulting service where I become your fractional CMO, and you leverage my expertise however you see fit. Flexible, cost-effective, and you retain all IP!

SPEAKING & TRAINING — Whether it is speaking at your event or hands-on training for your team, I can help.

nealschaffer.com/contact/

SUBSCRIBE TO MY NEWSLETTER

Every week I provide updates to my readers on the world of Digital Threads, including:

- **The latest digital marketing news**
- **Updates on search engine optimization**
- **Strategies for successful email marketing**
- **Trending topics in social media marketing**
- **The newest AI technologies and tips for marketing**
- **My latest YouTube video, podcast episode, and blog posts**

In addition, this is the best way to find out about my new books, speaking events, and free educational webinars and other resources that I provide!

Subscribe here:
nealschaffer.com/newsletter/

Acknowledgments

As you learned in the introduction, this book began where my last book, *The Age of Influence*, ended.

My father proudly displayed his copy of the book on the stand next to the sofa, where he and my mom would watch countless hours of television, right before the beginning of the coronavirus pandemic. Since then, I lost both of my parents, but they continue to inspire me to help educate and empower others.

In fact, the creation of a workbook for this book comes straight out of the playbook that my father, a true content entrepreneur, had when he created his first workbook, *Fun and Games with Reading*, that would launch his educational publishing company. If only I can be as lucky with *Digital Threads*!

Writing this book has been a remarkable journey, one paved with challenges, insights, and immeasurable support from a group of amazing individuals. Their faith in my vision and encouragement has been the north star guiding me through this ambitious project.

To my loving wife and children, your unconditional love and support have been the foundation of not just this book, but of everything I aim to achieve. The sacrifices you've made, those quiet moments given up so that I could write, have not gone unnoticed. Your belief in me gives me the courage to chase my dreams.

I want to express my sincere gratitude to my parents in heaven and my older brothers and sisters. Your advice has always been a lantern in the dark, guiding my steps.

A special thank you goes to the exceptional talents of my international team, who have helped bring this book to life. Developmental editors Jason Kenny for *Digital Threads* and Bob Cochrane for *Digital Threads Companion Workbook*, copy editor David Aretha, graphic designer Shumona Mallick, book cover artist Tatiana Villa, book interior formatter Damian Jackson, photographer Takehiro Patrick Kokura, and hair makeup artist Mai Koga have been crucial in bringing this book to life. Your professionalism, attention to detail, and dedication have helped to ensure that we put together a quality product.

My Digital First Mastermind Community, both past and present members, deserves a special mention for their continuous inspiration and boundless support. Our shared knowledge and the collective wisdom we've built together have been invaluable. The instances of support, the brainstorming sessions, and the never-ending encouragement have been a pillar of strength.

I am grateful for my incredible Digital Threads Launch Team, whose invaluable feedback and unwavering support made this journey possible. Thank you for believing in this project and helping to bring Digital Threads to life: Ashley Smith, Mellissa Green, Mattie Murrey-Tegels, Jen Vazquez, Bill Ashton, Ted Schachter, Mary Beth McCabe, Wendy Jae, Koehler Slagel, and Jennifer Radke.

Finally, to all those who have followed my work—buying my previous books, subscribing to my newsletters, reading my blog posts, listening to my podcasts, watching my YouTube videos, and engaging with me on social media—your enduring support has been the fuel for my creativity and dedication. Each interaction, every word of encouragement, has been a source of motivation. I am overwhelmed with appreciation for this collaborative spirit and shared journey we are on.

This book is a testament to the power of community, friendship, professional collaboration, and personal bonds. Each of you has left a mark on not only this project but on my life. I am forever indebted to you all for being a part of my story, and I hope to mirror your trust and support you have shown me in everything that lies ahead.

Neal Schaffer

Endnotes

1. The New Digital Landscape of Today

1. Toni Fitzgerald, "Major Milestone: Digital Ad Spending Will Pass Non-Digital This Year," *Forbes*, February 20, 2019, https://www.forbes.com/sites/tonifitzgerald/2019/02/20/major-milestone-digital-ad-spending-will-pass-non-digital-this-year/
2. "eMarketer Releases New Global Media Ad Spending Estimates," *eMarketer*, May 7, 2018, https://www.emarketer.com/content/emarketer-total-media-ad-spending-worldwide-will-rise-7-4-in-2018
3. "Survey: The Ever-Growing Power of Reviews (2023 Edition)," *PowerReviews*, last modified April 2023, https://www.powerreviews.com/power-of-reviews-2023/
4. "Survey: The Ever-Growing Power of Reviews," *PowerReviews*, accessed May 17, 2024, https://www.powerreviews.com/power-of-reviews-survey-2021/
5. Aisha Malik, "TikTok Aims to Grow Its TikTok Shop US Business Tenfold to $17.5B in 2024, Report Claims," *TechCrunch*, January 4, 2024, https://techcrunch.com/2024/01/04/tiktok-aims-grow-tiktok-shop-u-s-business-tenfold-17-5b-2024/
6. "The Suspicious Undertaker Who Caused 200,000 Women to Lose Their Jobs," *Destination Innovation*, accessed May 17, 2024, https://www.destination-innovation.com/the-suspicious-undertaker-who-caused-200000-women-to-lose-their-jobs/
7. Robert Williams, "90% of People Buy from Brands They Follow on Social Media," *Retail Dive*, May 5, 2020, https://www.retaildive.com/news/90-of-people-buy-from-brands-they-follow-on-social-media/
8. Jamia Kenan, "Social Media Customer Service Statistics to Know in 2024," *Sprout Social*, December 13, 2023, https://sproutsocial.com/insights/social-media-customer-service-statistics/
9. Katie Hansen, "Nearly Half of US Consumers Say They Have Made a Purchase through Social Media," *Mintel*, April 20, 2023, https://www.mintel.com/press-centre/nearly-half-of-us-consumers-say-they-have-made-a-purchase-through-social-media/
10. Eve Rouse, "43 Statistics About User-Generated Content You Need to Know," *Nosto*, April 7, 2022, https://www.nosto.com/blog/42-statistics-about-user-generated-content-you-need-to-know/

2. The New Marketing Infrastructure of Today

1. "How to Control When Your Customers Buy – The Zero Moment of Truth," *Grammar Factory Publishing*, accessed May 17, 2024, https://grammarfactory.com/writing-for-entrepreneurs/how-to-control-when-your-customers-buy-the-zero-moment-of-truth-zmot/
2. "What is the AIDA Model?" *Lucidchart*, accessed May 17, 2024, https://www.lucidchart.com/blog/what-is-aida-model

3. Joe Pulizzi, "What is Content Marketing?" *The Tilt*, November 7, 2020, https://www.thetilt.com/content/what-is-content-marketing
4. Simon Kemp, "Digital 2023 Deep-Dive: How Much Time Do We Spend on Social Media?" *DataReportal*, January 26, 2023, https://datareportal.com/reports/digital-2023-deep-dive-time-spent-on-social-media
5. Neal Schaffer, "What is a Good Average Open Rate for Email Marketing?" *Neal Schaffer*, last modified April 4, 2024, https://nealschaffer.com/average-open-rate-for-email-marketing/
6. Elena Cucu, "[STUDY] 2024 Social Media Benchmarks: Performance Data Across 22 Industries," *Socialinsider*, February 5, 2024, https://www.socialinsider.io/blog/social-media-benchmarks/

3. Rethink Search

1. Michal Ugor, "How Long Does It Take to Rank on Google? Here's What the Data Says In 2024," *AuthorityHacker*, last modified February 29, 2024, https://www.authorityhacker.com/how-long-to-rank-on-google/
2. Joan E. Solsman, "YouTube's AI is the Puppet Master Over Most of What You Watch," *CNET*, January 10, 2018, https://www.cnet.com/tech/services-and-software/youtube-ces-2018-neal-mohan/

4. Rethink Email

1. "100% Pure Returns to Klaviyo and Blows Past Goal to Drive 20% of Revenue with Email," *Klaviyo*, accessed May 17, 2024, https://www.klaviyo.com/customers/case-studies/100pure-email-revenue
2. Aastha Sirohi, "What is the Average Email Marketing ROI?" *Constant Contact*, last modified November 17, 2023, https://www.constantcontact.com/blog/what-is-the-roi-of-email-marketing/
3. "How Do You Calculate Email Marketing ROI?" *Campaign Monitor*, accessed May 17, 2024, https://www.campaignmonitor.com/resources/knowledge-base/how-do-you-calculate-email-marketing-roi/
4. Eli Overbey, "The List Building Strategies That Grew 251,000 Subscribers," *Help Scout*, November 29, 2022, https://www.helpscout.com/list-building/#the-awesome-power-of-segmentation
5. Justin Ellis, "How The Skimm's Passionate Readership Helped Its Newsletter Grow to 1.5 Million Subscribers," *NiemanLab*, August 18, 2015, https://www.niemanlab.org/2015/08/how-the-skimms-passionate-readership-helped-its-newsletter-grow-to-1-5-million-subscribers/

5. Rethink Social Media

1. *Simple Pin Media*, https://www.simplepinmedia.com/
2. "Chinese Ethnic Groups," *The University of North Carolina at Chapel Hill*, accessed May 17, 2024, https://guides.lib.unc.edu/china_ethnic/

Endnotes | 265

3. "How Instagram is Changing: Instagram CEO Adam Mosseri on 20VC," *20VC* (on TikTok), January 4, 2024, https://www.tiktok.com/@20vc_tok/video/7320284169601322245 [Note: You originally erroneously had this in Chapter 6]

6. Be Found

1. Danny Sullivan, "What Site Owners Should Know about Google's August 2019 Core Update," *Google Search Central*, August 1, 2019, https://developers.google.com/search/blog/2019/08/core-updates
2. Chris Nelson, "What Creators Should Know about Google's August 2022 Helpful Content Update," *Google Search Central*, August 18, 2022, https://developers.google.com/search/blog/2022/08/helpful-content-update

7. Be in Touch

1. "History of the Sears Catalog," *Sears Archives*, accessed May 17, 2024, http://www.searsarchives.com/catalogs/history.htm
2. Solon L. Goode, *The American Farmer* (Google Books, 1907), https://books.google.com/books?id=Vb7G-Py9UNQC&pg=RA3-PA5&lpg=RA3-PA5
3. "History of the Sears Catalog," *Sears Archives*, accessed May 17, 2024, http://www.searsarchives.com/catalogs/history.htm
4. Kayla Hollatz, "How Bethany from Primally Pure Generated $100,000+ from an eCommerce Quiz," *Interact*, accessed May 17, 2024, https://www.tryinteract.com/blog/ecommerce-quiz-interview-with-primally-pure/
5. *Bullet Journal*, https://bulletjournal.com/
6. *Morning Brew*, https://www.morningbrew.com/money-scoop/challenges/subscribe

8. Be Seen

1. Simon Kemp, "The Changing World of Digital in 2023," *We Are Social*, January 26, 2023, https://wearesocial.com/us/blog/2023/01/the-changing-world-of-digital-in-2023/
2. Amanda Natividad, "Zero-Click Content: The Counterintuitive Way to Succeed in a Platform-Native World," *SparkToro*, July 25, 2022, https://sparktoro.com/blog/zero-click-content-the-counterintuitive-way-to-succeed-in-a-platform-native-world/

9. Build Connections

1. Brian Dean, "Google's 200 Ranking Factors: The Complete List," *Backlinko*, last modified March 24, 2024, https://backlinko.com/google-ranking-factors
2. Brian Dean, "We Analyzed 11.8 Million Google Search Results: Here's What We Learned about SEO," *Backlinko*, last modified March 24, 2024, https://backlinko.com/search-engine-ranking
3. Brian Dean, "We Analyzed 11.8 Million Google Search Results: Here's What We Learned about SEO," *Backlinko*, last modified March 24, 2024, https://backlinko.com/search-engine-ranking

4. "Study - Outgoing Links Used as Ranking Signal," *Reboot Online SEO*, last modified April 2020, https://www.rebootonline.com/blog/long-term-outgoing-link-experiment/
5. Brian Dean, "We Analyzed 11.8 Million Google Search Results: Here's What We Learned about SEO," *Backlinko*, last modified March 24, 2024, https://backlinko.com/search-engine-ranking
6. "Growing the Domain Rating from 3 to 50 for Branded Merchandise Agency," *Respona*, accessed May 17, 2024, https://respona.com/case-studies/prg/

10. Build Paths

1. Helen Holovach, "101+ Email Marketing Statistics You Should Know In 2024," *Snov.io*, January 23, 2024, https://snov.io/blog/email-marketing-statistics/
2. Maryam Mohsin, "Email Marketing Stats You Need to Know in 2023," *Oberlo*, December 4, 2022, https://www.oberlo.com/blog/email-marketing-statistics
3. Lisa Ross, "Important Welcome Email Statistics and Trends," *Invesp*, last modified February 1, 2024, https://www.invespcro.com/blog/welcome-emails/
4. Gregory Ciotti, "Building a Newsletter Welcome Series from Scratch," *Help Scout*, August 13, 2015, https://www.helpscout.com/blog/autoresponder-series/
5. "Welcome Email Series with 54% Sales Rate," *GetResponse*, accessed May 17, 2024, https://www.getresponse.com/customers/landcafe
6. Naomi Murray, "Case Study: How This Lead Nurturing Program Converted 28% of Its Leads," *Brief Media*, May 29, 2020, https://blog.briefmedia.com/case-study-how-this-lead-nurturing-program-converted-28-of-its-leads/
7. "B2B Content Marketing: 2016 Benchmarks, Budgets, and Trends—North America," *Content Marketing Institute* and *MarketingProfs*, accessed May 17, 2024, https://contentmarketinginstitute.com/wp-content/uploads/2015/09/2016_B2B_Report_Final.pdf
8. Rieva Lesonsky, "Holiday Spending Predictions: 2023 Looks Bright for Small Businesses," *Forbes*, November 20, 2023, https://www.forbes.com/sites/allbusiness/2023/11/20/holiday-spending-predictions-for-2023-look-bright-for-small-businesses/?sh=cb649956b469

11. Build Visibility

1. Fahad Muhammad, "What is User-Generated Content & How to Use It on Your Landing Pages," *Instapage*, accessed May 17, 2024, https://instapage.com/blog/what-is-user-generated-content/
2. Megan DeGruttola, "Stackla Survey Reveals Disconnect Between the Content Consumers Want & What Marketers Deliver," *Business Wire*, February 20, 2019, https://www.businesswire.com/news/home/20190220005302/en/Stackla-Survey-Reveals-Disconnect-Content-Consumers-Marketers
3. Eve Rouse, "43 Statistics About User-Generated Content You Need to Know," *Nosto*, April 7, 2022, https://www.nosto.com/blog/42-statistics-about-user-generated-content-you-need-to-know/
4. Todd Kunsman, "36 User-Generated Content Statistics That You Can't Ignore,"

EveryoneSocial, last modified February 26, 2024, https://everyonesocial.com/blog/user-generated-content-statistics/

5. Shivbhadrasinh Gohil, "30+ User Generated Content Statistics You Need to Know," *Meetanshi*, accessed May 17, 2024, https://meetanshi.com/blog/user-generated-content-statistics/
6. Todd Kunsman, "36 User-Generated Content Statistics That You Can't Ignore," *EveryoneSocial*, last modified February 26, 2024, https://everyonesocial.com/blog/user-generated-content-statistics/
7. Farjad Taheer, "25+ Powerful FOMO Statistics to Skyrocket Sales," *OptinMonster*, March 18, 2024, https://optinmonster.com/fomo-statistics/
8. Rob Reed, "The Year of the Instagram Strategy," *HuffPost*, November 4, 2013, https://www.huffpost.com/entry/the-year-of-the-instagram_b_4171833
9. "What Do 'Hashtags' and 'Instagrammable' Mean? [Q.「ハッシュタグ」や「SNS映え」って何ですか？]" *Chieneta*, December 6, 2019, https://flets-w.com/chienetta/hobby/cb_otherl48.html [NOTE: JAPANESE CHARACTERS]
10. "Creating an Impact Without Saying a Word," *Social Media Today*, July 16, 2014, https://www.socialmediatoday.com/content/creating-impact-without-saying-word
11. Sara Sousa, "Lust for Lulu: An Examination of Lululemon Athletica's Marketing Authenticity and Branding," *California Polytechnic State University, San Luis Obispo*, June, 2016, https://digitalcommons.calpoly.edu/cgi/viewcontent.cgi?article=1242&context=comssp
12. Tharin White, "Disney is Hiring Influencers to Join Marketing and TikTok Team," *Attractions Magazine*, February 20, 2023, https://attractionsmagazine.com/disney-is-hiring-influencers-to-join-marketing-and-tiktok-team/
13. Brian Honigman, "Why Companies Like Nerf and Olipop are Hiring TikTok Creators to Run Their Accounts," *Fast Company*, August 11, 2022, https://www.fastcompany.com/90777834/companies-hiring-tiktok-creators-nerf-olipop
14. "Revel Nail," *Pixlee TurnTo*, accessed May 17, 2024, https://web.archive.org/web/20240131133834/https://www.pixlee.com/case-studies/revel-nail

12. Grow Content

1. "Tips for Getting Discovered in the Reels Tab," *Instagram Creators*, February 9, 2021, https://www.instagram.com/p/CLFMSunBRX1/
2. Travis McKnight, "Study: How Blog Post Updates Affect Keyword Growth in 2022," *Portent*, May 5, 2022, https://www.portent.com/blog/content/study-how-blog-post-updates-affect-keyword-growth-in-2022.htm
3. Brian Dean, "Repurposing Content," *Backlinko*, last modified November 14, 2023, https://backlinko.com/hub/content/repurposing
4. Brian Dean, "Repurposing Content," *Backlinko*, last modified November 14, 2023, https://backlinko.com/hub/content/repurposing
5. Jessica Tee Orika, "Hootsuite's Billion-Dollar Content Repurposing Menu," *Foundation*, last modified April 3, 2024, https://foundationinc.co/lab/hootsuite-content-repurposing
6. Jessica Tee Orika, "Hootsuite's Billion-Dollar Content Repurposing Menu," *Foundation*, last modified April 3, 2024, https://foundationinc.co/lab/hootsuite-content-repurposing

7. Gary Vaynerchuk, "The GaryVee Content Model," *SlideShare*, July 24, 2018, https://www.slideshare.net/vaynerchuk/the-garyvee-content-model-107343659
8. Peter Craven, "Content Repurposing – Turning 4 Case Studies into 45 New Videos," *BlueSky Video Marketing*, November 10, 2022, https://blueskyvideomarketing.com/blog/content-repurposing-turning-4-case-studies-into-45-new-videos/
9. "Metadata's Journey from Virtual Event to Podcast Powerhouse," *Content 10x*, accessed May 17, 2024, https://www.content10x.com/case-study-metadata/

13. Grow Conversations

1. "National Client Email Report 2013," *Data & Marketing Association (DMA)*, accessed May 17, 2024, https://dma.org.uk/uploads/National%20Client%20Email%20Report%202013_53fdd7e6684de.pdf
2. "Average Industry Rates for Email as of April 2024," *Constant Contact*, last modified May 9, 2024, https://knowledgebase.constantcontact.com/email-digital-marketing/articles/KnowledgeBase/5409-average-industry-rates?lang=en_US
3. "What are Good Open Rates, CTRs, & CTORs for Email Campaigns?" *Campaign Monitor*, accessed May 17, 2024, https://www.campaignmonitor.com/resources/knowledge-base/what-are-good-email-metrics/
4. "Transactional Email for Marketers (with Examples)," *Campaign Monitor*, last modified April 2019, https://www.campaignmonitor.com/resources/guides/transactional-email/
5. Claudiu Murariu, "How to Measure the True Impact of Transactional Emails," *Inner Trends*, accessed May 17, 2024, https://www.innertrends.com/blog/how-to-measure-true-impact-transactional-emails
6. "49 Cart Abandonment Rate Statistics 2024," *Baymard Institute*, accessed May 17, 2024, https://baymard.com/lists/cart-abandonment-rate
7. "What is the Average Conversion Rate for Cart Abandonment?" *Campaign Monitor*, accessed May 17, 2024, https://www.campaignmonitor.com/resources/knowledge-base/what-is-the-average-conversion-rate-for-cart-abandonment/
8. Tiffany Regaudie, "The Abandoned Cart Benchmarks Eeport: 2024 Data to Inform Your Strategy," *Klaviyo*, May 15, 2024, https://www.klaviyo.com/blog/abandoned-cart-benchmarks
9. Davis Tucker, "Email Marketing List Churn: The Silent Campaign Killer," *60 Second Marketer*, November 17, 2017, https://60secondmarketer.com/2017/11/17/list-churn-silent-campaign-killer/
10. "How Premier Achieves a 12% Click Rate Using the Price Drop Trigger," *Klaviyo*, accessed May 17, 2024, https://www.klaviyo.com/customers/case-studies/premier-price-drop-trigger

14. Grow Influence

1. Bea Smith, "George Clooney Really Made $40 Million Selling Coffee," *TheThings*, October 27, 2022, https://www.thethings.com/george-clooney-nespresso-deal-details/
2. Courtney Goudswaard, "Zero to 3,500 Ambassadors: Caraway's Influencer

Marketing Program Driving Explosive Growth," *Kynship*, April 18, 2023, https://www.kynship.co/blog/caraways-influencer-marketing-program-case-study
3. Mack Collier, "Case Study: Why GE Started an Employee Brand Ambassador Program to Solve One Specific Business Problem," *Mack Collier*, February 6, 2020, https://mackcollier.com/case-study-why-ge-started-an-employee-brand-ambassador-program-to-solve-one-specific-business-problem/

VI. Scale

1. Colin Scotland, "The Marketing Mix: A New Old Definition," *Colin Scotland*, accessed May 17, 2024, https://colinscotland.com/the-marketing-mix-a-new-old-definition/

15. Scale Influence

1. "Charli D'Amelio and Dunkin Donuts: A TikTok Influencer Marketing Case Study," *Influence Hunter*, June 15, 2022, https://influencehunter.com/2022/06/15/charli-damelio-and-dunkin-donuts-a-tiktok-influencer-marketing-case-study/
2. Julie Cauville, "How Tabs Chocolate Bet Everything on UGC with TikTok," *Bigblue*, April 14, 2023, https://www.bigblue.co/blog/how-tabs-chocolate-bet-everything-on-ugc-with-tiktok
3. "Taylor Stitch Streamlines Partner Discovery to Achieve 1,700% Return on Ad Spend," *Impact*, accessed May 17, 2024, https://go.impact.com/rs/280-XQP-994/images/CSdownload-PC-ED-Taylor-Stitch-Hawke-Media-Case-Study.pdf
4. "Buffer," *LATKA SaaS Database*, accessed May 17, 2024, https://getlatka.com/companies/buffer

16. Scale Budget

1. "ChicMe: Reaching High-Value Customers with Facebook Lookalike Audiences," *Meta*, accessed May 17, 2024, https://www.facebook.com/business/success/4-chicme
2. "Kensington Market Sourdough: A/B Test Clarifies Which Facebook Ad Objectives Drive Strongest Sales," *Meta*, accessed May 17, 2024, https://www.facebook.com/business/success/kensington-market-sourdough
3. Melissa Otto, CFA, "Global Digital Advertising Revenues – A Look at the Big Three: Alphabet (GOOGL), Meta Platforms (META), Amazon.com (AMZN)," *Visible Alpha*, May 17, 2023, https://visiblealpha.com/blog/global-digital-advertising-revenues-a-look-at-the-big-three-alphabet-googl-meta-platforms-meta-amazon-com-amzn/

17. PDCA

1. Danny Wong, "What Science Says About Discounts, Promotions and Free Offers," *HuffPost*, last modified May 22, 2019, https://www.huffpost.com/entry/what-science-says-about-discounts_b_8511224

2. "How Was the Deming Prize Established," *Union of Japanese Scientists and Engineers*, accessed May 17, 2024, https://www.juse.or.jp/deming_en/award/
3. "Order of the Sacred Treasure," *Wikipedia*, accessed May 17, 2024, https://en.wikipedia.org/wiki/Order_of_the_Sacred_Treasure
4. "How Data-Driven Insights Drove 12X ROAS Growth for Ikecho," *Digivizer*, accessed May 17, 2024, https://digivizer.com/blog/case-study/12x-roas-growth-for-ikecho/

18. Scale People

1. Rohit Shewale, "Freelance Statistics 2024 – Number of Freelancers & Insights," January 3, 2024, *DemandSage*, https://www.demandsage.com/freelance-statistics/
2. Milan Urosevic, "30 Mind-Boggling Freelance Statistics," *Website Builder*, December 27, 2021, https://websitebuilder.org/blog/freelance-statistics/
3. Tina Johnson, "How This U.S. Digital Marketing Agency Saves 70% in Monthly Operating Costs by Outsourcing to the Philippines: A Case Study," *The Marketing Folks*, October 16, 2023, https://themarketingfolks.com/how-this-us-digital-marketing-agency-saves-70-in-monthly-operating-costs-by-outsourcing-to-the-philippines-a-case-study/

19. AI & Marketing

1. "Marketing AI: Forge the Future of Smart Marketing," *Gartner*, accessed May 17, 2024, https://www.gartner.com/en/marketing/topics/ai-in-marketing
2. "Generative AI," *IBM*, accessed May 17, 2024, https://developer.ibm.com/technologies/generative-ai/
3. "Deepfake," *Brittanica*, last modified May 13, 2024, https://www.britannica.com/technology/deepfake
4. Leslyn Felder and Jaycie Nesbit, "How Goosehead Insurance Revamped Its Marketing Strategy with Jasper and Boosted Performance," *Jasper*, accessed May 17, 2024, https://www.jasper.ai/case-studies/goosehead-insurance
5. Lauren Petrullo, "Mongoose Media Grows Traffic 166% in two months with Jasper," *Jasper*, accessed May 17, 2024, https://www.jasper.ai/case-studies/mongoose-media
6. Scott Mathson, "Unleashing the power of AI with Jasper: Amplitude's Content Marketing Revolutionized," *Jasper*, accessed May 17, 2024, https://www.jasper.ai/case-studies/amplitude

Index

A

ActiveCampaign, 155, 247
ad creatives, 199, 251
Adobe Express, 146, 172–175
advocacy, 23, 119, 127, 155, 175, 212
The Age of Influence, ix, xi, 16, 61, 63, 192
Ahl, Kate, 52
AI:
   audio, 230–231
   ethics, 239
   generated content, 106, 228–229, 239–240
   generative, 5, 64–65, 225, 227, 230–240, 242, 251
   hallucinations, 234
   marketing, 71
   policy, 239
   static image, 228
   technology, 33, 196, 227, 231, 242, 251
   textual, 227, 241
   tools, 81, 147, 227, 229, 248–249, 251
   visual, 240–241
AIDA marketing funnel, 13
algorithm, 8, 10, 15–16, 18, 90, 115, 117, 119, 195–199, 213
Alice's Adventures in Wonderland, 141
Amazon, 4, 17, 22, 27, 36, 62–63, 228–229, 251–252
   ads, 198, 251

Amplitude, 238
analytics, 124, 145, 236–238, 246, 249–252
Arrested Development, 34
audio:
   AI, 230–231
   content, 234–236, 244
   editing, 231, 235, 245
authenticity, 98–99, 129–130, 133, 139, 186, 239, 251

B

A/B testing, 247
backlinks, 30, 106–117, 191, 243
   audit, 117
   benefits of, 106–108
   definitive study, 108
Bacon, Francis, 208
Baddeley, Mike, 186
Bezos, Jeff, 47
Blackberry, 4
Blockbuster, 4
blogging, 33, 35, 61, 63–64, 70, 107, 110, 112, 117
blogs, 12, 31, 69–71, 73, 109–110, 145, 181, 187, 189
Borden, Neil, 177
brand ambassador program, 166, 168–170, 184, 192, 209, 212
brand ambassadors, types of, 169
   affiliate ambassadors, 170, 187
   customer ambassadors, 169, 171
   employee ambassadors, 169–170

expert ambassadors, 170
Brocato, Oliver, 186
B2B, 80, 116, 124–125, 130, 134, 201–202, 214, 247
B2C, 134, 137, 153, 163, 202
Buffet, Warren, 177
Building a Story Brand, 120
Buzzsprout, 230, 235

C

carousel, 98, 146, 149–151, 200, 218, 220
case study, 214
CD Baby, 158
ChatGPT, 131, 225–227, 248
cheat sheets, 83
checklists, 83
Clooney, George, 166–167
Coca-Cola, 206
collaboration, 53–54, 57, 114, 167, 169, 182–188, 190, 192, 220, 222, 251
communication:
   automated, 45, 114, 152, 159
communication pathways:
   educational content, 124–125
   events, 43, 86, 125, 139, 147, 160, 162, 169, 187
   holidays and seasonal promotions, 125
   lead nurture sequences, 122–123
   newsletter, 123–124
   promotional broadcast, 125–127
   welcome emails, 121–122
companion workbook exercises, xii, 11, 24, 38, 46, 57, 73, 83, 87, 102, 117, 127, 140, 151, 164, 175, 192, 204, 215, 223, 241, 243, 252

computer-generated imagery (CGI), 227, 232
consumer:
   approach, 5
   culture, 4
   digital consumer, ix
   during the pandemic, x, 4, 9–10, 81
   modern consumer, 4, 7, 194
contact scoring, 247
content:
   chain, 22, 98, 150
   consistency, 50–51
   educational, 124, 173
   evergreen, 29
   library of content, 66–73, 145–146, 166, 194, 209, 243
   marketing, 18–21
   platform authentic, 96–102, 128–129, 145, 165, 191, 249
   publishing content, 173, 236–237
   repurposing, 80, 83, 99, 144–151, 235–236, 244–245
   timely, 73
content creator, x–xi, 52, 55–57, 129, 133, 191, 201, 220, 249–250
Content Management System (CMS), 155, 236
Content 10X, 143
contests, 84, 134–135, 250
Culliton, James, 177
custom audiences, 195, 200
customer:
   acquisition, 160
   lifecycle, 160, 164, 249–250
   reviews, 5, 36, 132, 134, 137–138, 158, 181, 187, 218–219, 249

D

DALL-E, 226
D'Amelio, Charli, 183–184
Data & Marketing Association (DMA), 152
Dean, Brian, 148
decision-making process, 46
Deming, W. Edwards, 205, 207
digital first:
  marketing, x, xii, 8, 12, 20, 24, 135, 162, 213, 217, 227, 242
  mastermind group, 40
  world, xi, 6, 8–9, 11, 119, 121, 254
digital marketing containers, 17, 20, 24
  content marketing, 18–20, 41, 71, 110, 116
  email marketing, xi, 18, 20
  influencer marketing, xi–xii, 20
  search engine(s), 17–18
  social media marketing, 19
  website, 17
digital relationship funnel, 14
digital threads, 3, 6–7, 10, 20, 25, 59–60, 72, 78, 87, 95, 139, 141–142, 146, 148, 163, 177–178, 180, 191, 193–194, 203–212, 215, 224, 227, 232, 252–254
Digivizer, 214
direct-to-consumer (DTC), 78, 139, 153, 214
directories, 111
discoverability, 28–29, 38, 62–63, 105, 244
Disney, 132–133
domain authority, 31, 33, 62, 67–72, 77, 111–117

domain rating (DR), 27, 52, 116
Dr. Seuss, 27
Dunkin' Donuts, 183–184, 188
Duolingo, 97

E

Eckhart, Meister, 59
Ello, 238
email:
  list, xii, 18, 40–42, 44, 159–160, 162, 196, 209, 211
  list retention, 160
  marketing, xi, 18, 20, 39–40, 159, 161–163, 246–247, 252
  marketing software, 44–45, 152, 155–156, 161, 246–247
  newsletter, 23, 31, 42–46, 76, 121, 126, 144–146, 191, 245
  sequence, 122–124, 127, 159–160
  strategy, 75
email, types of:
  abandoned cart emails, 155–156
  account activation emails, 157
  "How was everything?" emails, 158
  order confirmation email, 156–157
  promotional, 126
  re-engagement, 162
  shipping confirmation emails, 157
  transactional emails, 153–155, 158–159, 163
  triggered emails, 153, 159–160, 163
  welcome emails, 121–122
employee-generated content (EGC), 139
engagement, x, xii, 23, 28, 31,

144–146, 152–154, 247–248, 250–251
Eves, Derral, 100
experiment, 55, 197–198, 212

F

Facebook, 23, 28, 31, 48–49, 82, 193, 197, 199–201, 215, 228, 244
   Ads, 193, 228
Ferriss, Tim, 216
Fiverr, 217–222
The Four-Hour Work Week, 216
Fractional CMO:
   clients, xi, 40, 86, 116, 198
   consulting services, 68
freelance marketplaces, 217–218, 222
freelancers, 110, 137, 217–223
funnel, 13–15, 18, 21–22, 160, 195, 202–203, 210–211, 213
   awareness, 202–203
   consideration, 202–203
   conversion, 202–203

G

gap analysis, 108, 111
Gekko, Gordon, 60
giveaways, 84, 134, 187
Google:
   Ads, 18, 30, 40, 197–198, 228
   Gemini, 248
   Helpful Content Update, 64
   Plus, 238
   search, 33, 35, 64, 105, 108, 112, 114, 238
   shopping, 198
   trends, 225
Goosehead Insurance, 238
GoPro, 96
Grammarly, 229

guest blogging, 110, 112
guestographic, 112

H

Harris, Sydney J., 39
hashtag, 134–136, 138, 140, 149, 188, 248, 250
   branded, 135–136, 138, 250
Help a Reporter Out (HARO), 111
Herbert, George, 242
Hopkins, Claude, 206, 208
Hormozi, Alex, 192
The House at Pooh Corner, 103
HubSpot, 105

I

inbound leads, 180
influencer marketing, xi–xii, 20, 23, 141, 180–181, 184, 187, 190–191, 249–250
   agency, 35–36
   definition, 35
   external influencer, 20, 24, 54, 92, 137, 141, 171, 179–181, 184, 188, 191–192, 209, 250
   platform, 35
   tools, 250
influencers, x, xii, 6, 20, 24, 33, 171, 179–192, 208–209, 250
Instagram, 22–23, 27–28, 48–50, 52, 144, 146–150, 215, 228, 244
   marketing, 71
Instagrammable, 129, 133–134, 136, 140

J

Jack Daniel's, 137
Jasper, 228, 238
Jefferson, Thomas, 61

K

Kennedy, John F., 152
Kensington Market Sourdough, 197
Key Opinion Leader (KOL), 170
keyword research, 31–33, 38, 108, 243, 251
Kizart, Willie, 25
Klaviyo, 155–156
Kodak, 4

L

lead magnets, 76, 78–80, 83–87, 118, 145, 160, 203, 245–246
   creation tools, 246
   distribution tools, 246–247
lead magnets, ideas for, 78
   assessment, 83–84
   case studies, 85
   checklist, 83
   contests, 84
   coupon, 79
   discounted service, 79
   e-book, 80, 83
   email course, 82
   free online course, 83
   free trial, 85
   giveaway, 77, 84
   guides, 80
   infographic, 85
   online challenges, 82
   in-person consultation, 79
   quiz, 78–79, 83–84
   resource list, 81
   templates, 85
   test, 84, 86
   video training, 81
   virtual summit, 81
   webinar, 81, 83
   white paper, 80
   workbook, 83

Lewis, E. St. Elmo, 13
link in bio, 99–100
link reclamation, 114
LinkedIn, 28, 48, 62, 98, 100–101, 129, 217–218, 220, 228, 244
   content creator, 220
   style article, 146
livestream, 9, 125, 147, 150, 187, 244

M

marketers, x–xi, 13, 47, 92, 99, 107, 129–130, 144, 172, 227, 246
marketing:
   affiliate, 54, 170, 187, 250
   automation software, 159, 247–251
   digital marketing strategy, xii, 15
   infrastructure, xi–xii, 12–13, 15, 17, 19, 21, 23
   marketing budgets, percentage of, 4
   omni-channel marketing automation, 247
   word-of-mouth, 7, 20, 47, 53, 75, 158, 179
marketing channels, xii, 13, 20, 22, 137
   blogs, 12, 31, 69–71, 73, 138, 145, 181, 187, 189
   customer experience, 133, 140, 153
   email, 22–24, 41, 43
   livestream, 9, 125, 147, 150, 187, 244
   online presence, 5, 17
   search, 22
   social media, 22

videos, x, 5, 13, 28, 37, 52, 235, 237–238, 246, 250
Maximize Your Social, 91, 178
McCauley, Kathryn, 136
McDonald, Jason, 48
Melville, Herman, 105
Mencius, 118–119
Meta, 51, 197, 199–203
metadata, 149
micro-influencer, 33, 181, 185–186
Miller, Donald, 120
Miller, Henry, 25
Mongoose Media, 238
Morgan, J. P., 1
Motorola, 4

N
nano-influencer, 181, 185–186
Natividad, Amanda, 97
Nespresso, 166–167
Newman, Paul, 34
Nike, 191
Nokia, 4

O
Omnisend, 155
OpenAI, 33, 226
outsourcing, 112, 217, 222, 245

P
paid collaboration, 186
paid media, 7, 191, 193–195, 197, 202–203, 208, 211, 213–215, 251
tools, 251
paid search, 197
products, 197
paid social, 7, 19, 23, 91–92, 170, 193, 199
media products, 199

pandemic, ix–x, 4–10, 81, 88, 99, 103, 168, 181, 214
Covid-19 restrictions, ix
digital marketing challenges, 5–6
digital marketing opportunities, 5–6
effects on companies, x–xi
lockdown, ix–x, 4–5
online communication, 12
online reviews, 5
remote work, 4
Pastreez, 71–72
PDCA, 205–215, 237–238
cycle, 209, 213, 215
PDCA Social, 208
Penney, James Cash, 216
PeoplePerHour, 218
personally identifiable information (PII), 239
Picasso, Pablo, 74
Pinterest, 52–53, 63, 101, 200, 202, 228
Plautus, 193
Plumbs Veterinary Drugs, 123
podcasters, 63, 107, 113, 137, 189, 231
podcasting, 113, 230
Primarily Pure, 78
promotion, 6–8, 10, 37, 39, 43, 152, 154, 166, 171, 201, 235–236
promotional broadcast, 125
promotional emails, types of, 126
new products, 126
sales and discounts, 126
time-bound discounts, 126
publishing content, 173, 236–237
distribute/promote content, 236
schedule/publish content, 236

Pulizzi, Joe, 19, 41

R
reconnaissance, 100–102, 188
Reddit, 52, 63, 202
relationships:
   building, 8, 14–16, 21–22, 27, 45, 93, 107, 117, 127, 144–145, 182, 189, 202, 223, 253
research topic, 234
resource pages, 111
retargeting, 194–195, 204
Return on Investment (ROI), 39, 127, 131, 148, 154, 187, 197, 199, 203–204, 210, 213, 249–250
Rosemond, Anthony and Yami, 71

S
SaaS, 80, 85, 130, 149
Schweitzer, Albert, 128
Scientific Advertising, 208
search:
   demand, 29–32, 35, 67–69, 72, 225, 243
   intent, 32–36, 38, 68–69, 198
   search engine results, 28, 35, 64, 72, 114, 146, 150
   search engines, xi, 7–8, 17–18, 36–37, 40, 61–67, 110, 115–117, 145–146, 150, 189, 193, 198, 210, 219–220, 243, 245
search engine optimization (SEO), 19–20, 31, 35, 37, 67, 69, 71–72, 106–110, 114–117, 146, 148, 191, 228, 235, 237, 243–244, 252
   dashboard, 243
   dominance, 146
   search tools, 243, 250
   tool, 35, 67, 69, 71–72, 108–109, 115, 237, 243, 252
   YouTube, 244
Sears, 4, 74–75, 120
segmentation, 41–42, 46
SES:
   channels, 63
   framework, 13, 20–25, 47, 54, 57, 154, 210–211, 252
Shopify, 155, 222, 236
skyscraper technique, 113
Social media:
   content creator, x–xi, 52, 55–56, 185–187, 191, 201, 220, 249–250
   engagement, 130
   marketing, 6, 19, 39, 47, 71, 92
   tools, 248
Social Tools Summit, 242
SparkToro, 97
Starbucks, 134, 191
storytelling, 43, 46, 120
Strowger, Almon Brown, 8
StumbleUpon, 238
Supple, Steve, 143
SwagDrop, 116

T
Tabs Chocolate, 186
targeting, 29, 33, 115, 160–162, 172, 195–197, 199–201, 204
   audiences, 195–196
   keywords, 197–198
   user interests, 195–196, 203
   user options, 200
Taylor Stitch, 187
Tesla, Nikola, 165
testimonials, 85, 137–138
threads, 97–99, 146–147, 150

TikTok, x, xii, 5, 7, 18, 22, 27, 34, 181, 186, 197, 201, 228, 244
Total Addressable Market (TAM), 22
trust, building, 17, 45, 48, 67, 69, 136
Tsu, 238
TubeBuddy, 244
Turing, Alan, 224
Twitter. *See X (social network)*
Tyson, Mike, 3

U

Upwork, 217–218, 220–222
User-Generated Content (UGC), 9, 33, 53, 84, 92, 181, 184–186, 191, 201, 212, 249–250

V

Vaynerchuk, Gary, 149, 191
video creation, 244–245
  tools, 245
video editing, 235, 244
videos, short-form, x, 235
VidIQ, 244
visibility gap, 194

W

Wachler, Brian Boxer, 52
Warhol, Andy, 12
We Are Social, 94
webmasters, 107, 110
WhatsApp, 12, 200–201, 247
Wikipedia, 105, 116
Winfrey, Oprah, 88
Wolf, Macia, 186
Woods, Amy, 143
WordPress, 155, 189, 222, 236, 243

workflow, 223, 231–232, 236, 238, 241, 243, 249, 252

X

X (social network), x, 23, 28, 47, 94, 96–101, 146–148, 150, 160, 188, 202, 210–211, 228, 244

Y

YouTube, 5, 7, 18, 22, 27–28, 36–37, 149–150, 181, 197–199, 244–245
  marketing, 101
The YouTube Formula, 100–101
YouTubers, 97, 137, 244

Z

zero-click content, 97
Zero Moment of Truth (ZMOT), 13, 15, 24, 119
Ziglar, Zig, 179

About the Author

Neal Schaffer stands at the forefront of the digital marketing revolution, an innovative Fractional CMO and acclaimed authority whose insights and strategies have catalyzed the growth of businesses worldwide. With a career that spans over a decade and crosses four continents, Neal has solidified his reputation as a global thought leader in digital, content, influencer, and social media marketing.

Neal's passion for education and empowerment in the digital space comes to life through his roles as an instructor at prestigious institutions, including UCLA Extension and Rutgers Business School, where he covers crucial topics like personal branding, influencer marketing and social media branding. His commitment to nurturing the next generation of marketers extends beyond the classroom to the global stage, having delivered keynotes at hundreds of events worldwide.

Author of five pivotal sales and marketing books, Neal's publications such as *Maximize Your Social*, *The Age of Influence*, and his newest *Digital Threads* have been instrumental for professionals seeking to leverage the power of digital-first marketing. These works, acclaimed for their practical insights and forward-thinking strategies, underscore Neal's expertise and influence in the marketing domain.

Beyond his books, Neal enriches the digital marketing conversation with his Your Digital Marketing Coach podcast, offering weekly inspiration and actionable advice to help businesses and professionals stay ahead in the rapidly evolving landscape. Neal's blog at nealschaffer.com further establishes him as a leading resource, hosting hundreds of posts that serve as a vital toolkit for the business community.

With a storied career as a Fractional CMO and marketing consultant for an extensive array of brands, both large and small, Neal Schaffer's contributions to the marketing world are unmatched. His strategic vision, combined with a genuine dedication to empowering others, makes Neal Schaffer not just an expert in digital marketing, but a true pioneer reshaping the industry's future.

Made in the USA
Middletown, DE
12 March 2025